SPENSER

FOWRE HYMNES
EPITHALAMION

SPENSER

FOWRE HYMNES
EPITHALAMION

A STUDY OF EDMUND SPENSER'S
DOCTRINE OF LOVE

By ENID WELSFORD

BASIL BLACKWELL
OXFORD
1967

Printed in Great Britain or BASIL BLACKWELL & MOTT, LTD.
by A. R. MOWBRAY & CO. LIMITED in the City of Oxford
and bound at the KEMP HALL BINDERY

ACKNOWLEDGMENTS

My thanks are due to the Shakespeare Head Press for permission to use the text of *Fowre Hymnes* and *Epithalamion* contained in their edition of *The Works of Edmund Spenser*.

I have also to thank the Editor of *University of Missouri Studies* for the use of some small extracts from S. R. Jayne's translation of Ficino's *Dialoghi d'Amore*.

I am grateful to Professor Geoffrey Shepherd for some valuable criticisms and suggestions.

I am deeply indebted to the unremitting kindness of my cousin, Anne Welsford, whose skill both as nurse and secretary enabled me to complete this book during a period of illness.

I am much indebted to Sir Basil Blackwell and it is a pleasure to record my gratitude for the forbearance and skill of all those concerned in the publication of this book.

E. E. H. W.

LIST OF ABBREVIATIONS

CUP	Cambridge University Press
EPITH	*Ephithalamion.*
FH	*Fowre Hymnes.*
FQ	*Fairie Queene.*
HB	*An Hymne of Beautie.*
HHB	*An Hymne of Heavenly Beautie.*
HL	*An Hymne of Love.*
HHL	*An Hymne of Heavenly Love.*
JEGP	*Journal of English and German Philology.*
MP	*Modern Philology.*
OUP	Oxford University Press.
PMLA	Publications of Modern Language Association of America.
SP	Studies in Philology.
STh	*Summa Theologica.*
VarMP	Variorum Edition of Spenser's Minor Poems.

CONTENTS

INTRODUCTION

I. THE THEME

THE choice of poems for this edition calls for explanation. *Epithalamion* is of course an acknowledged masterpiece of English lyrical poetry, but up till now the *Fowre Hymnes* have excited more scholarly discussion than literary appreciation and although, as I believe, their beauty has usually been underestimated, nevertheless they are unquestionably minor poems. Nor is there any very obvious similarity of theme, for although they all treat of love there seems to be little in common between the triumphal ode in which the bridegroom celebrates his marriage as an occasion for both sacred and secular rejoicing, and the hymns in which the wooer seeks to assuage his unsatisfied desire and only turns to heaven when his earthly hopes have failed him.

It is, however, this very discrepancy of outlook which has suggested their inclusion in one volume, for since love is a major theme of Spenser's poetry all his thoughts on the subject deserve our attention and it is just this striking contrast between the wedded love of *Epithalamion* and both the earthly and the heavenly love of the *Fowre Hymnes* that makes comparison between our poems so illuminating. Illuminating but not easy; for since we are comparing works of art, we are bound to ask ourselves how we are meant to focus them. Are they lyrical in the modern sense of the word? Is Spenser giving us an outpouring of personal emotion in *Epithalamion* and an exposition of his personal philosophy of love in the *Fowre Hymnes*? This question involves further questions about sources, dating, and biography. A brief account of the textual history of our poems and references to further authorities are given in Appendix I, but unfortunately the known facts are scanty.

In 1595, William Ponsonby published *Amoretti* and *Epithalamion*, and dedicated the volume to Sir Robert Needham, because in September 1594 that gentleman had returned from Ireland in the same ship which had carried 'these sweet conceited sonnets' to Spenser's native land. Spenser has made the connection between them very clear. *Amoretti* differs from the usual Petrarchan

sonnet-sequence in that the lover's suit is successful. Sonnet 74
gives the lady's name as Elizabeth, and in the opening of *Epithalamion* the poet announces that he is about to celebrate in verse his
own wedding-day. Even if, as some scholars suggest, the sonnets
were composed at different periods and originally addressed to
different women, the fact remains that they were presented to the
public in 1595 as a planned whole and are obviously meant to be
taken as a poetic record, with the time sequence carefully marked,
of a protracted wooing culminating in the poet's happy marriage
to Elizabeth Boyle. The contents of the 1595 volume therefore
(with the possible exception of the unoriginal and not very distinguished 'anacreontics') can be taken as forming in one sense a
continuous narrative with at least some autobiographical reference, the wooer of the *Amoretti* becoming the bridegroom of the
Epithalamion and the two works representing different stages in a
love-story which ends happily. The case with *Fowre Hymnes* is
very different.

In 1596 William Ponsonby published *Fowre Hymnes* together
with a new edition of *Daphnaïda*, which he had first published in
1591. This latter poem is given a separate title page and has no
connection with the preceding *Fowre Hymnes*. The relationship of
the hymns to one another is more difficult to determine. On the
one hand the poet has linked them together so closely that one can
hardly avoid treating them as a complex but unified work of art;
on the other hand, both in the poems themselves and in the prose
dedication to the Countesses of Cumberland and Warwick,
Spenser insists that the Hymns to Love and Beauty were written
in his youth and that the Hymns to Heavenly Love and Heavenly
Beauty have been composed 'by way of retractation' of a point of
view which the Countesses regard as unedifying and which he
himself now repudiates.

Are we to believe him? It seems odd that only a year after the
appearance of *Epithalamion* Spenser should have published this
repudiation of human love and adopted the role of a disillusioned
and disappointed man; but, of course, noble patronesses have to
be honoured; the use of the first person may be merely a poetic
artifice, and the 'I' who speaks may not be Spenser the man, but
Spenser the Petrarchan poet following the same tradition which
prompted Sidney to write 'Leave me, O Love that reaches but to

dust'. It is indeed because they raise problems of this kind that it is useful to consider our poems in connection with one another and even (since the dates of composition are uncertain) to disregard the order of publication in our consideration of them. Even if they do not describe his personal experience *The Fowre Hymnes* may express a serious point of view and we may well ask ourselves whether the poet is exhibiting aspects of love which differ but are not ultimately irreconcilable, or whether we should regard the asceticism of the fourth hymn as Spenser's final word on the subject. The question is an important one for it may affect our interpretation not only of these poems but of the *Faerie Queene* itself. It can hardly be answered without some preliminary study of Spenser's intellectual background and, therefore, a general account of it is given in this Introduction, and annotations to the texts provide more detailed references to certain passages from Neo-Platonic and other sources, which help to elucidate the meaning of a difficult poet, whose literary conventions and modes of thought differ widely from our own.

II. The Intellectual Background

a. Introductory

OF recent years there has been an increasing unwillingness to draw hard and fast distinctions between the Middle Ages and the Renaissance. The 'Elizabethan World Picture', as the late Dr. Tillyard pointed out in a book under that title, was a simplified version of mediæval cosmology, which in its turn was derived from 'an amalgam of Plato and the Old Testament, invented by the Jews of Alexandria and vivified by the new religion of Christ'.[1] For the elucidation of Spenser's poetry, however, it is more important to grasp certain differences between Elizabethan and modern modes of thought than to discriminate minutely between the mediæval and the renaissance elements in his intellectual background.

When we approach the work of a sixteenth-century poet, it is important to remember that he shared neither the modern horror of didacticism nor the modern cult of originality, that he prided himself on the truth rather than the novelty of his ideas and therefore would rejoice to concur, if not with the common

reader, at any rate with all readers at the same level of education
as himself. The 'furor poeticus' in which he sometimes expressed
belief inspired him with eloquence rather than peculiar insight.
Spenser would have been flattered rather than insulted on being
told that his *Epithalamion* was reminiscent of Latin and French
Epithalamia and that none of the ideas in the *Fowre Hymnes* were
peculiar to himself. The attitude of the philosophers was not
wholly different. Although they disagree on some points, Ficino,
Pico della Mirandola and other Neo-Platonists of the Renaissance
repeat one another incessantly because of their conviction that the
most important truths about the nature of things are already
known, and their chief task is to expound and arrange these
ideas with order and clarity, and to explain away all apparent
inconsistencies. To achieve an ordered synthesis of this kind was,
of course, the aim of the great scholastics who set out to Chris-
tianize Aristotle, but the Florentine Neo-Platonists went further
than they did. For some of them a true understanding of Plato's
teaching not only shows it to be consistent with the Christian
religion, but provides a clue by means of which the inner meanings
of all the great religions of the world can be first unravelled and
then reconciled; a point that should be remembered when Spenser's eclecticism is under discussion.[1] For this purpose myth and
allegory were safe and potent weapons, for allegorical gods need
constitute no threat to an historical religion and can be helpful to
the poets in their attempts to teach delightfully by embodying
abstract truths in concrete living forms. To put it like this,
however, is to over-simplify and possibly to cause misunderstanding.

– For Spenser and his contemporaries, and indeed for his
mediæval predecessors, to allegorize was not to reduce the vivid
three dimensional world to a dull, flat, abstract pattern, but to do
the very reverse. Was not the whole hierarchic universe both an
immensely extended metaphor of the Divine Perfections and also
the habitat of innumerable living creatures, visible and invisible?
Were not the Aristotelian 'Intelligences' and even some of the
pagan deities to be equated with the Angels? The Greek and
Roman gods re-entered the Christian imagination, not just as
personifications of human passions, though they were often that;
not just as traditional names for the complicated partitions of the

universe, though they were that at times; but also as the names of living forces actually at work in the world and in our personal lives, and frequently connected with the movements and positions of the Heavenly Bodies.

The Italian Platonists gave a new prominence to the classical 'daemons', elementary 'median spirits' midway between angelic and human nature, and intimately concerned with human affairs. The Love of Spenser's first hymn is ultimately derived from the Eros who in Plato's *Symposium* is affirmed to be not a god but a daemon; and in his commentary on that work, Ficino asserts that each of the gods or angels who control the seven planets is accompanied by a bevy of daemons, who convey to human beings the gifts appropriate to the star under which they were born. He even goes so far as to suggest that each human soul contains two, if not five, love daemons! When, therefore, Spenser tells us that lovers

> See through amorous eye-glaunces
> Armies of loves still flying too and fro,
> Which dart at them their little fierie launces,
> Whom having wounded, backe againe they go
> Carrying compassion to their lovely foe.

though his touch is light, he is not treating us to a mere elegant frivolity, for such a conceit would not necessarily seem trivial at a period when a would-be serious philosophical work could contain a chapter entitled 'On the Ranks of the Daemons of Venus, and How They Shoot the Arrows of Love'.[1] This, however, gives little help to the modern reader.

This thickly populated Neo-Platonic universe, where everything comes alive, must surely be reckoned among those 'false worlds' which, according to Bishop Sprat,[2] had to be demolished before the scientists of the Royal Society could construct a truer model of reality, for certainly it is the opposite of the dead, unmetaphorical world of colourless, soundless atoms which played such an important part in much of later philosophy. Indeed the work of demolition was so thoroughly carried out, that now it is very difficult to understand the language of our forebears or to focus their poems aright. Even when the anachronistic approach of nineteenth-century critics is abandoned, the result is not entirely satisfactory. We can retrace the pattern of thought; it is more difficult to recover the experience. To us the allegorical method seems more likely to reduce a Redcross Knight to abstract Holiness than to bring Holiness to life as a Redcross Knight; but to Spenser, though the Love of the first hymn is a personification and the Christ of the last two hymns is a person, since the mythical daemon Love is not *wholly* unreal, he can, in a sense, co-exist with the historical Saviour. And what is true of Love, is true of the mythical beings who take such a prominent part in the wedding celebrations of the *Epithalamion*.

It is illuminating to compare the arrival of 'the rosy-bosomed Hours, Fair Venus train' at the beginning of Gray's *Ode to Spring* with their appearance in Spenser's *Epithalamion*. Both poets are working within the same convention and are using admittedly legendary beings as a mode of rhetorical heightening and ornament; but whereas to Gray mythological beings are little more than attractive traditional figures of poetic diction, to Spenser they also play an important part in the social and imaginative life of his day and can symbolize a real element in personal experience. Moreover, since he could assume that he and his readers possessed a common fund of knowledge drawn from masque, pictorial art and mythological handbooks, he could expect intelligent appreciation of subtleties in his own particular way of handling this familiar material. Unfortunately, what was in his day common knowledge to educated persons is now very largely the preserve of specialists. In my notes, therefore, I have devoted considerable space to the elucidation of classical allusions; for although, like all great poetry, *Epithalamion* makes a direct impact, which does not depend on historical information, nevertheless our aesthetic enjoyment can be enriched by it.

The poetic merits of the *Fowre Fymnes* have, I believe, been underrated, but they are unquestionably inferior to the *Epithalamion*, and perhaps for that reason are more in need of a commentary not confined to the explanations of classical allusions. Without some knowledge of the Platonism current in Spenser's time there can be no serious discussions of the problems of interpretation presented by these poems, and many passages must remain unintelligible. The subject is a wide and complicated one, but I shall confine my attention to those ideas which affected Spenser's poetry. Since it is probable that his knowledge of Plato was not wholly derived from later commentators, one must begin by examining his debt to that philosopher.

b. The Platonic Treatment of Love

When Spenser opened *Timaeus*,[1] or some commentary on it, he found there an account of the origin of the universe very different from that given in the first chapter of the Bible, where God, having created all things by word of command, 'saw everything that he had made, and, behold, it was very good'; and where evil results not from the defects of matter, which is divinely created, but from the disobedience of created wills who have been given the power of choice. Plato's account is not only different from this but is meant to be taken in a different way. In the opening chapters of *Genesis* the authoritative ring of God's creative word is echoed in the majestic assurance with which His deeds are described. But Plato is not reciting a creed, he is engaging in philosophical analysis and expressing tentative conclusions in what he insists is only a myth, and the image he employs is that of a craftsman, who shapes his not wholly satisfactory material into as perfect a likeness as possible of a model which exists in his mind or before his eyes. So the divine Demiurge (well translated by Spenser as 'great Work-Master') shapes what would otherwise be mere chaos into as close a likeness as possible of that 'perfect living creature' who exists eternally as a mental Form discernible by the Divine Reason. The product of his activities is the cosmos, a living creature endowed with soul and body, spherical in shape and revolving endlessly through the circular movement of Time which is the moving image of Eternity.

About the exact interpretation of this myth there is much scholarly disagreement, which fortunately need not concern us here; but there are certain differences between the Platonic and the Biblical cosmology which are both obvious and relevant. Unlike the God of the Bible, the Demiurge is not an object of worship and is not omnipotent, for he creates neither the model nor the matter of the cosmos, and his benevolent purpose is to a certain extent thwarted by the existence in the universe of a permanent disorderly element of blind 'necessity' which is never completely mastered by the Divine Intelligence. The cosmos, therefore, has its 'higher' and 'lower' regions, and the visible, tangible objects of our world are but shadowy imperfect copies of the intelligible forms contemplated by the heavenly gods and by human souls prior to their incarnation in physical bodies. Nevertheless, owing to the activities of the Demiurge, the physical world of becoming is a copy, albeit an imperfect one, of the eternal world of being, and although the fall into a body entails forgetfulness, whenever a human person sees a visibly beautiful object his memory is awakened, he begins to desire his former home and—as Plato puts it in the *Phaedrus*—his soul grows wings and if he restrains physical desire and pursues philosophical wisdom he eventually regains his vision of the Real, for 'the natural function of the wing is to soar upwards and carry that which is heavy up to the place where dwells the race of the gods'.[1] For Plato, therefore, evil is caused by a permanently recalcitrant element in the universe, and so 'sin' consists not in pride and disobedience, but in the ignorance and sensuality, which hinder the upward movement of the human spirit towards a life of disembodied contemplation. This upward movement is brought about by Eros, or Love, the nature of which is examined in the *Phaedrus* and in greater detail in the *Symposium*,[2] a favourite text of the humanists and, together with *Timaeus*, the ultimate source of Spenser's first two Hymns.

In the introduction to the *Symposium* we are told how the guests at that famous banquet decided to entertain themselves with philosophical discussion instead of excessive wine-drinking and to take Eros as their theme of discourse. One after another they deliver their eulogies. Phaedrus praises Eros as the most venerable and most beneficent of the gods and the inspirer of virtuous deeds. Pausanus maintains that there are two loves: the baser, popular Eros, who accompanies the popular Aphrodite, is concerned with physical union, which can be either hetero-sexual or homo-sexual; the Heavenly Eros, who accompanies the Heavenly Aphrodite unites members of the same sex in a nobler spiritual friendship. Eryximachus, the doctor, agrees that there are two Loves; but he suggests that they are not merely concerned with human relationships, but are great cosmic forces at work in everything which exists: the Heavenly Love produces order and harmony, the

Popular Love produces disease, destruction and many other evils. Aristophanes, as might be expected, makes a speech which is not meant to be taken too seriously, but after his comic account of the matter, Agathon the rhetorician resumes the theme in a more serious vein and eulogizes Love as the youngest, the most blissful, the most beautiful of the gods. His eloquence evokes loud applause which dies away as Socrates ironically remarks that he had foolishly supposed that one ought to speak the truth about the person eulogized, and then proceeds to give an analysis of the nature of Love, based, he maintains, on the teaching given him by a certain prophetess called Diotima. The gist of this lady's instruction was that Eros is to be identified not with the beloved but with the lover; and that since Love desires Beauty he cannot be already beautiful nor can he be a god, for desire implies lack and the gods lack nothing. But because Love is not beautiful it does not follow that he is ugly; because he is not a god, it does not follow that he is a mortal; he is, in fact, a daemon, one of those intermediary spirits who make intercourse possible between gods and men. This analysis of Love's nature is illustrated by an allegorical myth which was to become a favourite text of the Florentine Neo-Platonists.

When Aphrodite, the goddess of Beauty, was born, the gods made a great feast to celebrate the event, and Resource, son of Cunning, who was one of the guests, got drunk and went into the garden of Zeus to sleep it off. While he was asleep in came the beggar-woman Poverty and lay down by his side and conceived Love. So Love is desirous of Beauty, on whose birthday he was born: he is poor because he wants the beautiful and is resourceful because he schemes to obtain it. This account of the matter is, however, modified, or at any rate supplemented, by Diotima's account of the nature of Love's resourcefulness. Love, she explains, not only desires to possess beauty, he desires to possess it for ever. Love, therefore, desires immortality, but the nearest mortal lovers can get to this is by generation. Love, therefore, is not so much love of the beautiful as love of engendering and begetting upon the beautiful by means both of the body and the soul. The sight of a beautiful body stirs up this love, and to those dominated chiefly by physical desire it will lead to intercourse with women and the begetting of children. But the soul is higher

than the body and when two men love one another in the right
way they beget spiritual offspring; they are stimulated to write
great poems; to make good laws, and by various ways to achieve
immortality in the memory of their descendants. For the Heavenly
as distinct from the popular Eros is progressive: ' "Beginning
from obvious beauties he [i.e. the lover] must for the sake of the
highest beauty be ever climbing aloft as on the rungs of a ladder,
from one to two, and from two to all beautiful bodies; from
personal beauty he proceeds to beautiful observances, from
observances to beautiful learning, and from learning at last to
that particular study which is concerned with the beautiful itself
and that alone; so that in the end he comes to know the very
essence of beauty. In that state of life above all others, my dear
Socrates", said the Mantinean woman, "a man finds it truly
worth while to live as he contemplates essential beauty" .'[1]

This is the first appearance of that famous ladder of love which
was to play such an important part in the thought of the Renaissance, and there has been much disputing as to whether any such
ladder is to be found in Spenser's *Hymnes*. Is the lover of the last
two poems following the Heavenly Eros, or is he turning his
back on that guide and walking in the lowlier footsteps of the
Christian Love, which the New Testament writers called Agape?
The question cannot be answered without some further examination of the nature of these two Loves and of the contrast
between them.

In spite of its derivation, our adjective 'erotic' conveys a misleading impression of the Platonic Eros; for, as Anders Nygren
points out in his classic work *Agape and Eros*, both these Greek
words could designate ideals of love which are differentiated, not
by contrast between physical and spiritual desire, but by the
contrast between altruistic and egoistic motives or—in a theological context—between egocentric and theocentric religion.[2]
'We love him because he first loved us.'[3] God takes the initiative.
Our own love for God and for our fellow-men are products of
His love for us, and the Creator's parental love is concerned with
the creature's need of Him not with any need of His for the
creature. Christian love, therefore, unlike the Platonic heavenly
Eros, originates in God, not in man, and its most characteristic
manifestation is self-sacrifice rather than self-fulfilment. It is, to

use C. S. Lewis's terminology, 'gift-love', not 'need-love'. Both these loves play an important part in Spenser's poetry, and although he himself does not designate them as Agape and Eros, the terms will be used throughout this book as convenient and well known names for the love that descends to give and the love that ascends to get. For the moment our concern is with the latter deity.

c. The Neo-Platonic Treatment of Love

The Socrates of the *Symposium* betrays no interest in the theories of Eryximachus, but concerns himself solely with love as a mainspring of human conduct; later Platonists, however, did not limit themselves in this way, but were influenced by Aristotle's theory that the cosmos is a nest of endlessly rotating concentric spheres set in motion by love and desire, desire to attain to the perfection of the Divine Mind which, being immaterial, fully actualized and entirely self-sufficient, is unaware of any existence outside its own selfconsciousness. This unloving, unmoved Mover of the universe is very different from Plato's active Demiurge, the supreme Rational Soul, who ordered the cosmos because being good and therefore unenvious he 'desired that all things should come as near as possible to being like Himself'.

During the last centuries B.C. and the first two centuries A.D., Neo-Platonists made attempts to reconcile these apparent irreconcilable cosmologies, and in the third century A.D., Plotinus in his *Enneads*,[1] presented an ordered hierarchical structure of spiritual reality, which exercised a deep and lasting influence on Christian theology and was the most important source of Florentine-Neo-Platonism. For Plotinus, the First Principle which heads the hierarchic universe is too transcendent to be called Mind or even Being. It is the One and so far beyond our thinking that it can only be described by negation or suggested by metaphor. Just as all things are made visible by the natural brightness of the sun, which blinds us if we look at it directly, so all the varied orders of existence radiating from the One are the result, not of willed creation, but of necessary emanation. But although the emanation is necessary, the cosmos is no dead piece of mechanism but alive and organic. The first moment of emanation produces the Divine Mind, full of the Forms and Archetypes of *all* existence, including individuals; the second produces the World-Soul, the principle of life and movement, the intermediary between the higher world of Mind, and the lower world of corporeal Nature. This downward movement involves ever-increasing multiplicity, until, just as rays of light disappear into darkness, so emanation from the One ends in Matter: mere potentiality, formlessness, non-being. As mere potentiality matter comes near to being the principle of negation and of evil, and, therefore, though the visible, material world, being the product of soul and itself ensouled is beautiful and good, nevertheless it occupies the lowest rank in the hierarchic cosmos; and although sexual loves that serve the procreative purposes of Nature are innocent and right, nevertheless spiritual progress consists in intellectual contemplation involving increasing detachment from worldly and bodily preoccupations. Plotinus who is said to have experienced mystical union with the One, is also said to have been ashamed of being in a body.

For emanation is not the only kind of movement in the universe. Besides the downward movement by which the higher generates the lower without any loss to itself and as a 'necessary reflex action of its own contemplation' there is also a reverse and more consciously willed movement of return, ascent, and simplification by which the soul passes upwards through the various stages of existence until it achieves union with the First Principle. Sometimes Plotinus interprets emanation as a process by which the lower proceeds from the higher in a merely potential condition and only attains its full actuality by contemplation of the higher source from whence it came. This energizing act of loving contemplation which plays an important part in the Neo-Platonism of the Renaissance, displays very clearly the difference between Eros who ascends because he needs the beloved, and Agape who descends because the beloved needs him. The Socratic Eros is too imperfect to be even *a* god; *the* God of Christianity *is* Agape. Neither term can be applied to the ineffable One of Plotinus.

d. The Mediæval Tradition of Romantic Love

The Neo-Platonism of the first centuries of our era was a mystical philosophy which was taken seriously by theologians; the Neo-Platonism of the Renaissance was very largely a product of the court, a theme for secular discussion and relevant to the conduct of the cultivated man of the world. When therefore Ficino and his friends considered the nature of Eros, their meditations were bound to be affected not only by the New Testament conception of Agape and the Christianized Platonism of later days, but also by the cult of Romantic hetero-sexual love which originated in eleventh-century Provence and, as C. S. Lewis has stressed in his classic work on the subject,[1] brought about a revolutionary change of sentiment and made a lasting impress on our literature and social life.

In the New Testament marriage is regarded as an honourable estate, but—in St. Paul's opinion, at any rate—inferior to celibacy. St. Paul's attitude seems to have been partly due to his belief that the end of the world was at hand; but reverence for Christ's mother and the rise of monasticism reinforced the conviction that virginity was *essentially* superior to wedlock. This view persisted up to the time of the Reformaton and is still the doctrine of many Christians. As regards the moral status of the married couple there was a certain ambiguity in the attitude of the theologians. Marriage was a sacrament[2] and marital intercourse lawful insofar as its purpose was procreative, but owing to the Fall the carnal pleasure of coition was tainted with evil, so that as Professor Lewis points out 'according to the mediæval view passionate love itself was wicked, and did not cease to be wicked if the object of it were your wife'.[3] The object of it however was more likely to be the wife of another man, for in feudal society marriage was more often a business contract than the culmination of a passionate love affair, and it was probably in reaction against this utilitarian disregard and religious disapproval of sexual passion that the troubadours of twelfth-century Provence, having dissociated courtly love from matrimony, invested it with spiritual dignity and at times transformed it into a kind of secular religion. As a wife the mediæval lady was—theoretically at any rate—subject to her husband; as the object of courtly love, she was the acknowledged superior of her 'servant', who offered her not only passionate adoration but also an obedience more complete and abject than that of a vassal to his overlord. Although concealment of the lady's name formed part of the convention, it is uncertain to what extent courtly love involved actually illicit relationships; but the important and novel characteristic of this *fin' amors*, 'fine love', was that it was a hetero-sexual love involving heart and mind as well as physical instinct and exacting from the lover a vow of lasting fidelity.

The attitude of the courtly lover was modelled not only on that of a feudal vassal but also on that of a religious devotee. His religion consisted in the worship of Amor, the presiding deity of Ovid's flippant and ironic *Art of Love*, and frequently took the form of a parody of Christian belief and ritual, often emphasizing the antagonism between the ecclesiastical and courtly ideals of conduct. Gestures of defiance, however, do not necessarily indicate complete repudiation, and the mediæval love poet often concludes his work with an expression of repentance for his past follies.

When in the thirteenth century the troubadour love lyric reached Italy it began to change its character: the feudal element diminished, the poet worshipped his mistress less as his liege lady and more as an inspiring paragon of beauty and virtue, and although some tension remained, the opposition between courtly love and Christian ethics became less pronounced. For instance in Guido Guinicelli's influential and beautiful ode *Al Cor Gentil*, love and the gentle (i.e. noble) heart are said to be inseparable, and this nobility of heart—which is a matter not of birth but of inner God-created excellence—is fully manifested only when stimulated by love for a noble woman. This being so, argues Guinicelli, should not his lady bestow upon her servant the essence of her own nobility, just as God bestows on the company of heaven the vision of His unveiled face? When at the day of judgment God reproaches the poet for this daring comparison he will have his excuse ready:

> As though from Thee he came,
> Love wore an angel's face
> Lord, if I loved her, count it not my shame.[1]

No more is said, but one is left with the impression that the plea will not be rejected.

Equally famous, but very different in style and temper, was Guido Cavalcanti's *Canzone d'Amore*[2] ('Donna me prega . . .'), which is not, properly speaking, a love lyric but an analysis of 'fine love' intended for educated readers well versed, it would seem, in scholastic psychology. The interpretation of this obscure

poem has occasioned much controversy; but it seems pretty clear
that for Cavalcanti 'fine love' when fully actualized is physical,
emotional and intellectual. Its first object is a mental image
embodying the idea of perfect female beauty, which the intellect
has abstracted from its memories of actual visible forms. When
a man meets a woman who has some affinity with him he identifies
her for a time with this mental image and his ideal love is transformed into a passionate desire, which is both spiritual and sensual
and by its very nature non-moral, impermanent, and very painful.
Cavalcanti was held in high repute by later love poets and philosophers, who continued to assert, as he had done, that the object
of 'fine love' is partly at least a creation of the lover's mind.

At the end of the thirteenth century, Dante Alighieri produced
Vita Nuova,[1] a collection of thirty-one love lyrics accompanied
by a prose commentary analysing their structure and telling the
story of his love for Beatrice Portinari, a love which began in
childhood, outlasted her early death in 1290, and ultimately
inspired *La Divina Commedia*.

Dante was a friend of Cavalcanti, and his love lyrics show
signs of his influence; nevertheless his deepest affinity was with
Guinicelli, whom he calls 'il padre mio', my (poetic) father, and
whose attitude to love he endorses:

> Amore e'l cor gentil sone una cosa
> Si come il saggio in suo dittare pone,
>
> Love and the gentle heart are one same thing
> Even as the wise man in his ditty saith. . . .[2]

Dante, however, went further than Guinicelli in the idealization
of 'fine love'. Even in his childhood the ever-present image of
Beatrice 'this youngest of the Angels . . . was of so perfect a
quality that it never allowed me to be over ruled by Love without
the faithfull counsel of reason', and throughout his lady's short
life he did homage to her as to a holy being, 'the destroyer of all
evil and the Queen of all good' and found his utmost beatitude in
her salutation.

Unlike Guinicelli, Dante anticipates no divine reproach for his
glorification of a human girl; on the contrary, he tells in his
greatest poem how ten years after her death Beatrice was sent

down from heaven to ensure his salvation and to guide the 'process of ascending from heaven to heaven'[1] that was to culminate
in a first vision of God Himself. Before he could begin this
upward flight, however, Dante had to undergo a journey through
Hell and Purgatory under the guidance of Virgil, and when
Beatrice met him in the Earthly Paradise her first words to him
were words of reproach, because after her death he had forsaken
her for others and pursued false visions of good.[2]

What was the nature of Dante's apostasy? The question,
which has given rise to much discussion, raises issues of considerable interest to the reader of the *Fowre Hymnes*.

A year after the death of Beatrice, Dante, so he tells us, was
sitting in his room alone grieving over his lost lady, when looking
up he saw that a beautiful young woman 'was gazing upon me
from a window with a gaze full of pity'[3] and felt himself attracted
towards her. The ensuing 'battle of doubts' between his old and
new loves was ended by a vision of Beatrice as she at first appeared
to him in her ninth year, 'and then, this evil desire being quite
gone from me, all my thoughts turned again unto their excellent
Beatrice'.[4] There is nothing in the *Vita Nuova* to suggest that the
compassionate lady was not a real woman who for a while interrupted Dante's devotion to the memory of Beatrice. That,
however, is not the end of the matter.

About eleven years after the completion of the *Vita Nuova*
Dante began to compose a vernacular work entitled *Il Convivio,
The Banquet*,[5] because it was intended to provide a feast of learning
for men and women unacquainted with Latin. Like the earlier
work, it contains both prose and poetry, but the love lyrics are
interpreted allegorically and the whole work is written in praise
not of a human woman but of a personified Wisdom or Philosophy
whom, strangely enough, Dante identifies explicitly with the lady
of the *Vita Nuova*, whose appearance at the window occasioned
such a severe inner conflict between the old and the new love.
Her philosophical counterpart also started a similar conflict but
with a different result. In the *Vita Nuova* Dante's temporary
inconstancy is overcome by a 'strong visible phantasy' of the
child Beatrice,[6] in the *Convivio* love for philosophy gradually predominates over the thoughts of that 'blessed Beatrice who liveth
in heaven with the angels and on earth with my soul'.[7]

It is surprising that Dante gives no explanation of this discrepancy, but perhaps he felt that he had said all that was necessary
in his introductory chapter. 'And if in the present work . . . the
handling be more virile than in the *New Life* I do not intend
thereby to throw a slight in any respect upon the latter, but rather
to strengthen that by this; seeing that it conforms to reason that
that should be fervid and impassioned, this temperate and virile. . . .
And in that I spoke before entrance on the prime of manhood,
and in this when I had already passed the same.'[1] *Mutatis mutandis*,
the relationship between *Vita Nuova* and *Il Convivio* presents an
interesting parallel to the relationship between Spenser's last two
hymns and the earlier pair written 'in the greener time of my
youth', a parallel which is all the more striking because Spenser's
Sapience and Dante's Philosophy are both identified with the
personified Wisdom of the Bible.

— Whatever the nature of Dante's 'apostasy' may have been, it is
clear that as a poet he solved not only his own conflict but the
conflict between courtly and Christian love when he identified
the soul of Beatrice with the highest wisdom and made her an
agent of Divine Agape. Later generations of love poets, however,
were more influenced by Petrarch than by Dante, and Petrarch,
who never quite succeeded in reconciling his human desires with
his religious aspirations, made a different use of the troubadour
tradition.

There is no reason to doubt that the Laura whom Petrarch first
met on Good Friday 1327 was a real woman; but her identity is
unknown and there is no conclusive evidence that she was married. For some reason, however, she rejected the poet's advances,
and although Petrarch praises her virtue and beauty and recalls
moments of great happiness, many of his odes and sonnets are
filled with complaints of her cruelty, of the pains of unsatisfied
desire and the resultant pangs of an uneasy conscience. After her
death in 1348 Laura, like Beatrice, visits her lover in his dreams
and encourages him to follow her to heaven; but, unlike Dante,
Petrarch does not regard this heavenly visitation as a fulfilment
of an earthly love which was always pure and noble; on the contrary in his prose dialogue *Secretum*[2] he makes St. Augustine
reproach him for having loved Laura in the wrong way from the
start. In his *Trionfi* Amor seems more like the Ovidian deity

whom Christians should renounce than that 'lord of terrible aspect' who sacrificed Dante's heart to Beatrice and finally enabled him to be guided by her up to the highest heaven. In one of his sonnets Petrarch tells us that it is only now after ten years of mourning for his dead mistress that he can begin to turn seriously to religion in order to correct his life:

> I am tired
> Of so much error, which could well nigh thwart
> All virtue's growth; and humbly with what part
> Is left me to serve God I have desired.
> Now for lost years I sorrow and repent,
> Of which a better use I should have made. . . .[1]

As a scholar Petrarch recognized the importance of Plato, but he climbed no Platonic ladder and he helped to transmit to later poets the mediæval tradition of adding a repentant postscript to their love poetry. In their different ways, however, both Dante and Petrarch helped stimulate that revived interest in Plato which led to the formulation of the Renaissance theory of Love.

e. Neo-Platonism in the Renaissance

The history of the Florentine Platonic Academy begins in 1452, when Cosimo di Medici gave a villa at Careggi, near Florence, to Marsilio Ficino on the understanding that he would devote himself to the study of Plato and attempt a reconciliation between Platonism and Christianity. The 'Academy' which flourished under Medicean patronage was not an organized society with a rigid constitution, but a group of prominent *littérateurs*, artists and professional men who enjoyed discussing the new ideas with Ficino and with one another and formed a habit of meeting annually on November 7th, to celebrate Plato's supposed birthday by a banquet modelled on his *Symposium*. Ficino's *De Amore* (completed 1474 or 1475) is professedly an account of one such reunion, when the *Symposium* was read and expounded by seven of the assembled guests, who, unlike their prototypes at the Athenian banquet, were chiefly concerned to explain away all apparent disagreements, not only between the original Greek banqueters themselves but also between them and later Platonists. *De Amore*, therefore, throws little light on Plato, but it sets out the main tenets of Renaissance Neo-Platonism and is the chief source of later Neo-Platonic treatises and love lyrics.

God, who is at the head of the hierarchy of being, is naturally regarded as the Creator of Hebraic and Christian tradition; but He also appears to possess some of the characteristics of Plato's Demiurge and the Ineffable One of Plotinus. Being perfectly simple, He cannot be said to have the archetypal ideas separately within His mind, but He causes them to exist in the Angelic Mind, the world of Pure Intelligence, which is the primary and, according to some, the only direct creation of God. The substance of the Angelic Mind is dark and formless, a *chaos*; but because it is born of God it possesses an innate desire to return to its source, and in so returning it becomes illuminated and formed into a world, a cosmos, 'for God, who is omnipotent, created in the Angelic Mind as it cleaved to Him the forms of all things to be created'.[1] This provides an answer to the question suggested by discussion of Plato's *Symposium* namely: 'Why Phaedrus said that Love was older than Saturn and Jupiter but Agathon said that Love was younger'. Ficino's answer is that God created the Angelic Mind out of beneficent Love and 'this mind as soon as it is born recognizing its parent, loves Him'. The Creator's love for His child is, of course, older than the creature's love for its parent. 'However, the Angelic Mind did not receive from its father the ideas of the planet Saturn and the others [i.e. the other planets] until it was attracted towards His countenance by innate love. . . . Thus therefore the love of that Angelic Mind for God is partly older than the ideas which are called gods and partly younger.'[2]

This process, which begins in the Angelic Mind, is repeated down the scale of Being. The World Soul which comes next in the hierarchy is primarily chaotic, but turning in love to the Angelic Mind it thence receives ideas which it converts into the concepts of all the varied objects of the physical world. For unlike the Angelic Mind, the World Soul is mobile. It has the power not only of reasoning, but of sensation and generation, and it is this generative power of the Soul, sometimes called Nature, which turns concepts into 'seeds' and so produces all those shapes which are really mere shadows and images of the real archetypal ideas existing in the Angelic Mind. The third grade of Being is therefore the World Body. Matter itself hardly counts as a grade of Being since it is a mere potentiality for the reception of form. The Florentine Neo-Platonists sometimes describe this cosmic process as circular, sometimes as a descending and ascending movement but the underlying idea is much the same in either case. Each order of Being imparts, without loss to itself, something of its properties to the order below it, and each order of Being changes from chaos to cosmos by turning in love to the order above it. So Love or Eros is the great power which animates, orders and beautifies the whole universe.

It is on this Neo-Platonic cosmology and particularly on Ficino's interpretation of Plato's myth of the birth of Eros in the light of it, that the first part of Spenser's *Hymne of Love* is based. Since, according to Ficino, the 'double Venus' of the *Symposium* is to be interpreted as the power of Intelligence in the Angelic Mind and the power of Generation in the World Soul, it follows that the birthday of Venus means the day when the Angelic Mind and the World Soul were born of the majesty of the supreme God, and the statement that the gods were feasting on that occasion is a way of saying that the supreme God was pre-existent to that event. Love was born of the union of Porus and Penia, that is to say of Plenty and Poverty, for 'Porus is the Son of Thought. . . . By "the garden of Jupiter" Diotima means the richness of the Angelic life into which, when Porus, that is the light of God, . . . descends and mixes with Penia, that is the former lack of the light, he creates love. In the beginning, the Angelic Mind exists and has its being through God, . . . It has, moreover, the power of understanding, which we call Venus. Power of this sort is of its very nature formless and dark unless it is illuminated by God, just like the strength of the eye before the arrival of the sun.'[1]

Ficino's interpretation of the Platonic myth is based on that of Plotinus who interprets Porus as 'the lavishness, the abundance of beauty',[2] an interpretation which alters its meaning in a very significant way. In the *Symposium* it is clear from the context that the Greek word πόρος should be translated as 'contrivance' rather than 'abundance', and that the Father of Eros is more accurately described as Resource the son of Cunning than as Plenty the son of Thought. Plato's Love lacks beauty but knows how to acquire it, Ficino's Love knows the way to acquire and spread beauty because he is already in partial possession of it.

'Therefore since lovers partly have and partly have not what they seek, it is very true that love is a combination of a certain poverty and plenty. For this reason that heavenly Venus [i.e. the Angelic Mind], aroused by the first sensation of the divine light itself, is drawn by love to the whole richness of the full light, and by this force clinging more closely to her parent, she glows immediately with His fullest light. . . .'[1]

It is important to recognize that for Ficino Venus is a personification of the Angelic Mind, whereas 'Beauty is the Splendour of the Divine Countenance' and consequently is more or less identical with Porus 'which is the light of God'. Ficino explicitly contradicted Pico and those who held that beauty consists in a harmonious disposition of parts and consequently denied that beauty can exist in God who is One. On the contrary, there can be a beautiful simplicity 'so the simple light of the One Itself in everything is infinite beauty. . . . So the light and beauty of God, which is pure, free from all things, is called, without the slightest question, infinite beauty. But infinite beauty demands a vast love. . . .' This love is due to God from men but it is also given by God to Himself: 'And so the source of all beauty and love is God. . . . God is never so deceived as to love the shadow of His own beauty in the Angelic Mind and to neglect His own true beauty.'[2]

Ficino's interpretation, or misinterpretation, of the Platonic Porus, by stressing God's initiative brought his cosmology nearer to the Christian doctrine of creation; nevertheless it was derived from Plotinus and it remains more akin to earlier Neo-Platonic doctrines of emanation, doctrines which imply that the downward movement towards multiplicity and materiality is a movement for the worse and that the 'fall' of man is the fall into a body. On this subject indeed Ficino is not always consistent, but there is little doubt that for him and still more for some of his followers the rise of man is a flight away from the physical world, and that the highest form of love is a desire for intellectual beauty which leads to the love of God.

The ascent of this ladder of love which is touched upon in the last speech of Ficino's *De Amore* is the main theme of Girolamo Benivieni's very obscure poem *Canzone dell' Amor Divine* and Pico della Mirandola's more lucid prose commentary on it. A particularly clear account of the lover's upward progress is given by Pico in Book 3 Ch. 10 of this work.[1] The ascent takes place in six degrees. At the lowest rung of the ladder, the lover loves the physical beauty of a particular person. At the second step he forms a mental image of the beloved and by thus separating it from matter brings it a little nearer to ideal beauty. His third step is to realize that the mental image of perfect physical beauty cannot be associated with one particular person and he proceeds to consider the universal nature of corporeal beauty, which is the highest degree the soul can reach while she goes no further than sense perception. But now the turning point comes, and at the fourth step the soul withdraws from the outward object and engages in introversion. Having reflected that everything founded in matter is particular, she concludes that this universality proceeds, not from the outward object, but her own intrinsic power, and begins to love the image of Ideal Intellectual Beauty which she discovers in her own mind. But she cannot rest there. No particular human intellect can comprehend the fullness of beauty, so the lover seeks to identify himself with the angelic Mind, the dwelling-place of ideal beauty, and, when he is successful, he reaches the sixth and last step, where he enjoys the angelic vision of God and is united to Him as closely as it is possible for a creature to be.

Since Ficino and Pico are professing to expound a philosophy, they naturally place human love in a cosmic setting. For them the ladder of love, which exists in the individual mind, is analogous to, even partially identical with, the great ladder which extends from top to bottom of the universe. Their system was accepted as Neo-Platonic orthodoxy and their ideas were constantly repeated in the Love-treatises of the Renaissance. There were, however, important differences of mood and tone. Both Pietro Bembo's *Gli Asolani* and Baldassare Castiglione's *Il Cortigeano* (*The Courtier*) are ostensibly based on recollections of actual conversations; but, unlike the banqueters in *De Amore*, the speakers express their ideas not by a series of learned disquisitions, but by social talk in an attractive courtly environment.

The conversations recorded by Bembo are supposed to have taken place in the grounds of the Castle of Asola during the marriage festivities of a favourite maid of honour of the Queen

of Cyprus. Three of the young men present, Gismondo, Perot-
tino, and Lavinello, decide to spend their siestas discussing the
nature of love. The setting is idyllic, the account is obviously
idealized and at least partly fictitious.

After Love has been praised and dispraised on two successive
days, the proceedings culminate on the third afternoon, when
Lavinello gives an eloquent disquisition on the true nature of Love
derived—so he claims—from the instructions of a spiritually
gifted hermit. According to that holy man love of beautiful
women is justified in so far as it leads on to the more satisfying
love of the beauty of the universe and its Creator. As a means of
passing from human to heavenly Love the hermit advises a sustained contemplation of the ordered beauty of the Ptolemaic
universe, 'But your delight and wonder will be even greater,
Lavinello, if you can pass from these heavens which you see
to those which are unseen . . . ascending from one to another until
you raise your desires to that beauty which surpasses them and
every other beauty . . . beyond this sensible material world of
which I have spoken . . . there lies another world which is neither
material nor evident to sense, but completely separated from this
and pure; a world which turns round this one and is both sought
and found by it, wholly divided from it and wholly abiding in
each part of it; a world divine, intelligent and full of light'. A
world which contains all that our world contains but in more
perfect form, a world which surpasses itself more and more as 'it
draws nearer to its Final Cause'. Lavinello's friends then will do
well, 'remembering that they are in a temple', to court God as
hitherto they have courted their mistresses and having cast aside
'false earthly mortal love . . . clothe themselves in that which is
true, celestial and immortal'.[1]

Castiglione begins his *Courtier* by a charming description of the
intellectual and artistic and highly civilized life that prevailed in
the palace of the Duke of Urbino; and his book professes to be a
record of a series of evening entertainments, when a distinguished
company of men and women discussed the nature of the perfect
courtier. When the character of this perfect gentleman has been
completed, discussion turns on his social function and the question
arises as to whether the elderly courtier can be a lover as well as a
valuable councillor of his prince. An affirmative answer is put

into the mouth of Pietro Bembo and made the occasion for a long
and enthusiastic exposition of the Ladder of Love. The implied
cosmology is that of Ficino and Pico and of *Asolani*; but, as is
natural in the circumstances, Bembo is here seen to be more
concerned with the emotions and experiences of men in the world
than with the ascent to the Angelic Mind and, although he is in
earnest, he is so far from being disconcerted by the witty comments of his listeners that he joins in their laughter and can
descend from the heights of contemplation and ecstatic prayer, to
return a gallant answer to the Lady Emilia with an unselfconscious
ease which could only be possible in a highly sophisticated society.
'When Bembo had hetherto spoken with such vehemencie that a
man woulde have thought him (as it were) ravished and beside himselfe hee stood still without once moving, holding his eyes towards
heaven as astonied: when the Ladie Emilia, which together with the
rest gave most diligent eare to this talke, tooke him, by the plaite of
his garment, and plucking him a little saide. Take heede (Maister
Peter) that these thoughts make not your soule also to forsake the
bodie. Madam, answered Maister Peter, it should not be the
first miracle that love hath wrought in me.'[1]

The ability to veer without embarrassment from high seriousness to gallantry and mock gravity is a recurrent feature of
sixteenth-century poetry, and disregard of it can lead to misinterpretation. Spenser was influenced by the *Canzone dell' Amore* and
sometimes practically translates from that poem; but in attitude
and tone his *Hymne of Love* is nearer to the flexible urbanity of
Castiglione than to the stiff metaphysical solemnity of Benivieni.
One must not, however, exaggerate differences. The spirit of the
Florentine Academy seems to have been not altogether unlike
that of the delightful court of Urbino. The Renaissance gentleman
did not have to leave the court in order to contemplate God or
talk philosophy; still less did he have to enter a cloister.

- But if he intended to progress, he had to part company with the
devotees of the popular Eros. Castiglione does not expect much
spiritual improvement during youth, but if the old courtier wants
to be respected as a lover he must emancipate himself from sensual
desire. Does this mean that the lover can only reach the top of the
ladder by detaching himself from the beloved human being who
started him on the upward way? The question is very important to

the reader of Spenser's *Fowre Hymnes* but it is not easy to answer. On this subject the Neo-Platonists are neither consistent nor unanimous. In the *De Amore*, Ficino makes 'Pausanius' disapprove not of physical love itself but only of its abuse. The dignity of love is profaned when a man neglects contemplation because he is too eager for procreation and when he prefers the beauty of the body to that of the soul. The true lover will, of course, value bodily beauty, but only because it reflects the more excellent beauty of the soul. 'Moreover, he performs the function of generation and coition within the bounds prescribed by natural law and civil laws drawn up by men of wisdom'.[1] At other times, however, Ficino speaks less moderately: 'Love and the desire for physical union are not only not identical impulses, but are proved to be opposite ones'.[2] Pico holds much the same opinion. The desire for the coitus, though not exactly condemned by him, is depreciated as something that we possess in common with the brutes and cannot properly be called human love.

Sometimes, however, ascent of the Ladder seems to involve increasing detachment even from human love. Pico, as we have seen, tells us that at the third step the lover turns away from the particular image of his beloved to adore the idea of universal beauty, which has been created by the 'intrinsical power' of his own mind. It is this awareness of his ability to generalize, which convinces him of the superiority of mind over matter and enables him to achieve his quest and unite himself with the Divine Beauty.

Most of the Neo-Platonists agree in affirming the importance of this moment of introversion; but Ficino has also much to say of the spiritual creativity which results from the marriage of minds, and in his *Dialoghi d'Amore* (*c.* 1502) Leone Ebreo lays great stress on the unifying function of love, which is manifest not only in the love of the inferior for the superior, but even more in the love of the superior for the inferior, which is supremely manifested in the paternal love of the Creator for his Creation.

– Leone Ebreo's philosophy was derived from that of Ficino and theoretically, no doubt, most of what he said could be squared with orthodox Neo-Platonism; but his emphasis is markedly different and he reverses the usual account of the lover's progress, by asserting that spiritual love precedes and generates physical

desire. When in the *Dialoghi d'Amore* Sophia accuses Philo of
placing the goal of love in the sense of touch, the latter replies:
'I do not admit that this is the end of perfect love; but I have
been telling you that this act, far from dissolving perfect love,
rather confirms and integrates it. . . . Furthermore, when two
spirits are united in spiritual love, their bodies desire to enjoy
such union as is possible, so that no distinction may persist, but
the union be in all ways perfect . . . a corresponding physical
union increases and perfects the spiritual love. . . .'[1] This account
of the love which unites particular human beings both in soul
and body is applicable *mutatis mutandis* to the love which unites
God to the universe. Having asserted that, since to give is nobler
than to gain, the love of the higher for the lower is nobler than
the love of the lower for the higher, Philo has to meet two
objections: firstly that since desire presupposes lack of that which
is desired, this lack, or defect, must be in the lover rather than in
the beloved; secondly: 'that the beloved, *quâ* beloved, is of greater
worth than the lover; for love is of the good, and the beloved is
the end and purpose of the lover, and the end is nobler than that
which subserves it. How then can the imperfect be loved by the
perfect?' Is the universe then of greater worth than God, because
it is the object of his love? The answer is that the ultimate object of
the Divine Lover is the Universe perfected and united to Himself
by Divine Love. No father can be satisfied while his son is imperfect. The cause loves its effect and by delivering it from imperfection delivers itself. 'Thus there is reason, not only in the love of
the inferior for the superior and desire to be united therewith, but
no less in the love of the superior for the inferior and desire to unite
therewithal, to the end that each may in his degree be perfect without flaw and that the Universe may be progressively united and
bound with the bond of love which unites the corporeal with the
spiritual world and the lower with the higher: this union with all
diversity co-ordinated and all plurality unified being the chief end
of the supreme Artificer, Almighty God, when he created the
world.'[2] No doubt many Neo-Platonists agreed with this in
theory, but their emphasis is very different. They usually describe
the birth of love as taking place not in the Divine, but in the
Angelic Mind, and the consummation that interests them is not

the fulfilment of Divine love in a perfected creation but the fulfilment of human love in a union with God which amounts to
apotheosis. 'I, from an inferior thing do change me to a god' is
a characteristic declaration of one of the 'Heroic Enthusiasts' in
Giordano Bruno's *De Gl' heroici furori*, a work which illustrates in
an extreme form this kind of spiritual ambition.[1]

De Gl' heroici furori (1585) was the last of six philosophical
dialogues written in Italian, but composed and published during
Bruno's visit to England and dedicated by him to Sir Philip
Sidney. It consists of a number of allegorical love sonnets, a few
of them the work of other authors, but all of them interpreted by
means of prose dialogues in which one of the interlocutors
obviously expresses the view of Bruno himself.

The prefatory argument opens with a violent repudiation of
'Petrarchanism'. His own poems, Bruno insists, are addressed to
no woman alive or dead. 'Heroic Fury' is indeed a madness, but
it is a madness springing from love of God not from 'submission
to the tyranny of a stupid, imbecile, unworthy and dirty piece of
dung'.[2] Bruno, so he assures Sidney, is not frigid, he is no
enemy to generation or sexual passion, but he maintains that
women should be loved not as goddesses but as women, and the
only use of women is to satisfy physical desire and to bear children.
Similar views are voiced in the treatise itself, though in more
moderate terms. The final object of all heroic love is the Divine
Beauty and Goodness, but corporeal beauty can be an index of
spiritual beauty, a shadow of Divinity and the higher and lower
forms of love sometimes co-exist. Even the heroic lover cannot
always remain on the heights: 'he commonly wanders and trans-
ports himself, now into one, now into another form of the double
Eros; therefore, the principal lesson that Love gives to him is,
that he contemplate the divine beauty in shadow, when he cannot
do so in the mirror, and, like the suitors of Penelope, he entertain
himself with the maids when he is not permitted to converse with
the mistress'.[3] But only those of a barbarous nature will confine
themselves to the enjoyment of physical love: 'to say the truth,
that object, which beyond the beauty of the body has no other
splendour, is not worthy of being loved otherwise than to make
the race; and it seems to me the work of a pig or a horse to
torment oneself about it, and, as to myself never was I more

fascinated by such things than I am now fascinated by some
statue or picture to which I am indifferent.'[1]

Whereas most of the Neo-Platonists lose interest in feminine
beauty at a certain stage of their journey, Bruno disdains it from
the start. His use of imagery suggests that he envisaged heroic
love as the flight of a bird, the hunting of a prey, a conflict, even
an Icarian fall rather than the systematic climbing of a ladder.
Bruno's doctrine of love is indeed deliberately paradoxical. He
divides the lovers of God into two kinds: the first being simple
or ignorant men directly inspired or rather possessed by the
Divine Spirit; the second being men of intelligence whose quest
for God is prompted by will and guided by reason. The first
kind possess the Divinity, the second kind are superior because
they *are* divine: 'in the first the divinity is contemplated as an
object of admiration, worship and obedience, in the second it is
the excellence of their own humanity which is contemplated'.[2]

The heroic enthusiast, however, manifests the limitations as
well as the excellence of human intelligence. His love is agonizing
because infinite desire for infinite beauty can never be fully satisfied. There are indeed moments of illumination and ecstasy when
the lover recognizes his divinity and becomes one with the object
of his love; but even these moments have a tragic quality, because
to live as a god is to die as a human being. The myth of Actaeon
who saw Artemis naked and was changed into a stag and killed
by his own hounds is a symbol of this experience. 'Actaeon
signifies the intellect intent on the pursuit of divine wisdom and
the apprehension of divine beauty.' His hounds signify his
thoughts and his fate a mystic death which enables him to live
'the life of the gods, fed on Ambrosia and drunk with Nectar'.
Actaeon begins by hunting for an external goodness and wisdom;
but when he has found what he sought he is wrapt out of himself
and 'perceives that he himself has become the desired prey of his
dogs, his thoughts, and that having contracted the deity into
himself it is no longer necessary to seek outside himself for it'.[3]

Spenser could hardly have failed to be acquainted with Bruno's
works, and certain passages in *The Fairie Queene* and *Colin Clout's
Come Home Again* may show signs of their influence; but Miss
Lilian Winstanley's contention that Bruno is one of the main
sources of the *Fowre Hymnes* is not convincing. The Actaeon

sonnet and its prose exposition furnish a striking example of a
fervent humanistic pride which pervades the whole of *De Gl'heroici
furori* but is totally absent from the *Fowre Hymnes*. Spenser's
temper of mind is nearer to that of Leone Ebreo than to that of
Bruno, and since the *Dialoghi d'Amore* was frequently translated
and reprinted during the sixteenth century he may very well have
known it. When, therefore, in the third hymn he identifies Love
with the divine Agape rather than with the human or daemonic
Eros he is not necessarily repudiating every form of Renaissance
Neo-Platonism. On the other hand some scholars suggest that he
may be speaking not as a Platonist of any kind, but as a Protestant.

f. The Influence of Protestantism

For Spenser, as for all his contemporaries, the struggle between
Roman Catholicism and Protestantism had all the urgency and
the confusing complications that the struggle between Democracy
and Communism has for us today. It is impossible here to give
even a superficial account of the ramifications and cross-currents
of the theological controversy or of Spenser's attitude to it. But
some consideration of the implications of the central Protestant
doctrine of 'Justification by Faith alone' is an essential preliminary
to the study of the *Fowre Hymnes*—especially if the Lutheran
scholar, Bishop Nygren, is right in supposing that the conflict
about faith was really a conflict about love, and that Luther's
fundamental aim was to shatter the mediæval doctrine of *caritas* —
(i.e. the love of men primarily for God and secondarily for one
another), in order to free the Christian theocentric Agape-love from
its unholy alliance with the pagan anthropocentric Eros, which
had been initiated by St. Augustine and maintained (though not
without tension and conflict) throughout the middle ages.

From the Protestant point of view, this doctrine of *caritas*—
especially as interpreted by mediæval mystics—was open to two
main objections: firstly, its teaching that men ought to desire God
as their supreme good implied approval of egocentric Eros-
love; secondly its teaching that God had granted men some
power to co-operate willingly with His prevenient grace suggested that men could acquire merit, could contribute something
at least to their own salvation. Certain passages from John
Ruysbroeck illustrate this point very clearly, and indeed it is

the fundamental premise of his mystical treatise *The Adornment of the Spiritual Marriage*. 'Prevenient grace', says Ruysbroeck, 'is common to all men, Pagan and Jew, good and
evil. By reason of His common love, which God has toward
all men, He has caused His name and the redemption of human
nature to be preached and revealed to the uttermost parts of
the earth. Whosoever wishes to turn to Him can turn to Him . . .
for God wishes to save all men and to lose not one.' If a man
does all he can to respond to prevenient grace, God bestows
upon him efficacious grace that makes possible the free conversion of the will. 'Of these two things—that is to say, the
grace of God and the free conversion of the will enlightened
by grace—charity, that is Divine love, is born.'[1] According to
Nygren both Ficino and Luther desired to shatter this mediæval
synthesis between pagan and Christian thought but with different
ends in view. Ficino's attempt to reconcile Platonism and Christianity was really an attempt to free Eros from Agape in order to
uphold the dignity of man; Luther was concerned to free Agape
from Eros in order to proclaim the generosity of God. For if, as
Nygren maintains, any recognition of worth in the beloved
object renders love for it acquisitive, it follows that man's love
for God must be egoistic, and conversely, since God's love for
man is necessarily altruistic, it must therefore be not only uncaused by any human merit, but the sole cause even of the faith
and gratitude with which some men receive it. The grim corollary
to this is that since some men exhibit neither faith nor gratitude it
must be because God has chosen to limit His generosity.

Bishop Nygren's views have not passed unchallenged, but his
learning is unquestionable. It is true, as Bishop Nygren acknowledges, that Luther himself did not speak of a conflict between
Agape and Eros, but he did claim to be attacking the paganism
of the Roman Church and recalling Christians to the original faith
of the Gospel, and although in *The Bondage of the Will* he asserts
the omnipotence and inscrutability of God's will rather than His
loving kindness, nevertheless in *The Freedom of a Christian* he
speaks most movingly of Christ's self-sacrificing love and of how
our good works should spring from gratitude for grace received
rather than from a self-regarding desire to acquire it. It is therefore arguable that in his two last hymns Spenser is speaking as a

good Protestant and is recanting not youthful passion but pagan
spirituality.

The problem which faced the sixteenth-century Reformers was
not a new one; indeed it was almost coeval with Christianity,
for the influx of Gentile converts inevitably raised the question of
the relationship of the Christian Church to Judaism on the one
hand and to Graeco-Roman culture on the other. The question
has never been settled. 'Hebraism and Hellenism', explains
Matthew Arnold, 'between these two points of influence moves
our world. At one time it feels more powerfully the attraction of
one of them, at another time of the other; and it ought to be,
though it never is, evenly and happily balanced between them.'
How indeed could it be if 'the uppermost idea with Hellenism is to
see things as they really are' while it is the 'essential bent of
Hebraism to set doing above knowing'.[1]

Arnold's diagnosis of the tension in Western culture is different
from but not incompatible with that of Bishop Nygren, for the
insistence on obedient conduct and disinterested love can both
be traced back to the belief that God is not the Absolute Being
discovered by the philosophic mind, but the living Creator who
acts through history, and reveals to the Prophets and the inspired
authors of the Bible truths that the human intellect could not
discover for itself. These truths of revelation concern the requirements of God's will, the inability of fallen man to meet those
requirements, and God's gracious action on his behalf. Sin is
rebellious self-assertion, therefore no man can save himself,
because it is precisely his will to be saved that has become corrupt.
To rescue him, God enters history and in the person of Christ
performs an act of utter self-sacrifice, that *demonstrates* that God is
Agape, and inaugurates a new relationship between God and man
open to all those who believe the good news of God's forgiveness
and enter the Christian Church.

But what of the unbelievers, the unconverted, the good Pagans?
Why does not God save everyone? One answer, as we have
seen, is that God offers his grace to all, but leaves men free to reject
or accept it, and some choose to reject it. To quote Ruysbrock
again: 'The prevenient grace touches all men, God bestowing
it upon all men. But not all men give on their part the conversion
of the will and the purification of conscience; and that is why

so many lack the grace of God, through which they should merit
eternal life.' The difficulty here is that even this limited freedom
detracts from God's omnipotence and omniscience and even the
smallest contribution by men to their own salvation impairs the
uncaused, creative character of God's love. The answer formu-
lated by St. Augustine was that since God is omnipotent and
omniscient and his grace irresistible, the division between Elect
and Reprobate has been decreed by His Will. Since all men
without exception deserve damnation, God leaves some to their
deserts in order to manifest his justice; but others he saves out of
purely gratuitous mercy and excites in them a love of Himself.
As soon as you love God the moral conflict is won. 'Love and
do what you like', because you only like to do the will of your
beloved. What is the nature of this love which God's grace makes
possible to chosen souls? It is *caritas*, an ordered love that seeks
to enjoy God as the supreme good and to love its neighbours in
and for Him. This is Eros-love because the soul is seeking to
satisfy its needs; on the other hand it is not selfish because it leads
us to find our good not in our isolated selves but in God, and
finally brings us to the Heavenly City where jealousy is unknown
and we rejoice in our allotted place in God's order because our
wills have become one with the Divine Will. None of this is our
doing, for God gives us Himself not only as the object of our love
but as the love with which we love Him. So the Divine Agape
stirs up in us an Eros-love which, when it reaches its goal, is
indistinguishable from Agape. But all this applies only to the
Elect, for it is God's will to withhold his grace from the Reprobate
and abandon them to the outer darkness which all men have
deserved.[1] St. Augustine had a powerful and lasting influence on
later theological thought; but a milder interpretation of the works
of God's grace was never completely banished and could equally
well serve as a basis for the doctrine of *caritas*.

The theological problem of Salvation was connected with more
practical problems of culture and education. Had the Fall impaired
man's reason as well as his will? Was pagan philosophy entirely
valueless? Was there no valid knowledge of God apart from
revelation? Though the debate continued intermittently for
centuries, it did not prevent the Church from absorbing classical
culture. Our concern, however, is not with history, but with the

problem of the relationship of faith and reason as it presented
itself to men in the sixteenth century.

According to St. Thomas Aquinas 'the divine rights of grace
do not abolish the human rights of natural reason'.[1] By exercising
their reason aright men could arrive at important ethical and
religious truths, and both the existence of God and a universally
binding moral law could be proved by rational argument. Reason,
however, was not enough to procure salvation, and the saving
truths of revelation had to be accepted by faith. But, although
faith teaches us supernatural truths, it neither supersedes nor
contradicts the findings of our natural reason and there is no
need to reject all pagan culture. If the Bible is divinely inspired
and the Aristotelian philosophy intellectually sound, there can be
no radical incompatibility between them, and so St. Thomas
Aquinas proceeds to construct a philosophical synthesis, built on
the foundation of a Christianized Aristotle. Although St. Thomas
believed in predestination, his doctrine of the validity but limited
scope of human reason corresponds well with belief in the real
but limited power of human free will, and both doctrines are
deducible from the Catholic belief that the Fall has seriously
damaged but not wholly destroyed the Divine Image in Man.

It was the assertion of some worth, some vestige of good, some
power of co-operation with the unmerited Divine Grace which
evoked the opposition of the Reformers and led them to lay an
ever-increasing stress on the doctrine of Predestination and that
in its severest form. We are justified, not by any religious works,
but by faith and trust in God's gift of grace; but this justifying
faith is also God's gift, and He has decided from all eternity to
grant it to some and withhold it from others—even the Fall of
Adam having been pre-ordained. As William Perkins put it:
'Now we know this, that man's creation, and his fall in Adam,
are but means to execute God's predestination and therefore are
subordinate to it: but the end of God's decree, is the manifestation
of his glory, in saving some, and condemning others.'[2] Perkins
was a Calvinist, but Luther and Calvin are at one as to the arbitrary character of God's judgment. 'What God wills is not
right because He ought, or was bound, so to will; on the contrary,
what takes place must be right, because He so wills it'[3] says
Luther to Erasmus, and if Erasmus objects that Luther's God

seems 'to delight in the torments of poor wretches and to be a fitter object for hate than for love', he is reminded that human reason is not competent to judge the acts of God, and to presume to do so is an act of egoism and pride.[1] It is not surprising that Luther wanted to banish most of Aristotle's writings from the university curriculum: '. . . this defunct pagan has attained supremacy; impeded and almost suppressed the scriptures of the living God. . . . I cannot avoid believing that the Evil One introduced the study of Aristotle . . . his book on Ethics is worse than any other book being the direct opposite of God's grace and the Christian virtues.'[2] It is important, however, to remember that in this, as in other matters, there were considerable differences of opinion among Protestants, and that in Elizabethan England the doctrine of predestination, or rather the interpretation of it, was a subject of controversy within the national church, to which the Puritans were still supposed to belong.[3]

In the famous dispute between Hooker and Travers at the Temple, when 'the forenoon sermon spake Canterbury and the afternoon Geneva',[4] Travers, Hooker tells us, 'questioned about the matter of reprobation, misliking first that I had termed God a permissive and no positive cause of the evil which the schoolmen do call *malum culpae*; secondly that to their objection who say, "If I be elected, do what I will I shall be saved", I had answered, that the will of God in this thing is not absolute but conditional, to save His elect believing, fearing, and obediently serving Him; thirdly that to stop the mouths of such as grudge and repine against God for rejecting castaways, I had taught that they are not rejected, no not in the purpose and counsel of God, without a foreseen worthiness of rejection going though not in time yet in order before'. Hooker believed in justification by faith, and emphatically denied that we can of our own unaided free will do anything to merit salvation; but he also affirmed that God's grace was resistible and denied that any lost soul would ever 'be able to say unto God, Thou didst plunge me into the depth and assign me unto endless torments only to satisfy thine own will'.[5]

Travers objected not only to his adversary's opinions but to his method of defending them. When asked to produce his authority for his doctrine of predestination 'he answered me' says Travers, 'that his best author was his own reason'; but, of course, to

Hooker, who on this topic agreed with the schoolmen, his reason was to be respected not because it was his own but because it was the voice of God within. In his great apologia for the Elizabethan Establishment, Hooker traced the disputes between Episcopalians and Puritans to a fundamental disagreement about the Divine Will and the relationship between reason and revelation.

In the first chapter of *Laws of Ecclesiastical Polity* Hooker opens his argument 'with consideration of the nature of law in general', and gives reasons for applying the term to any kind of rule by which actions are directed towards a fore-conceived end, instead of restricting it to rule imposed by superior authority, and also for holding that, when the word is used in this larger sense, it can be rightly said that 'God is a law both to Himself and to all other things beside'. All things are created and governed by God's will; but God's will, though omnipotent, is not arbitrary: 'God worketh nothing without cause . . . that and nothing else is done by God which to leave undone were not so good . . .' and that helps us to understand why He created the universe. 'The general end of God's external working is the exercise of His most glorious and most abundant virtue. . . . Not that anything is made to be beneficial unto Him, but all things for Him to show beneficence and grace in them. . . . They err therefore who think that of the will of God to do this or that there is no reason besides His will nor is the freedom of the will of God any whit abated, let or hindered, by means of this; because the imposition of this law upon Himself is His own free and voluntary act.'[1] Hooker admits that for God's particular actions there are 'many times no reason known to us', but if the Divine Will acts in accordance with the Divine Reason, and if human reason is the voice of God within, why, then, it follows that human reason must be capable of reaching sound conclusions not only about purely secular affairs (that was never denied), but also about some questions of religion, moral doctrine and church policy.

Faith in the Christian revelation is indeed necessary to salvation, but true faith can neither contradict reason nor render it superfluous, and consequently the wisdom of the pagan philosophers is not to be despised: 'There is in the world no kind of knowledge, whereby any part of truth is seen, but we justly account it precious;

yea, that principal truth in comparison whereof all other knowledge is vile [i.e. Scriptural truth], may receive from it some kind
of light; whether it be that Egyptian and Chaldean wisdom
mathematical, wherewith Moses and Daniel were furnished; . . .
or that rational and oratorial wisdom of the Grecians, which the
apostle St. Paul brought from Tarsus; or that Judaical, which he
learned in Jerusalem sitting at the feet of Gamaliel: to detract
from the dignity thereof were to injure even God Himself, who
being that light which none can approach unto, hath sent out these
lights whereof we are capable, even as so many sparkles resembling the bright fountain from which they rise.'[1] Hooker comes
very near to achieving that balance between Hellenism and
Hebraism desired by Matthew Arnold.

Where did Spenser stand? He is often called a Puritan, but it
seems unlikely that the secretary of Bishop Young was an enemy
of Episcopacy. The fact that he was a partisan of Leicester is no
proof that he shared all his patron's religious views. He apparently
believed in predestination,[2] but there is no evidence that he held
the extreme Calvinistic form of this doctrine. Obviously the
author of the *Faerie Queene* and particularly of Book II did not
regard Aristotle's *Ethics* as a work of the Devil or distrust Reason
as a moral guide. The possibility that he shared Hooker's views
on other matters deserves consideration.

III. FOWRE HYMNES

a. The Problem

THE interpretation of the *Fowre Hymnes* has been the subject of
much inconclusive discussion. The questions at issue are fully
considered by Robert Ellrodt in his learned thesis *Neo-Platonism
in the Poetry of Spenser*. Here it is only possible to give the barest
outline of a most complicated debate.

Disagreement begins over the interpretations of the dedicatory
preface. Are we to believe Spenser when he tells us that the last
two hymns are 'retractations' of the first two, which were the
more frivolous products of his youth? For some time Spenser's
statement was accepted as literally true, but in the last half of the
nineteenth century, critics began to point out that all four hymns
are too similar in style to have been composed at widely different

periods; that since the Palinode was in fashion the designed contrast between the two pairs need not imply moral repudiation, and both the prose preface and the second and third stanzas of *An Hymne of Heavenly Love* might be chiefly intended to give structural unity to the whole composition. I find it hard, indeed, to believe that Spenser would have dared to publish a completely false statement about the attitude and behaviour of the noble ladies to whom his work was dedicated; but it is a plausible theory that he was referring to earlier versions of the two first hymns which had been drastically revised and 'reformed' in every sense of the word, brought up to date in style and purged of excessive sensuality. At this point further problems arise. Spenser recants in his poems as well as in his Dedication. Why should Spenser recant hymns which, whether reformed or unreformed, express a lofty and spiritual ideal of love between the sexes? What was he recanting, and why? Are the first hymns Petrarchan or Platonic? Are the last hymns Platonic or Protestant? Are all four hymns Platonic and intended to depict various stages of the Ladder of Love, or were they all from the start written from a strictly orthodox point of view and planned to emphasize the contrast between Christianity and Neo-Platonism?

Before attempting to answer any of these questions, it is well to remind ourselves that since Spenser is writing poetry not versified philosophy, much of his meaning will be conveyed by style, structure and the use of literary conventions; and it is, therefore, important to consider the poetic and *fictitious* character of these hymns and the nature of the genre to which they belong.

The history of the hymn is complicated and obscure, but for our purpose it is sufficient to recall that it originated in ancient Greece and was closely connected with religious cult. In its specific sense it denoted a song to a divinity and consisted in an invocation to a god, a prayer for his favour, and it usually included stories concerned with his birth, his achievements and the propagation of his cult. During the heyday of Greek lyric poetry, hymns were often sung in unison by a procession of choristers as they marched towards the temple and stationed themselves around the altar.[1]

When the ancient hymn was revived in Renaissance Italy its ritual character could naturally not be recovered. Some of the

extant hymns of the Hellenistic and Roman periods, however,
were already purely literary and philosophical in character, and
in others references to rites, processions and festive ceremonial
could and did influence the style and content of later poetry.
Spenser's first two hymns show unmistakable traces of this
ritualistic influence but also owe much to Benivieni's *Canzone
d'Amore* which, in spite of its title, must be classified as a philosophic hymn.[1]

It should not, however, be overlooked that they also owe something to mediæval tradition. In employing the seven-lined stanza
known as rhyme-royal, Spenser was following the example of
Chaucer; and, in the first two hymns, the poet's tongue does at
times seem to be that of the troubadour rather than that of the
Neo-Platonic philosopher.

b. *An Hymne in Honour of Love*

The *Hymne of Love* begins with the customary invocation and
prayer. The poet is preparing a song of praise as a propitiatory
offering to his god and we are asked to suppose that the description of the birth of Love and the extension of his power is intended
to be chanted by a procession of devotees. Muses, Nymphs,
beautiful Virgins are all summoned:

> Prepare yourselves, to march amongst his host,
> And all the way this sacred hymne do sing
> Made in the honor of your Sovereign King.

In his choice of genre Spenser was not only following a literary
fashion, he was also expressing something fundamental in his own
imaginative life; for, besides sharing the contemporary taste for
pageantry, he had an unusually profound consciousness of the
connection between religious and social ritual and the rhythmic
sequences of nature. *Amoretti* and *Epithalamion* illustrate this very
clearly; and it is arguable that the first hymn is the most poetically
successful and owes its success largely to its ceremonial quality.
Spenser could set his secular love-chant into a mythical, ritualistic
framework, but when writing Christian hymns he had 'to versify
the truth not poetize', a procedure perhaps less congenial to him
than to his contemporary Samuel Daniel. In this connection it is
illuminating to compare *An Hymne of Love* with Benivieni's

Canzone d'Amore, a poem which Spenser obviously knew well and which in some ways may have served him as a model.[1]

Both poets begin and end with a direct address to Love, under whose sway they have for long been living; both poets distrust their own powers, but expect Love himself to inspire them and enable them to sing the strange nature of his birth, his progress, his mighty powers, his influence on human and on cosmic life. For both poets, the movement of Love is an upward movement initiated by the desire for beauty, and both poets praise Love as a beneficent as well as a powerful creative force. Besides these general resemblances, there are detailed verbal resemblances which can hardly be accidental. The differences between the two poems are, however, more significant than the resemblances, and a comparison between them makes it clear that the ritualistic quality of Spenser's *Hymne of Love* was not derived from the *Canzone*. Benivieni, it is true, invokes Love as a divine personage and speaks of him in mythological terms, but the personification seems little more than a literary convention; his Love is a metaphysical idea rather than a personality, he uses mythology as a useful storehouse of symbols, metaphors and obscure conceits, and when his language is decoded, we find that he is saying no more to us in poetry than Ficino and Pico are saying to us in more intelligible prose. Spenser, on the contrary, makes hardly any use of metaphor, his descriptions are direct and lucid, he uses classical learning as a source of myth rather than of obscure symbolism and Love moves throughout his poem as a masculine personage, powerful, imperious, purposeful, cruel at times yet ultimately beneficent. Apart from stanza 8, there is nothing confused in the description of Love's cosmic action. We watch him as he wings his way upwards like an eagle; ordering, pacifying, kindling creative fire in the 'barraine cold', transforming chaos into cosmos. This is far more vivid than the elaborately allusive accounts of Love's movements given in the *Canzone d'Amore*. Moreover the approach is significantly different. Love is forcing a very reluctant Benivieni to reveal the high mysteries which he has inwardly experienced, and the revelation is intended for an audience, though only for an audience of the initiated; for, as the last stanza makes clear, the poet is acting in accordance with a current critical theory which regarded poetry as a beautiful veil

D

for philosophy, transparent to the few but opaque to the many.
Spenser, on the other hand, is following another critical theory of
the day: the theory that poetry, like rhetoric, is intended to
persuade, to move the will, to influence conduct. He wants to
compose a poem which will help him to get his own way, and
consequently he makes no mention of any readers but addresses
Love alone, hoping by flattery to cajole him into softening the
heart of an obdurate mistress.

The comparison with Benivieni shows very clearly that here
Spenser is speaking not as a philosopher, but as a Petrarchan lover,
and, like other sixteenth-century poets, has no scruples about
using Neo-Platonic philosophy as a kind of lover's language,
veering from high seriousness to mock-gravity and back again in
a way that can be confusing to a modern reader. Hardly has he
completed his description of Love's birth and growth than he
transforms the mighty god who orders the cosmos and delights
in the cruel rage of lions and tigers into a Cupid who shoots out
poisoned arrows through coy feminine glances and again into a

> . . . Lord of truth and loyalty
> Lifting himselfe out of the lowly dust,
> On golden plumes up to the purest skies

Such modulation of tone, reminiscent of *The Courtier* rather than
of the *Canzone*, might well be misunderstood by 'light wits' and
pious ladies. It is important to remember this when at the end of
the poem we watch the God of Love leading his votaries through
Purgatory to Paradise: a Purgatory where jealousy is not a sin
but a cleansing pain; a Paradise where '*Venus* dearlings' enjoy not
the Beatific Vision but the fulfilment of sexual desire in an innocent
Bower of Bliss. We are not told whether the couples are legally
married, but we are assured that their sports are harmless, their
pleasures 'devoid of guilty shame', their Heaven the due reward
of painful but ennobling experience and prolonged discipline.
Since Spenser states emphatically that mere physical desire is not
love but lust, we must surely assume that even when the lovers
have come to 'feede on Nectar heavenly wize' and 'lie like Gods in
yvorie beds' their thoughts are still quite unlike the 'dung-hill
thoughts' of 'base-borne mynds'; but also, it must be confessed,

not very like the thoughts of dedicated Christians or aspiring Neo-Platonists. Leone Ebreo, it is true, maintains that physical union can perfect spiritual love; but he denies that he is thereby making coition the lovers' final goal, and that is just what Spenser seems here to be doing. Or if that is to put the case too strongly, he is, at least, suggesting that Love's Heaven is an earthly Paradise of 'joyous happie rest' which provides no incentive to further travel. These lovers are not standing on any rung of the Platonic ladder; they have settled down into a home which leaves nothing further to be desired.

To ask whether Spenser means us to approve of their situation is to ignore the structure and fiction of the poem and to forget that the poet is speaking under the mask, not of a teacher, but of a wooer, whose one aim is to achieve complete union with the woman he desires and is using rhetoric to gain his ends. Rulers like to be congratulated on their power, and power is often manifested by the infliction of pain; but since good rulers desire the good of their subjects, Love's cruelty can only be apparent and his greatest power—or so the poet would persuade him—is manifest when, after having purified lovers by suffering, he brings their courtship to a happy conclusion. The ascent hymned in this poem is not the ascent from physical to spiritual love, but the ascent from the pains of wooing to the bliss of consummation.

The theme is announced in the opening stanzas. Love has so weakened the poet that he cannot even prepare a propitiatory offering without the help of his tormentor. But to call on him for help is to believe in his benevolence. The god who sits on Venus' lap and enjoys her 'ambroisiall kisse' is a god who can overshadow his votaries with 'gentle wing' and inspire them with 'gentle furie'. Muses, Nymphs, and youthful Beauties are summoned to share Love's triumphs, because they can bear witness that his cruel smarts are kindly and that feminine coldness need not last forever.

The first stanza of the hymn proper stresses Love's force rather than his gentleness, but the following verses show that this force is directed against the hostilities, the barrenness and ugliness of chaos, and is productive of warmth and fertility and cosmic order. For the sub-human world this process is natural and painless, the trouble begins with human beings; who, since they possess

immortal souls, desire something more than procreation and are
therefore harder to satisfy, more likely to be frustrated. At this
point the poet seems to be interrupting the choral hymn as he
recalls his own plight and for a moment doubts the goodness of
his god. If Love is really:

> The world's great Parent, the most kind preserver
> Of living wights, the soveraine Lord of all

why does he torture his devoted follower and harden the heart
of the Dame who rebels against his authority? But, like other
religious believers, the poet refuses to think evil of his god. All
is really for the best. The song of praise is resumed. Purgatory
leads to Paradise, and with the description of this Paradise the
hymn proper ends. The last two stanzas form an Envoy in
which the poet presents his gift and makes a final attempt to
wheedle Love: at present he can only offer a 'simple song'
expressive of his hopes, but if only Love would admit him into
that happy port, why then he would worship him with a hymn
such as the Angels sing in Heaven.

As one reads the Envoy, the misgivings of Spenser's patronesses
become understandable, for here, and indeed throughout the
poem, he seems to be speaking with the tongue of the troubadour
and making an almost blasphemous use of Christian phraseology.
Without the grace of Love one cannot worship Love; whom Love
loveth he chasteneth, in Heaven Love will become the sole object
of adoration. Is not this to place the Ovidian Amor on the throne
of the Christian God? Yes, but not necessarily with any impious
or defiant intention. The references to Heaven in the Invocation,
the Hymn and the Envoy are all part of an attempt to influence
Love's behaviour by suggesting that he discloses his *essential*
nature most fully, when his restless Eros-action brings about a
restful Hymeneal joy which includes both soul and body.

In itself, this is neither heretical nor sinful. Both Platonists and
Christians could find a place for Hymen in their systems and the
Protestants of Spenser's day regarded marriage as a more honourable estate than 'religious' celibacy, at any rate for laymen. We
may conclude from his other works that much of what Spenser
says about the ennobling nature of love is meant to be taken
seriously. Rhetoric is not necessarily false. From the Christian

standpoint the weakness of Love's Heaven is not that it includes *bodily* enjoyment, but that it puts a stop to further progress by treating *temporal* enjoyment as the final end of endeavour. This is idolatry; but it is an idolatry almost inseparable from passionate desire.

Whether Spenser is or is not speaking in his own person is an unimportant problem. What is important is to focus the poem aright; and we can only do so if we remember that within the fiction of the poem Spenser is inviting us to listen not to the revelation of a Diotima but to the studied, purposeful rhetoric of a man in love.

c. An Hymne in Honour of Beautie

The first four prefatory stanzas link the second hymn to its predecessor. Inspired by Love's 'gentle furie' the poet has offered up his 'simple song' full of wishful thinking, and has promised to produce a triumphal 'heavenly Hymne' if Love will make his hopes come true. The result of this coaxing is unexpected and ironical: the poet's wishes are not granted but he is compelled to write another hymn. Love's gentleness was deceptive, and now instead of slaking his raging fire he adds more fuel to the flame. Love was invoked to come softly down from his secret, blissful resting place on the lap of his mother Venus; his answer is to drive the poet upwards towards the vision of Venus herself and so force him to frame a hymn in honour not of Love himself but of his mother. Love has been praised as the active and effective pursuit of Beauty. Beauty must be praised as the magnet which both originates and worthily rewards the activities of Love.

Both poems are constructed on the same general plan. In the opening lines of the *Hymne of Beautie* the poet seems to be making a fresh start; but the apparent break has only been a pause; unsatisfied passion is still the source of his poetic inspiration, and once more he invokes the subject of his poem to help him in composing it and to reward him when it has been composed. In the hymn proper he honours Beauty (as he had formerly honoured Love) both as a cosmic force and as a potent influence on human life in general and his own heart in particular. Again he insists that bodily beauty is meant to reveal spiritual beauty and that both kinds are most clearly manifested in the celestial harmony of Love. In both Envoys he asks to be rewarded by success in his suit.

Spenser has been careful to construct his poems in such a way that the obvious similarities make the subtle dissimilarities particularly significant. Each poem, for instance, contains a vivid image suggesting a ritual setting; but the images are differently placed and conjure up different pictures. At the opening of the first poem we are invited to imagine Love's hymn being chanted by a band of devotees, marching forward with their victorious Lord after the manner of a Roman triumph. In the Envoy of the second poem we are made to see Beauty more clearly than her devotees. From some high central spot she waves her flag of victory, and draws up towards herself a host of chanting worshippers who approach her from all quarters of the world. A similar distinction is made in a more intellectual way, when in the Invocation to the second poem the poet prays not for inspiration but for enlightenment. Inspiration suggests life, movement, a driving impulse felt within and spurring on to achievement; illumination suggests light shining from without and increasing vision and understanding. The second hymn, therefore, is the quieter and more contemplative of the two; for, whereas Love the inspirer is born and grows and moves up towards his goal, absolute Beauty is always absolutely perfect in Herself, though her radiated light grows fainter as it streams down through the created universe. This main distinction drawn between the two hymns is in accord with Neo-Platonic teaching; but Platonic ideas are naturally more fully expounded in the second hymn, where the poet describes his vision, than in the first hymn where he is more preoccupied with his feelings.

The second hymn begins in the traditional manner, with an account of the 'birth' of the deity who is being celebrated. 'Birth', however, is an inaccurate word in this context, for Spenser stresses the mysterious origin of Beauty and identifies her with the 'goodly Paterne' which the 'great workmaister' used in modelling the Universe. Obviously, the account of Creation given in lines 29–40 is derived neither from Genesis, nor from the elaborate systems of the Florentine Neo-Platonists, but directly or indirectly from Plato's *Timaeus*. Spenser, however, is following the Neo-Platonists rather than Plato when he equates

the Pattern contemplated by the Demiurge with the Idea of
Beauty which is the final goal of the philosophical lover of Plato's
Symposium.

Since, to a greater or lesser extent, every earthly thing partakes
of Beauty's radiance it follows that visible beauty cannot be completely explained as an attractive composition of colours and
shapes, and although feminine beauty is first experienced through
sight, nevertheless the true lover, as distinct from the voluptuary,
is really in love with the lady's immortal soul which is imparting
something of its radiance to her mortal flesh.

All this is Neo-Platonic commonplace, and Spenser is following
even the more daringly unorthodox views of Ficino, Benivieni,
etc., when he asserts that souls, descending from their native
planets, actually shape their own bodies so that they may be
suitable dwelling-places for their spirits. This helps to solve the
recurrent problem of the good but ugly woman. By an unhappy
chance she has descended into unusually tough matter which just
cannot be moulded into a suitable shape. As for the bad but
beautiful woman, Spenser asserts emphatically that her evil conduct is entirely due to the misuse of her will and in no sense
detracts from the goodness of her beauty, nor can it even (an
unorthodox sentiment this) totally deprave her soul. Whether
or no Spenser derived this theory from a Neo-Platonic source I
do not know, but he seems to express his own genuine sentiments
when he shows as much or more concern for the spiritual wellbeing of beautiful women as for that of their lovers. They must
loathe disloyal lust as a foul blot that will dim their glory; on the
other hand (here possibly the poet is not wholly disinterested in
his advice), to respond to 'gentle Love, that loiall is and trew'
will add fresh lustre to it. But they must choose their lovers
carefully. If lovers are to be joined in a 'celestiall harmonie' they
must be united by spiritual affinity as well as physical attraction,
an affinity which comes from having been born under the same
star and having known one another previously in those 'heavenly
bowres' whence they have descended. True love is not a quick
superficial response to physical beauty; on the contrary the
genuine lover pierces through the external loveliness of his lady
to the inner spiritual source of that loveliness and separates it in

his mind from any physical defect which may happen to mar or dim it.

In all these stanzas Spenser is following his Italian models very closely, and indeed some of his verses sound almost like a paraphrase of Ficino's account of spiritual affinity. He explains how of two souls born under the ascendancy of the same star, one may have a much more beautiful physical body than the other; nevertheless they love each other because their etherial forms and inmost natures are similar. The lover, however, has the power of beholding in the beloved her true and original nature, and therefore of constructing in his mind's eye the etherial form which is far more beautiful than the physical body; it is this image which he always sees and this image which he loves, and therefore lovers so often believe each other far more beautiful than they are. Here certainly Ficino asserts that this mental image is not merely subjective; nevertheless he is usually more impressed by the creative power of the lover's mind than by the spiritual beauty of his beloved. 'So love that image which your soul *created* and that soul itself its creator . . .,'[1] and as we have seen, Benivieni, Pico and Bruno make the same point with even more insistence. Spenser, also, delights in his ability to fashion a mental image of his lady which is more beautiful than the so-called reality; but strictly speaking this skill is *perceptive* rather than *creative*. Pico and the rest desert the beloved to explore their own mental powers, Spenser uses his mind to explore the spiritual beauties of the lady and, so far from deserting her to climb the Ladder, he obviously expects that by journeying together in sweet sympathy, the lovers will not only work 'ech other's joy and true content', they will also enhance one another's spiritual experience.

But the lover's interest in his lady's soul does not entail forgetfulness of her body. On the contrary, here, as in the former poem, Spenser can change from Neo-Platonic to conventional sonneteering language without embarrassment or sense of incongruity. The sharp-sighted lover sees not only the 'inly faire', but also the 'thousand Graces masking in delight' on his lady's forehead, for charms such as these are the means by which Beauty seeks to attract all men to herself. In fact (though no doubt Spenser would have disliked this way of putting it) physical beauty is sacramental,

and the true lover is like a Catholic whose belief in transubstantia-
tion only increases his reverence for the outward and visible
vehicles of an inward and spiritual grace, and here, as in the
Hymne of Love, Spenser affirms that this is most fully understood
when love is reciprocated, and concludes his act of praise with a
prayer for personal success. His concluding prayer is addressed
to Venus and is followed by a similar address to 'Venus' dearling',
his own coy mistress.

This double-Envoy corresponds to the double dedication of the
Hymne of Beautie, but its final stanza concludes not that poem only,
but both Hymns taken together. In the first hymn the poet-lover
speaks directly to the God of Love and gives no hint of any other
audience; for the Muses, Nymphs, etc., are invoked not as listeners
but as performers. In the second hymn he speaks first to Love
and then to Love's Mother and offers up a new hymn which is
intended both for her and for his own mistress and also for a
wider public. The poet is still asking for reward; but he claims
that now his chief aim is to praise Beauty for her own sake and
to reveal her nature to all the world.

This widening of outlook might seem to lend some support to
those who would find the Ladder of Love in the *Fowre Hymnes*;
for has not the poet now reached Pico's third rung, the rung
where the lover considers 'the universal nature of corporeal
beauty'? The answer must be 'No', for although the poet professes to be chiefly concerned with Beauty Itself, there is no sign
that he means to deflect his attention from the particular example
of beauty he has in mind. On the contrary, she is included in this
very invocation, and the last stanza of the Envoy suggests that
the 'fearefull lines' are primarily intended for her perusal and that
the meditations on universal love and beauty are persuasive
compliments intended to win her favour.

This does not mean that they are false or frivolous. Throughout both poems, human love is described as an ennobling experience which should lead to a joyful and permanent uniting of
souls and bodies, and we know from the rest of his work that
this was one of Spenser's serious convictions. In the *Hymne of
Love* the emphasis naturally is on consummation; in the *Hymne of
Beautie* on the value of that which is desired, but there is no progress
from particular to general, from physical to spiritual, and if there

is any ascent, it is ascent from awareness of the self to awareness
of the other, an awareness which is the exact opposite of the
introversion recommended by most of the Neo-Platonists. The
last stanza, indeed, suggests that there has been no ascent, but
only a shift of attention, and that the poet remains preoccupied
with his own needs and their possible satisfaction.

Extraversion may bring enlightenment, but apparently it
lowers rather than raises the poet's spirits. The *Hymne of Love*
closes on a note of hopeful anticipation. The lover feels that he
has won the right to enter into his reward and sooner or later
expects to do so. At the end of the *Hymne of Beautie* he has lost
self-confidence, his talk is no longer of Purgatory and Paradise
but of death and damnation, and he pictures himself not as a
conquering hero, but as a helpless slave, nay, a lifeless corpse
utterly dependent on the miraculous saving power of his lady's
pity.

The semi-blasphemous prayer for redemption from death is in
the court-of-love tradition, and is obviously voiced by a Petrarchan
not a Neo-Platonic lover. The Petrarchan lover was traditionally
doomed to frustration; but by ending his two life-affirming hymns
with the ominous word 'death' Spenser prepares us for the conversion, the *volte-face* that is to follow.

d. *An Hymne of Heavenly Love*

Whatever the past history of the first two poems may have been,
it is obvious that the *Fowre Hymnes* as published in 1596 were
meant to form a poetic whole, and the poet emphasizes the
relationship between the two pairs by the same methodical use of
correspondences, contrasts and connecting stanzas which he employs to link Love with Beauty, and Heavenly Love with Heavenly
Beauty. The pattern is symmetrical and, as Ellrodt points out,[1]
is best seen as a diptych. The two leaves of the main diptych are
on the one hand Love and Beauty, on the other hand Heavenly
Love and Heavenly Beauty; but each of these leaves contains a
corresponding but smaller diptych whose leaves are Love and
Beauty, Heavenly Love and Heavenly Beauty, respectively. It is
difficult to see how a plan of this sort can include any indication
of a continuous 'scala' or ladder.

Whatever Spenser's private sentiments may have been, the first three stanzas of *An Hymne of Heavenly Love* have to be accepted as part of the structure of the poem. Once again, the poet invokes Love and begs him to inspire a Hymn in his own honour; but the Love whom he now addresses is not the pagan 'daemon' who had inspired him with many 'lewd layes' . . . 'In praise of that mad fit which fooles call love'; no, he is the 'god of Love, high heavens king', and the repentant poet has now entirely changed his tune. As we read the first stanza, we are surely meant to recall the last stanza of the *Hymne of Love*, where the poet promises to sing a heavenly hymn in his praise, provided he will admit him into the lover's paradise. His prayer has not been answered and now that his heat is quenched he prepares a truly heavenly hymn in praise, not of the Ovidian idol Amor, but of the true and living God. It has been suggested that the 'lewd layes' may refer to early love poetry now lost; but surely if Spenser had not meant us to identify them with the first two hymns, he would not have repeated in verse what he had already said in prose to the Countesses of Cumberland and Warwick. Spenser is not just continuing a steady ascent, he is turning round and taking a different path. I do not see how the introductory stanzas can be interpreted in any other way, especially since in the final stanzas of the *Hymne of Heavenly Beautie* the poet clinches the matter by reverting to the theme of renunciation.

Even if the introductory stanzas are dismissed as merely conventional, it is still very difficult to fit the main body of the poem into a Neo-Platonic mould. The Neo-Platonic lover does, as we know, leave his lady behind, but he never ceases to seek a personal satisfaction which he hopes to attain by his own efforts. His lord is not Agape but Eros. In the third hymn this situation is reversed because the object of devotion has changed, and this is made clear from the outset.

When Spenser once again traces Love back to its source, he no longer envisages a naked Babe on its mother's lap, that grows in power and stature as it wings its way upwards; for he has now discovered that Primal Love is not a stirring of desire in the heart of chaos or in the hearts of men; it is the reciprocal movement within the Divine Nature itself, it is the eternal life of the Blessed Trinity and within that life Love and Beauty are eternally one.

'It lov'd it selfe because it selfe was faire'. These words may have a
Platonic ring but their Platonism is a Platonism which influenced
Christianity from very early days; the Beauty of God having
constantly been a theme for Jewish and Christian meditation.

It has been maintained that the account of the creation is
Platonic rather than Christian because it suggests, heretically,
that the Son and the Holy Spirit and the Cosmos all *emanate* from
the Primal Deity. I do not think that Spenser's words need be
construed in this way; but, in any case, a poet can hardly be
expected to speak with the precision of a trained theologian, and
our knowledge of Spenser should be sufficient to assure us that
any lapse from orthodoxy was quite inadvertent and a matter of
style rather than of meaning. I see no reason to doubt that he
intended to versify the creed, not of Neo-Platonism, nor, as some
scholars surprisingly suggest, of Calvinism, but of what Professor
Lewis describes as 'mere Christianity', and this, I think, is true
not only of the account of Creation but of the whole contents of
the last two hymns.

The structure of both the Heavenly Hymns depends upon an
initial assertion, which is also the central Christian assertion,
namely that God is Love. That being so, it follows that true
Love is God and that love is essentially the life of the triune
Deity. Since, in the unity of the Godhead, Divine Love is
inseparable from Divine Beauty and consequently fully grown
from all Eternity it follows that its movement in time can only
be *downwards*. It overflows deliberately, and in so doing creates
the hierarchic universe, arranged in descending tiers of angels,
who, in their 'trinal triplicities' contemplate, praise and serve
God. When some of these angels refuse allegiance through pride,
their rebellion calls out another downward movement of Divine
Love and their place is filled by Man, whom God creates by taking
'clay, base, vile, and next to nought', shaping it in his own image
and breathing into it the spirit of life. When Man in his turn
rebels, the Parental patience is not exhausted; on the contrary,
his disobedience calls out the most extreme form of selfless love,
and the Divine Son Himself actually descends to earth and
assumes human flesh in order to lift fallen man up to Heaven.
Spenser did not have to resort to mythology to personify Heavenly

Love; for, as a Christian, he believed that Heavenly Love had personified Himself at a given moment of historic time.

The subject of the third hymn is the loving activity of God both in the Eternal Trinity and in Christ Jesus of Nazareth, the Incarnate Son. Of course, Jesus Christ, like the Love of the first hymn, grows and matures; but the story of his human life is the story of increasing suffering, culminating in an ignominious death. The inmost nature of the love that moves within the Trinity is revealed in Christ upon the Cross, sharing the death and bearing the sins of men and asking as the reward for this incredible generosity only that men should return this love and love their fellow-men for His sake. Even this desire for reward is altruistic, for it is only after this supreme manifestation of Divine Love has met with a due response of gratitude that the human soul can be enabled by Christ to rise up to the vision of Divine Beauty. As earthly love by increasing penetration enables the true lover to form a mental image of his lady which is more expressive of the spiritual reality than of her outward appearance, so devout and loving meditation on the gospel story enables the Christian to see and love the vision of the glorified Christ; and just as Earthly Love inspired the poet to sing the praises of Earthly Beauty, so now Heavenly Love inspires him with ecstatic love of Heavenly Beauty. The parallelism is obvious; but so also is the contrast.

The 'Platonizers' might well claim that at the end of the hymn to Heavenly Love, the poet, who now regards all 'earthes glorie' as 'durt and drosse', has reached that fourth rung of the ladder, where all forms of human beauty are left behind, and the lover presses upwards to reach the Angelic mind and there enjoy the vision of God. But the difference is greater than the resemblance. Half-way up the ladder the Neo-Platonic lover is spurred on to greater heights by delighted admiration of his own creative powers; the poet of the third hymn lies helpless on the ground and cannot begin to love truly until, 'humbled with meeke zeale', he gratefully recognizes his total dependence on the uplifting love of his Divine Rescuer. The essential difference can be put very briefly. In Neo-Platonic doctrine Heavenly Love usually means the love of man for God; in Spenser's third hymn it means primarily the love of God for man.

e. An Hymne of Heavenly Beautie

The parallelism of the two pairs is strikingly illustrated in the first stanzas of *An Hymne of Heavenly Beautie*. Here, as in the second hymn, little, if any, interval of time separates the poem from its immediate predecessor: Heavenly Love, like His earthly counterpart, inspires Spenser with a vision of Beauty, and just as in his unregenerate days the poet sought to win fresh devotees for Venus, so now, having contemplated Heavenly Love as manifested in Christ on the Cross, he desires to reveal the vision to his fellow-mortals in order that they too may be filled with love of Heavenly Beauty. Since Spenser is now concerned not with two mythological figures but with the Triune God of Christian faith, there are naturally differences as well as correspondences. Christ saves and enlightens him, but in both the Heavenly Hymns, the poet invokes the Holy Spirit to inspire his verse. It was, as we have seen, traditional to begin a classical hymn with the birth of a god, but since Love and Beauty are one in the Trinity, the origin of Heavenly Beauty has already been dealt with in the third hymn, and the fourth hymn starts not with a counterpart of the 'wondrous Paterne' of the second hymn but with 'th' easie vew of this base world'. It is only after he has mentally scaled the hierarchic universe that the poet comes into the presence of the mysterious and queenly Sapience, who sits in God's bosom and clearly corresponds to the Venus of the second hymn.

Of all four hymns, *Of Heavenly Beautie* is the one which appears to conform most closely to the usual Neo-Platonic pattern; for in it the soul soars further and further away from Earth until it arrives at a vision of perfect beauty and a condition of ecstatic love of God. Nevertheless, this upward movement is not really to be equated with the mounting of the Neo-Platonic ladder, for the journeys begin and end differently. The Christian mountaineer starts by admiring, not a particular woman, but the order of Nature, and when he arrives at his goal, he experiences not an apotheosis, but a prostrating sense of creaturely nothingness.

Nor is the mediæval mystic way to be found in the *Fowre Hymnes*. Purgation, Illumination, Unification are stages in a course of arduous training; Spenser is suggesting a method of meditation which could occupy an occasional quiet hour or a daily period of devotion practised throughout a lifetime: but he is not composing a typical spiritual biography. As a Protestant, Spenser would be suspicious, not only of Neo-Platonic apotheosis, but of the unitive way of monastic mysticism. [There is evidence in *The Fairie Queene* that Spenser believed that it is possible here on earth to enjoy moments of high contemplation, but such experiences are incomplete and transitory and the full Beatific Vision can only be enjoyed after death.] Perhaps this is why certain chosen souls are admitted into the presence of Sapience and apparently remain there, whereas the vision of God is too dazzling to be sustained, and the human soul is advised to take cover beneath the 'Lambes integrity', lest he should either see or be seen by God. The significance of Spenser's *Sapience* is, however, still a matter of acute controversy.

It is impossible to discuss all the various interpretations of Sapience which have been conveniently listed by Dr. Ellrodt,[1] and some can, I think, be dismissed without further ado. It is most unlikely that an Elizabethan Protestant would have identified Sapience with the Virgin Mary and there is no reason to suppose that Spenser resorted to the Gnostics or the Cabala, or even the Neo-Platonic treatises when all the information he needed was to be found in the Biblical Wisdom literature and most of it in *Proverbs*, Chapter 8, and the *Wisdom of Solomom*, Chapters 7 and 8. The female figure of Wisdom, 'more beautiful than the Sun, and over all the order of Stars', created by the Lord before all other things and greatly beloved by Him, presented Spenser with the perfect Heavenly Counterpart of his Earthly Beauty and one, moreover, which would already be familiar to every educated reader of the Bible.

But difficulties remain. Is this Wisdom a personification of a Divine Attribute, or is she one of the Persons of the Trinity and, if so, which one? Such questions had perplexed Christians from very early days. Some of the Fathers identified her with the Logos, others with the Holy Spirit, and no final conclusion had been reached. In the absence of authoritative definition, Spenser could choose the interpretation that best suited his artistic purpose; and his Sapience cannot be understood apart from the poetic context. The identification of Spenser's Sapience with the Holy Spirit is *artistically impossible*. In both hymns the Spirit is invoked to

infuse inward inspiration, whereas Sapience is an object of contemplation; she is enthroned, devotees are admitted to her
presence. Theologically Sapience may or may not be indistinguishable from the Spirit; in Spenser's poem she has a separate
existence.

In spite of Ellrodt's ingenious arguments, I find it equally
impossible to identify Sapience with the Logos. Spenser knew
perfectly well that the Logos was also the Son, Second Person of
the Trinity; whereas Sapience, though described as sovereign
and heavenly, is always distinguished from the Supreme Being,
who, in this context, is called God or Deity, not Sire or Father.
Whether Spenser was conscious of it or not, this is in accordance with various passages of the wisdom-literature, which
speak of her as an eternal but created being: 'Wisdom hath
been created before all things. . . . The word of God most high
is the fountain of wisdom; and her ways are everlasting com-
mandments. . . . He created her, and saw her, and numbered her
and poured her out upon all his works.'[1] The aesthetic argument
seems to me even more conclusive. The structure of the *Fowre
Hymnes*, the descriptive parts of the last two hymns, all suggest
a distinction between the active, masculine Christ-Love and the
stationary, feminine Sapience-Beauty. The imaginative impact of
this contrast is so strong that Spenser would have had to make
some strikingly clear pronouncements if he wished to counteract
it. No such pronouncements are made.

In these two hymns, Spenser's theme is God's dealings with
His creatures and, although it is a matter of revelation that Love,
Beauty, Wisdom, etc., are one in the mysterious life of the
Trinity, to us they manifest themselves separately. 'God so loved
the world that he gave his only Begotten Son. . . .'[2] That is the
theme of hymn three; 'for the invisible things of him from the
creation of the world are clearly seen, being understood by those
things that are made, even his eternal power and Godhead':[3] that
is the theme of hymn four; this clear-sightedness, made possible
by the redeeming grace of Incarnate Love, evokes such love of
the Divine Beauty that all other loves seem futile in comparison:
that is the theme of the two poems taken together.

But is not the vision of Sapience sitting in the bosom of God
identical with the idea of Christ's pure glory mentioned at the

end of hymn three, and are they not both manifestations of the Logos? Possibly, but only in the sense that two very different photographs may be taken of the same subject if either the subject or the photographer shifts his position. The picture of Christ's glory is a picture of the Incarnate Logos who has taken up humanity into God; Sapience, surely, represents the Idea or thought in accordance with which the Divine Reason has created the Universe.

The distinction between God (who includes the Logos, the Second Person of the Trinity) and Sapience in the bosom of God, governs the structure of the fourth hymn which consists of five parts:

(1) The invocation to the Holy Spirit.

(2) A mental ascent of the hierarchic universe, peopled by creatures who excel one another in beauty 'As to the Highest they approch more neare.'

(3) Consideration of the attributes of God (His truth, love, wisdom, bliss, grace, judgment, mercy), which, being essential parts of His nature, must be lovelier than the loveliest of His creatures, and lead to the contemplation of the ineffable overwhelming beauty of Him Himself. God's own beauty is, however, too dazzling to be directly experienced, and must, therefore, be contemplated in the mirror of His works, His attributes and particularly in His attribute of Beauty or Wisdom, as displayed in the Order of Creation.

(4) A description of the appearance, function and influence of Sapience. Her beauty, like the Divine Beauty whom she reflects, cannot be expressed by mortal tongue; but, unlike the essential Divine Beauty, it can here and now be continuously contemplated and enjoyed by chosen souls who for its sake despise all earthly gratifications.

(5) A kind of envoy addressed by the poet to himself, admonishing his hungry soul, to look up to the source of perfect beauty which kindles the love of God, suppresses love of the world and gives perfect satisfaction.

The eternal but *created* Wisdom of the Bible not only provided Spenser with a convenient heavenly counterpart to his earthly

E

Venus; it enabled him to represent the love of Divine Beauty as being even here on earth the most satisfying of all loves, without contradicting the doctrine—common among all Christians, but particularly emphasized by the Protestants—that the full vision of God can only be enjoyed in Heaven. The figure of Sapience is, there fore, a personification of a Divine attribute, but an attribute particularly associated with the Second Person of the Trinity, and an Attribute that tends to lose its distinctness for us, as we catch a partial transient glimpse of the beautiful and mysteriously rich simplicity of God. I do not wish to stress the point, but this does seem to me to be suggested by the ambiguity of the 'soveraine light' which may represent either the beauty of the Deity or the reflected beauty of Sapience; but in either case kindles the love of God.

Ellrodt notes with some regret that in the *Hymne of Heavenly Beautie* Spenser seems to have reverted to the Old Testament conception of an avenging Jehovah,[1] but it must be admitted that God's wrath against sin is not absent from the New Testament and, moreover, it was consonant with Spenser's theme. In the Bible Wisdom is frequently praised as a teacher of justice. She endows rulers with true discrimination and enables them to use their authority for the good of their subjects and the maintenance of God's law of righteousness. In a sinful world to do justice involves the punishment of evil-doers, and to such men law must appear hostile and justice be experienced as retribution. But, although pain may have to follow the infringement of it, the purpose of law is to maintain order and peace, and since beauty is a matter of order, proportion, harmony, law to the righteous man is both beautiful and delightful. But even the 'righteous' man, knowing himself to be a sinner, must approach the Divine Judge with fear and trembling, and it is only when he is covered 'with the Lamb's integritie' that he can recognize the the beauty as well as the terror of the law. Beneath the feet of God Enthroned are the instruments of His 'avenging yre'; but in His bosom sits His 'soveraine dearling', Sapience, a queen, a ruler, but also an object of love and joy to all regenerate men. Does not this suggest that Spenser's Sapience is not a representation of the Second Person of the Trinity, but a personification of the Eternal Law of God?

The first four books of *Laws of Ecclesiastical Polity* were published in 1594 and it is therefore possible, indeed probable, that
Spenser had read it before composing the heavenly hymns.
But even if Spenser left unread a book so learned and so relevant
to his own political and religious interests, it remains true that the
first book of Hooker's masterpiece throws considerable light on
An Hymne of Heavenly Beautie. The resemblance between Spenser's
Sapience and Hooker's First Eternal Law is remarkable, and both
are related to the Biblical Wisdom literature. Even if no direct
influence can be proved, it is instructive to hear the poet and the
theologian meditating on the same theme.

Hooker's fundamental premise is that law is essentially *not* a
sovereign decree but a rule made by which actions are framed so
that a desired end may be achieved; that God Himself is not an
Arbitrary Will; His Will and His Reason work together and the
first Eternal Law is 'that order which God before all ages hath
set down with himself, for himself to do all things by'. 'That
law eternal which God himself hath made to himself, and
thereby worketh all things whereof he is the cause and author;
that law in the admirable frame whereof shineth with most perfect
beauty the countenance of that wisdom which hath testified
concerning herself, "the Lord possessed me in the beginning of
his way, even before his works of old I was set up" (Prov. 8. 22);
that law, which hath been the pattern to make and is the card to
guide the world by; that law which hath been of God and with
God everlastingly; that law, the author and observer whereof is
one only God to be blessed for ever: how should either men or
angels be able perfectly to behold? . . . That little thereof which we
darkly apprehend we admire, the rest with religious ignorance,
we humbly and meekly adore.'[1]

The second Eternal Law springs from the first, for it is the
law which governs the whole created universe and is both
beautiful and reasonable, for it is imposed on the creatures of
God for their own sakes, and the ultimate purpose of the Divine
benevolence is that all created spiritual beings should find their
restless desires, fulfilled in the love and enjoyment of God Himself.
'Then are we happy therefore when fully we enjoy God, as an
object wherein the powers of our souls are satisfied even with
everlasting delight; so that though we be men, yet by being unto

God united we live as it were the life of God. . . . Whereas we now love the thing, that is good, but good especially in respect of benefit unto us; we shall then love the thing that is good only or principally for the goodness of beauty in itself. The soul being in this sort, as it is active, perfected by love of that infinite good, shall, as it is receptive, be also perfected with those supernatural passions of joy, peace and delight. All this endless and ever-lasting.'[1]

It is unnecessary to point out the parallels between the ideas expressed in these passages and those in Spenser's Fourth Hymn. Hooker helps one to understand the very structure of the poem. The poet traces the workings of the second Eternal law through-out the Universe until he arrives at the throne of the Deity and, like Hooker, sees Sapience, the Eternal Law, laid up in the bosom of God in the closest possible connection both with the Creator and the Creation and yet not exactly identical with either. Like Hooker, he finds the vision utterly satisfying and productive of an enduring love of God. It is not without interest that, in Book I, Hooker never identifies the first Eternal Law with the Logos, Word, or Son of God, and that, at the end of it he personifies Law as a feminine figure and summarizes his whole argument in a final paragraph which might serve almost equally well as a sum-mary of the argument of Spenser's last Hymn:

Wherefore that here we may briefly end: of Law there can be no less acknowledged, than that her seat is the bosom of God, her voice the harmony of the world: all things in heaven and earth do her homage, the very least as feeling her care, and the greatest as not exempted from her power: both Angels and men and creatures of what condition so-ever, though each in different sort and manner, yet all with uniform consent, admiring her as the mother of their peace and joy.[2]

Spenser did not have to go to the Cabala or the Italians for his Sapience who is also Beauty—nor, one might add, did he have to go to Calvin for his religion.

f. Conclusion

Since there is no generally accepted interpretation of *Fowre Hymnes* the conclusion of this study is bound to take the form of a somewhat dogmatic-sounding statement of personal views, and it was, therefore, reassuring to find, on reading Ellrodt's very learned thesis, that on a number of important points we had arrived independently at very similar conclusions.

The first conclusion to be drawn from a study of *Fowre Hymnes* is that it is a unified work of art constructed with meticulous care. To my mind, the dedication enforces the belief that in the first two hymns Spenser was rehandling earlier material, but I agree with Ellrodt that the stylistic, prosodic and structural uniformity of all four poems proves that this re-handling was very drastic and, indeed, amounted to fresh creation. The work we are concerned with is, therefore, the poem in four parts which was published in 1596 and quite probably written in 1595.

I need not repeat here the reasons I have already given for holding that although throughout the hymns the 'poet' makes a sympathetic use of certain familiar Platonic ideas; nevertheless in the first two he is speaking primarily as a 'Petrarchan' lover, in the last two as a devout Christian; that the Platonic Ladder is not to be found in the hymns whether examined singly or collectively; that the recantation must be taken seriously and that the whole poem is written from the Christian point of view.

To determine the exact nature of the recantation is a more difficult matter. To set two contradictory statements about love side by side for purposes of edification is not an exciting literary project, and Spenser was too accomplished an artist to follow fashion or please patronesses with insignificant work. Moreover, the fact that these very patronesses are addressed as 'the most excellent and rare ornaments of all true love and beautie, both in the one & the other kinde' suggests that in all four hymns Spenser is presenting ideals which are not wholly incompatible with one another. But if this is so, what are we to make of the recantation at the beginning of *An Hymne of Heavenly Love* and the renunciation at the conclusion of *An Hymne of Heavenly Beautie*? To find an answer to that question, we need to consider the fiction as well as the structure of the poem, for to quote from W. K. Wimsatt: 'The actual reader of a poem is something like a reader over another reader's shoulder; he reads through the dramatic reader, the person to whom the full tone of the poem is addressed in the fictional situation. . . . Even a short lyric poem is dramatic, the response of a speaker (no matter how abstractly conceived) to a situation (no matter how universalized). We ought to impute the thoughts and attitudes of the poem immediately to the dramatic *speaker*, and if to the author at all, only by an act of biographical inference.'[1]

If this is true—and it strikes me as self-evident—it is a mistake to dismiss Spenser's speaker as an insignificant bit of machinery and to regard the hymns as direct analyses of love which can be interpreted without any reference to the 'poet-lover' who is supposed to be composing them, the poet, it may be added, whom it is difficult to identify with the singer of *Epithalamion*. Ellrodt regards the dramatic framework of the first two hymns as 'Petrarchan in the worst sense: it repeats frigidly the Petrarchan commonplaces . . . but affords none of Petrarch's subtle notations of a lover's moods'.[2] But this, surely, is to disregard the purpose of Spenser's fiction. He is not trying to give 'subtle notations of a lover's moods', but to exhibit the nature of love, its diverse aspects and the different responses it can evoke. His lover repeats the Petrarchan commonplaces, because he is meant to be a fashionable Elizabethan gentleman, engaged in writing a poem for his mistress; much as a modern young man might be engaged in choosing a well-arranged bouquet in order to give pleasure both by the generally acknowledged beauty of the flowers and also by the trouble and expense they have cost him. Sixteenth-century sonneteers (see, for instance, Drayton, *Idea*, Sonnet XXI) expected their poems to be most effective, not when they were the 'spontaneous overflow of powerful feelings', but when they were the product of intelligent, painstaking craftsmanship. In this case our Petrarchan lover has drawn upon the most up-to-date philosophical theories in order to produce an attractive and convincing panegyric, and it is, therefore, quite possible that we are meant to accept his account of the value of human love, while deprecating his response to his situation.

The significance of the fictitious speaker becomes clearer when we turn to the last two hymns. The poet's suit has failed; his passion—or so he would persuade himself—has died down, he has turned his thoughts to religion and to versifying his meditations for purposes of edification. In the first two hymns his rhetoric was for the persuasion of his mistress, now it is for the persuasion of others but most of all for the persuasion of himself. It is to be noticed that at the end of the whole poem he still has to exhort himself: 'Ah ceasse to gaze on matter of thy grief.' It looks as though the opening stanzas of the third hymn were over-optimistic and that his 'straying thoughts' had never as yet been wholly brought to rest by the 'sweete enragement of celestiall love'.

Throughout the hymns, the poet seems to be standing just outside Paradise. He can contemplate the joys of 'Venus dear-lings' on their 'yvorie beds'; but his hardhearted mistress prevents him from sharing them; he can admire the incomparably more satisfying raptures of those who live in the presence of Sapience; but hankerings and regrets are holding him back from their company. To him, in this situation, earthly love is something to be renounced if heavenly love is to be enjoyed; but he braces himself with the thought that the bargain will prove a good one. Disillusionment awaits the earthly lover who fixes his mind wholly on the image of his lady 'That seemes in it all blisses to containe, In sight whereof, all other blisse seemes vaine', but to the more fortunate devotees of Sapience 'that soveraine light' is really so utterly satisfying that in comparison with it, not merely earthly beauty, but all honour, riches and mirth seem utterly valueless. Such a wholesale repudiation of ordinary human values can hardly be intended to be taken quite literally; but it should be noticed that the poet does not say that all earthly things are valueless in themselves, but only that they seem value-less in comparison with the pleasures bestowed by Sapience and that no 'fleshly sense or idle thought' of them can remain in a mind wholly preoccupied with the vision of Heavenly Beauty. Repentance of his past follies need not therefore involve the 'retractation' of everything that he has said in praise of earthly love. What then does he recant? It has often been remarked that the first two hymns cannot justly be termed 'lewd layes', but it must be remembered that the primary meaning of 'lewd' is 'unclerkly', 'ignorant', and that in Spenser's day it did not necessarily imply lasciviousness.

The lover of the first two hymns manifested his 'lewdness' in three ways: he desired his beloved for his own sake rather than for hers; he thought he could merit her favour; he thought he could find full and final satisfaction in a noble form of sexual love. His love for a woman could teach him that true love is incompatible with lust; only the love of Christ for him could teach him that the truest love is incompatible with self-regard, idolatry or pride.

But has the lover of the fourth hymn learnt the lesson? To look up to the 'soveraine light' and to scorn the world below is not that a Neo-Platonic rather than a Christian ambition, a prompting of that spiritual form of Eros-love which is so dangerously akin to the aspiration of Lucifer? There are two considerations which forbid this interpretation.

In the first place, the lover's spiritual development is a development in humility. Already in the first hymn he reveres his lady, by the end of the second hymn he seems to have lost self-confidence, throughout the last two hymns he regards himself as an abject sinner.

In the second place, the discovery that in his relationship to God he is the wooed, not the wooer, has effected a change of heart and a more enlightened attitude. Gratitude is not a selfish emotion, and by evoking his gratitude Christ has aroused in him at least the beginning of the selfless, Agape-love which is concerned to give rather than to get, and his desire for the vision of Heavenly beauty is the effect not the cause of this newly awakened love of Christ. It is only after he has loved Christ for His self-sacrificing love and tried to respond to it, that he learns that this Agape-love is beautiful in itself and the only source of infinite joy. His need to insist that to love God is actually pleasanter than to love the world shows that he has learnt a valuable truth, but is still somewhat of a novice in the art of Heavenly Love.

To sum up: In the *Fowre Hymnes* Spenser has set before us two ideas of love, both of which are shown to be good and true. It is an admirable thing that a man and woman should be joined together in a lasting union which includes both soul and body and is based on unselfish mutual love. Sexual love only becomes evil when it is based solely on physical desire or selfish possessiveness or treated as a substitute for religion. Whether they realize it or not, all men need to love God and to recognize in Him the goal of all activity, the source of all beauty, the final satisfaction of all legitimate desire, and the impelling motive for the love of one's fellow men.

Since love of one's fellow men includes love of one's husband or wife, it is clear that sexual love need not conflict with the love of God. But in this fallen world it often does, for human love is seldom quite unselfish, and the full vision of God is only to be enjoyed in Heaven.

In the *Fowre Hymnes* Spenser emphasizes the contrast between the two loves and only hints at a possible reconciliation. He puts songs of praise into the mouth of a man whose mind is restless and divided against itself, because here, as elsewhere, Spenser combines an intense appreciation of the goodness and joy of life with a sorrowful awareness of its transience and imperfection. As to the merits of the *Fowre Hymnes* opinions will no doubt continue to differ, but no opinion is worth consideration that is not based on careful attention to its structure and fiction, and the realization that Spenser has given us, not a versified treatise, but a dramatic poem.

IV. EPITHALAMION

THE date of composition of *Epithalamion* is not known. On November 19th, 1594, William Ponsonby entered on the Stationers' Register 'A booke entituled Amoretti and Epithalamion written not long since by Edmund Spencer' which he published in the following year. In *Amoretti* Sonnet 60, Spenser refers to himself as forty years old, and in Sonnet 80 claims the right to rest now that he has completed six books of *The Fairie Queene*. This is all the information we possess; those who wish to study the various conjectures that have been based on it should consult the *Variorum Spenser*[1] and for a sensible summary of the probabilities they should turn to Renwick,[2] who concludes that the poems contained in Ponsonby's volume probably cover a period from 1591 or 1592 to 1594, and that Spenser was married at Youghal or Cork in 1594. The known facts and many guesses about the marriages of Spenser and his bride are given in *Variorum*, loc. cit.

Elizabeth Boyle was a kinswoman of Sir Richard Boyle, first Earl of Cork and a distant relation of the Spencers of Althorp in Northamptonshire and of the poet himself. It has been suggested that when Spenser married her she was the widow of Tristram Peace; but her youthfulness makes this improbable though not impossible. After Spenser's death she was twice married, to

Roger Seckerstone before 1600, to Robert Tynte in 1613. She
died in 1622. When in *Amoretti* 74, Spenser praises the three
Elizabeths who have made him happy: his mother, his queen
and 'the third my love, my lives last ornament', he must surely
be referring to his bride. It is quite likely that Spenser was a
widower when he married Elizabeth Boyle and that the greetings
sent by Gabriel Harvey on April 23rd, 1580 to 'Domina Immerito,
bellissima Collina Clouta' were addressed to his first wife. We
need not, however, conclude with Douglas Hamer that Spenser
began to write *Epithalamion* as a celebraton of his first marriage;
but only managed to finish it in time for his second one.[1] It is a
relief to turn from biographical fact and fiction and attend to the
work of art.

   In the *Epithalamion*, as in the *Fowre Hymnes*, Spenser is using a
traditional form which was derived from classical literature and
originated in ancient custom. In the eighteenth book of the *Iliad*
Homer tells how Hephaistos depicted two cities on the famous
shield of Achilles: 'In the one there were marriages and feastings,
and by the light of the blazing of torches they were leading the
brides from their bowers through the city, and loud rose the
bridal song. And young men were whirling in the dance, and in
their midst flutes and lyres sounded continually; and there the
women stood each before her door and marvelled.'[2] The word
used here by Homer is ὑμέναιος (Lat. *hymenaeus*) a term which
referred specifically to the processional lyric, but in its acquired
generic sense could signify any type of bridal song. From later
accounts and from pictorial art we learn that the marriage ceremonies of ancient Greece and Rome were elaborate and prolonged
and included sacrifices and invocations of the gods, banquetings,
exchanges of gifts, the adornment of the bride by her attendant
women, the festive procession to the husband's house, the
preparation of the bridal chamber for her reception. The songs
accompanying the wedding procession were sometimes licentious,
full of 'merry fescennine raillery' and no doubt, like the literary
epithalamia, very frank about the carnal pleasure and procreative
purpose of matrimony.

   From the Hellenistic period onwards, 'epithalamion' (Latin
epithalamium) is used as a term for the nuptial ode. The word
which is derived from Greek ἐπι, before, and θαλαμος bridal

chamber, denotes specifically the song chanted outside the bed-room of the newly married couple, as distinct from the proces-sional song accompanying the bride to her husband's home and the drinking song sung by the guests at the wedding banquet. As in the case of 'hymenaeus', however, the term became generalized and the literary Epithalamion often included passages reminiscent of all phases of the marriage ceremony.

The literary Epithalamion developed in two main directions. The lyrical type, which could include a lyrical refrain such as 'Talassio' or 'Hymen O Hymenaeo', is meant to sound—at any rate for the most part—as though chanted by well-wishers in-volved in the proceedings. In one fragment from Sappho, how-ever, the bride herself takes part in the singing and in a passage from Euripides' fragmentary play *Phaeton* the husband sings his own wedding song as leader of a band of maidens. But these instances would seem to be exceptional; as a rule the epithala-mion was sung to, not by, the bride or bridegroom.

The remains of Greek hymeneal poetry are unfortunately very scanty. Our knowledge of the lyrical Epithalamion is mainly derived from short references, from fragments of Sappho, from episodes and descriptive speeches in Greek and Latin dramas, possibly from Theocritus' Idyll 18,[1] and above all from Catullus 61, 62.

Theocritus' *Epithalamion of Helen* (Idyll 18) is hard to classify. It is written in hexameters and is usually described as an epic piece; but it is lyrical in feeling and the narrative describing the arrival of a choir of Spartan maidens occupies only eight lines while the remaining fifty lines are devoted to the actual epithala-mion which was sung and danced by them outside the bridal chamber of Helen and Menelaus.

In Carmen 61 Catullus hymns the wedding of Manlius and Vinia in light short-lined stanzas which fall into groups corre-sponding to the successive phases of the marriage ceremonial, the changes being sometimes emphasized by variations of the refrain. The poet begins by invoking Hymen to be present at the wedding and summons unmarried maidens to add their persuasions to his by singing a hymn in praise of the Marriage God. During this hymn the refrain changes from 'O Hymenaeus Hymen, O Hymen Hymenaeus' to 'What god dare match himself with this god?' In the next section the song is evidently being chanted amid an expectant crowd gathered in front of the bride's house and the refrain is 'Come forth new bride'. After some delay she answers the summons, boys go before her waving torches and shouting 'Io Hymen', etc., and the procession makes its way to the accompaniment of 'merry fescennine raillery' until the hymeneal cry is raised for the last time and the bride steps over the threshold of her new home. Once inside the house the bride is escorted to the bridal chamber, the bridegroom is summoned and words of encouragement and praise are now addressed to him. After wishing them future happiness and a numerous and fortunate progeny the virgins leave the bridal couple to themselves: 'Maidens, shut the doors. We have sported enough. But ye, happy pair, live happily, and in your office exercise joyously your vigorous youth.'[1] It is not always easy to identify the speaker of the poem but probably we should regard the poet as the leading singer with virgins, boys, etc., joining in the chorus; though presumably the initial hymn to Hymen and the farewell verses in the bridal chamber are sung by the choir of virgins. However that may be, the effect of the poem is both lyrical and dramatic; we are not listening to a description, we are participating in an action.

This is still more true of Carmen 62, which is a singing match between a band of boys and a band of girls, the former praising marriage and the latter virginity. The competition begins as the evening star rises and the competitors appear to be awaiting the coming of the bride. All the stanzas which are written in hexameters close with the refrain 'Hymen, O Hymenaeus, Hymen, be present O Hymenaeus'.

In Carmen 64 Catullus gives in hexameters a lengthy and elaborate account of the wedding of Peleus and Thetis, but the most important examples of the epic Epithalamion are *An Epithalamium in Honour of Stella and Violentilla* of Statius[2] (*c.* A.D. 40–96); *Epithalamium of Honorius and Maria* (A.D. 398) and *Epithalamium of Palladius and Celerina* (probably A.D. 399) of Claudian.[3]

In these epithalamia the poet speaking undisguisedly in his own person as orator rather than as singer gives in hexameter verse a long rhetorical account of the nature of the occasion, eulogizes the bride and bridegroom and wishes them a happy and fruitful union. His compliments are conveyed chiefly by means

of an elaborate mythological fiction. The greater part, and sometimes the whole of the narrative, deals with the appearance, the
environment and the actions of certain deities—Venus, Love,
Hymen, etc.—who are concerned with the feelings of the lovers
and play a part in their wedding celebrations. Apart from some
references to the festal shouts and songs of the expectant crowds
little is said of the actual events of the wedding day, and there is
no real feeling for the ritualistic and numinous character of the
celebrations.

The Epithalamion, like other classical genres was revived at
the Renaissance, and in the sixteenth century its vogue spread
from Italy to other European countries. In his *Poetics* published
in 1561 the Italian critic Scaliger gives elaborate rules for its
composition.[1]

Firstly the poet describes the bride and bridegroom and their
affection for one another. Secondly he praises their country,
their family, their virtues of mind and body. Thirdly, he gives
them his blessing. Fourthly, he cracks some jokes and although,
of course, he must exercise restraint in his references to the bride,
he may permit himself a few amusing remarks about the approaching joys of the married couple. Fifthly he prophesies offspring
for the marriage. 'The last part contains an exhortation to sleep,
to sleep indeed for others, but for them of course wakefulness.'
At this point the bridal chamber itself should be praised and the
poet may suitably mingle a little 'fescennine railery' with his
eulogies. If he wishes to praise wedlock, he may resort to mythology and natural history. He may mention the weddings of
Peleus and Thetis, Dionysus and Ariadne, Hercules and Hebe.
He may derive Love and Friendship from the 'primordial rudi-
ments of the universe', showing how all the species spring from
the wedding of Heaven and Earth and continue to propagate
themselves by imitating their primal marriage act so that 'the
immortality denied them by the nature of their matter might be
procured by the ordered succession of their forms'. Provided
certain prudent omissions are made, arguments in praise of Love
can also be derived from Plato's *Symposium*.

Scaliger appears to be giving rules for the composition of an
oration rather than a song, but at the end of his chapter he
discriminates between the different types of Epithalamion and

offers a number of quotations from Catullus as inspiring models
for modern poets. Most of the writers of Latin epithalamia
follow the epic way of Statius and Claudian, but in France the
Pleiade poets did compose vernacular epithalamia in the lyrical
vein of Theocritus and Catullus.

In his *Epithalame d'Antoine de Bourbon et Jeanne de Navarre*,
Ronsard[1] begins by describing the arrival of twelve virgins who
sang some lovely verses to the bride and bridegroom as they
danced round their marriage bed. These 'lovely verses' are composed of delicate short-lined stanzas each of which ends in the
traditional refrain:

> O Hymen, Hymenée
> Hymen, O Hymenée.

Congratulations are offered, Muses and meadow nymphs are
invoked to take their part in the proceedings, Cypris and the
Graces are said to be arriving to bless the union and finally the
virgins take their leave with a farewell song.

In 1559 Rémy Belleau published an *Epithalame Sur le Mariage
de Monseigneur le Duc de Lorraine et de Madame Claude Fille du Roy.
Chanté par les nymphes de Seine et de Meuse*.[2] In this case the opening
nine stanzas are chanted by Apollo, who summons a choir of
nymphs in an invocation which also includes Venus, Love,
Hymen, and the Sky. The actual epithalamion is chanted in
alternate verses by the nymphs of the Meuse who praise the
bridegroom, and the nymphs of the Seine who praise the bride,
and it ends with the usual good wishes for the happiness and
fruitfulness of the marriage. Each stanza closes with the twice
repeated refrain 'Hymen, Hymen, Hymenaee'. The influence of
Catullus is evident throughout, but Apollo's invocation may owe
something in matter, though not in manner, to the mythological
pageantry of Claudian.

Joachim du Bellay[3] and Marc Claude de Buttet[4] both prepared
epithalamia for the marriage of Princess Marguerite of France
with Prince Philibert Emanuel, Duke of Savoy; but since, owing
to the death of King Henry II, the wedding had to be celebrated
quietly, du Bellay's masque-like piece was never performed and
de Buttet, who chose the epic genre, wrote a lengthy descripton
in alexandrine couplets of festivities which never took place.

It has been suggested that Spenser owes much to de Buttet, and certainly the French, like the English poet, claims to be tracing the events of the wedding day from morning to night. After he has eulogized the bridegroom and invoked Hymen, the sun rises. Paris is full of guests from all parts of the world, of rushing crowds, of the sound of the drums and fifes of the Swiss Guard. The royal cortège approaches and many notable personages are mentioned by name. [They go to the 'temple' and the bride is described in glowing terms. After a bare mention of the church service, the poet gives a long and very realistic account of the wedding banquet which was followed after sunset by a ball. At the sudden appearance of the evening star the guests disperse and the lovers are invited to retire to bed.] The imagery now becomes completely pagan and the poet's final prayer is addressed to the 'gods':

Ie prie, en inuocant, Votre eternel pouvoir;
Que dans trois fois trois mois nous bienheuriés de voir
Vn petit Telemach, qui tout resemble au pere,
Et, pour chanter leur faits, faites moi leur Homere.

[There is, no doubt, a certain similarity in ground plan, but in style, feeling and attitude there is no resemblance at all between the French and English poems, and I see no reason to agree with the view that 'Spenser owes more to the obscure Marc Claude de Buttet than to any other author in the composition of the Epithalamion'.[1]]

The first English epithalamion was written by Philip Sidney some time between 1577 and 1580 and was published in 1593 in the folio edition of *Arcadia*.[2] It is pastoral in setting. The shepherd Dicus who sang it 'with a cleare voice and cheerfull countenaunce' at the wedding of Lalus and Kala drew his imagery from country sounds and sights and invoked besides Muses and water nymphs 'Pan, Father Pan, the god of silly sheepe'. Sidney makes no attempt to imitate Catullus but employs for his lyrical epithalamion a nine-line stanza consisting of four pentameters, two trimeters, one pentameter, one trimeter and a final pentameter refrain: 'O Hymen, long their coupled joyes maintaine'. The rhyme-scheme is *ababbccdd*.

Both in matter and manner the song of Dicus bears a striking resemblance to *Arsilius his Carol for joy of the new marriage between*

Sirenus and Diana,[1] a poem contained in a translation made by Bartholomew Young of Gil Polo's continuation of Montemayor's romance *Diana*, which was not printed until 1598, but was completed in manuscript by 1583. It is interesting that Young's stanza-form is modelled on its Spanish original except that the rhyme-scheme is altered from *abbaaccdd* to *ababbccdd*; for apart from a freer use of feminine endings which reproduces more closely the rhythm of the Spanish poem, it is identical in length, metre and rhyme-scheme with that of Sir Philip Sidney.

[Spenser's *Epithalamion* stanza was not borrowed from either Sidney or Young, it was an original adaptation of the irregular canzone-stanza of Petrarch; nevertheless he may possibly have been encouraged by the example of one or both of his English contemporaries to compose his lyrical Epithalamion in fuller, more flowing stanzas than those favoured by Catullus and his French followers, and his treatment of the refrain may well have been suggested by that of Young whose:

Ring forth fair nymphs, your joyful songs for gladness

is changed in the last verse to:

End nymphs your songs that in the clouds are ringing.

It is unnecessary here to produce a detailed analysis of the *Epithalamion* stanza which every reader can examine for himself. [The conclusions drawn by Professor Hieatt from the fact that *Epithalamion* is the only poem of Spenser in which the stanzas vary freely in metrical structure, line-lengths and rhyme schemes are discussed in detail in Appendix II. Here I need only say that the twenty-four stanzas and three hundred and sixty-five long lines may or may not have been made to represent the diurnal and annual movements of the sun in order to symbolize the seasons of human life in relation to eternity; but no sensitive ear can doubt that Spenser's free variant of the canzone stanza is exquisitely fitted to express that mingling of joy and solemnity, of personal feeling, social revelry and stately ceremonial that is one of the great beauties of *Epithalamion*. In metrical experiment as in handling of his subject Spenser brings out of his treasure things new and old and a study of his sources can give valuable insight into the workings of his creative imagination.]

Spenser's most important deviation from tradition may have been suggested by Statius, who, after describing the wedding of Stella and Violentilla remarks: 'Such was that day: of the night let the bridegroom sing'.[1] However that may be, the fact that it is the husband who sings both of the day and the night, affects the whole structure and meaning of *Epithalamion.*

The presupposition of the whole poem, *including* the first and last stanzas is that the poet is describing the wedding as being recalled or, more probably, foreseen, in his own imagination; the pre-supposition of the marriage hymn proper, *excluding* the first and last stanzas, is that it is a kind of silent song, chanted mentally by him during the actual celebration and consummation of his marriage.

Since the poet is not professing to give an account of the nature of love but of a particularly happy experience of it, any attempt to distinguish matter from manner or to make a separate analysis of the thought is bound to fail; the only way to arrive at the meaning of the poem is to follow its movement.

The form of the opening is similar to that of the *Hymne of Love.* In the first stanza the poet is preparing to write his own marriage ode, and since as a happy bridegroom he needs aid not in courtship but in versifying, he naturally invokes not Love but the Muses for the gift of inspiration.

It is somewhat difficult to decide at what point the Invocation ends and the hymn proper begins. In stanzas 2, 3 and 4 the poet is still invoking the Muses and their accompanying Nymphs. On the other hand, the first stanza and the closing Envoy are the only verses completely detached from the hymn proper, which consists in a running-commentary on the feelings of the Bridegroom and the appearance and movements of the Bride from the moment of waking on the wedding morning to the falling asleep on the wedding night. In the first stanza the poet is still concerned with his poetic past and future and no exact indication of time or place is given; during the second stanza the future gives way to the present tense and in that and the following two stanzas, the Muses, together with all the Nymphs of the countryside are invited to enter the bride's bower and adorn her with bridal posies. It seems most natural, therefore, to confine the Invocation to the first stanza and to suppose that the poet's prayer is answered

F

and that under the inspiration of the Muses, with the first glimmer-
ing of the morning twilight he begins his hymn with a variant of
the traditional aubade or dawn-song. This gradual transition
from invocation to aubade is particularly suitable in a poem
which is being sung by the poet to himself and it is to be remembered that even within the fiction of the hymn proper, the poet
at this stage can only be present in thought in the bridal chamber.

These opening stanzas are beautiful instances of Spenser's
handling of traditional material. In ancient as in modern times,
the dressing of the bride was an important part of the day's proceedings and in pictorial art little winged Loves are sometimes
depicted as fluttering about her dressing-table while her human
attendants help her to get ready. It was an obvious method of
poetic heightening to transform bridesmaids and friends into
supernatural beings, especially those connected with love, marriage and poetic inspiration. Statius tells how the Muses, Apollo,
Bacchus, etc., left Helicon in order to attend the wedding of
Stella and Violentilla and how Venus, disguised as a Roman lady,
visited the house of the bride to be, led her out from her home
and prepared the bridal bed and sacred rites. In Claudian's epithalamion for the wedding of Honorius and Maria (A.D. 398)
Venus herself, arrives in a magnificent cortège and adorns the
bride with ornaments brought by her accompanying Nereids.
In both of these poems, divinities mingle freely with human
beings, their appearances are described in detail and their doings
treated as actual events of the wedding day. Nevertheless, the
accounts of them though vivid are unconvincing, they are there
only to adorn the tale, and do not excite even a momentary suspen-
sion of disbelief. Spenser's technique is very different. Since his
poem is a lyrical soliloquy, the question of belief does not arise,
for we are not asked to imagine the nymphs as existing anywhere
except in the poet's thoughts, and there they can function as
classic nymphs and Irish fairies and human bridesmaids. To the
loving fancy of a bridegroom, steeped in the lore of Greece and
Rome, Nymphs, Hours and Graces might well be the invisible
companions of the bridesmaids, since the Bride herself is as lovely
as Venus, Queen of Beauty, whom it was the duty of these Hours
and Graces to adorn.

When Spenser bade the Muses summon attendant nymphs, not from past literature, but from the very real woods, hills and rivers of the surrounding country and from 'the sea that neighbours to her neare', he was not discarding convention. Claudian, for instance, includes in the Fescennine verses for the marriage of the Emperor Honorius an invocation not only to Earth, but to the Plain of Liguria, the rivers Adige, Mincio, etc.,[1] and nymphs of the Meuse and Seine and of the meadows of the Loire play graceful parts in epithalamia in the Pléiade poets. The local divinities and personifications, however, serve purely decorative and complimentary purposes; whereas [Spenser though he is singing a song, not painting a landscape, conveys in his aubade both awareness of his environment and also a sense of its significance. As the sun rises above the horizon, the last verse of his aubade is drowned in the dawn chorus of birds; but as long as daylight lasts the woods will continue to answer and echo the human revellers. The refrain is not just a pleasant-sounding substitute for the traditional *Hymen Hymenaee*, it is a reiterated cry of joyous affirmation.]

[Marriage is an event which concerns the community as well as the individual, and as soon as the Bride's preparations are complete, Spenser, following the example of Catullus, makes his hymn keep time with the ceremonial of the wedding-day. The conjunction of minstrels with tabor and pipe, Biblical damsels smiting their timbrels and 'Roman' boys shouting 'Io Hymen' is anachronistic but not discordant; for an Elizabethan wedding was a lively affair which a poet could translate into classical terms, without losing all touch with reality. The people standing all about effect an easy transition from the excited 'Roman' boys to the Christian bride walking slowly and solemnly to the church, where the bridegroom is awaiting her. From now onward, of course, the poet imagines himself actually taking part in the events which he describes, acutely conscious of the passage of time and of his correspondingly changing moods. It does not, however, follow as some critics have suggested, that Spenser is solely preoccupied with his own feelings, and that the bride never comes alive, that 'It is his own ecstasy and rapture, his lifelong adoration of feminine beauty that he sings at his wedding-time'.[2]

Detailed characterization would be out of place in a marriage
hymn; but the restraint and tenderness, with which he describes
the scene in church surely suggest that he is looking at and feeling
for the timid girl who is standing by his side. The catalogue of her
physical charms given to the merchant daughters, which may be
influenced by various passages in *The Song of Solomon*, is admittedly
conventional and frigid and the effect of the Medusa-image in the
next stanza which has been compared to that of a grotesque
gargoyle on a Gothic cathedral, is not altogether pleasing. It is,
however, possible that our discomfort may be based on a misunderstanding. Spenser is not asking us to visualize the snakey-
haired head of the Gorgon, but to remember that the very sight
of it turned onlookers into stone. The living Medusa was an evil
monster; her severed head affixed to the aegis of Athena had
protective virtue and was generally interpreted as the shield of
chastity. In Du Bellay's epithalamion, for instance, the bride is
complimented on her militant virtue and likened to Minerva:

> Telle contre les vices
> Au milieu des delices
> Porte le chef vainqueur
> Ceste Minerve forte,
> Qui sur sa face porte
> Une chaste rigueur.
> Io, io, victoire
> Io triomphe & gloire.
>
> L'honneur est son pennache,
> La chastete, sa hache:
> Et l'amour vertueux
> Est sa Meduse enorme,
> Qui en pierre transforme
> Le vice monstreux.
> Io, io victoire,
> Io triomphe & gloire.[1]

Spenser was probably influenced by this passage; but he uses
the 'Medusa' image in a characteristically different way. For both
poets 'Medusa's' head symbolizes the potency of virtue, the connection between chastity and virtuous love, but whereas Du
Bellay's lines are rigid, austere, bellicose, Spenser's suggest the

richness and magnetic vitality of spiritual loveliness. Du Bellay's 'Medusa' petrifies the spiritual enemies of the bride, Spenser's 'Medusa' entrances her friends. It is the change from a negative to a positive conception of virtue. So far from being uninterested in his lady, the poet devotes four stanzas to showing how her demeanour and behaviour and bodily beauty are the effects and outward signs of a beautiful spirit. The virgins are reduced to silence by the sight of her physical charms, but if only they could see the heavenly beauty of her living soul, why, then, they would be struck not only dumb but motionless. But their trance would be that of ecstatic delight and would quickly give way to songs of praise.

The sudden silence which greets the appearance of the bride creates a dramatically effective pause between the cheers of the onlookers outside and the sacred music sounding from within after the church doors have been flung open. During this pause we are invited to suspend the use of our senses both of hearing and of sight while we contemplate the invisible, inward beauty of the lady about to partake of the sacred ceremonies 'the which do endlesse matrimony make'. The pause, the moment of silent recollection is both aesthetically and religiously right; but, as usual, Spenser allows no absolute opposition between the sacred and the secular. If the virgins can learn something of the bride's virtues by watching her outward behaviour, the Angels cannot refrain from peeping at her lovely face, and, in fact, behave very much like the little winged Loves, who, in classical art, are seen fluttering about the bride's dressing-table and in Spenser's poem will soon be seen fluttering round her bridal bed. Moreover, the woods echo indiscriminately the cheering crowds, the church music, the inaudible songs of the invisible angels, the jollity and carols of the wedding banquet. 'Endlesse matrimony' has its due place in the universal order.

Though Spenser is not a squeamish poet and is quite frank about the hearty hospitality of the wedding-feast:

> Poure out the wine without restraint or stay,
> Poure not by cups, but by the belly full;

he only devotes one stanza to the Bacchanalian revelry, and (no doubt with equal realism), describes how his first exuberant delight in it is followed by increasing weariness and impatience. By so doing, he provides a clear answer to Professor Hieatt's question: 'In particular, what would Spenser's purpose have been in alluding not simply to the day of the summer solstice, but also to the year, in a poem on a marriage day?' The coincidence of mid-year with mid-day intensifies the feeling that the brilliant climax of social rejoicing has now been reached and the bridegroom's taste for public festivities is beginning to decline. This holy saint's day, says the poet, is a holy day for me, and it is indeed fitting that my wedding should take place when 'the sunne is in his chiefest hight'. Yes, but these merrymakings are too protracted, should not a marriage be celebrated on the shortest rather than the longest day in the year? In stanzas three and five Spenser had already suggested a kind of connection between himself and Phoebus the sun, and between his bride and Phoebe the moon; the fact that the sun will shortly begin to weaken in heat and light, is obviously not meant to suggest that the bridegroom's passionate love will weaken during the ensuing year; but rather that, like the tired steeds of the sun, he wants to go home and longs for the nightfall which will leave him alone with his bride. The same impatient ennui marks his attitude to the bell-ringing and the Midsummer bonfires. Remembering, no doubt, Stephen Hawes' famous couplet:

> For though the day be never so longe
> At last belles ryngeth to evensonge:

he feels that the wedding bells which at first expressed for him the unique holiness and brightness of the day, would now chime in better with his mood if they were ringing for the evening service and by a poetic form of imitative magic he seeks to bring his wish to fulfilment. Similarly because dancing round the midsummer bonfires was a nocturnal custom, he wants the fun to begin and continue in daylight, not merely to while away the time with amusement, but magically to speed its passage.

The rising of the Evening Star, which was a traditional epithalamic theme, is used by Spenser to effect a beautiful transition from day to night, from sound to silence, from company to solitude à deux, and even, it is hinted, from earth to heaven. At the sight of it the poet's mood changes: the star twinkling from

above distances the noisy, happy crowd and enables him to take
his leave of the outside world with kindly cheerfulness, before
entrusting himself and his bride to the

> glorious lampe of love
> That all the host of heaven in rankes doost lead,
> And guydest lovers through the nightes dread.

During the ensuing brief hours of total darkness the marriage is
consummated.

Spenser is quite frank about sexual intercourse and its results.
He prays the Moon-goddess:

> t' effect our wishful vow,
> And the chast wombe informe with timely seed,

and his reticence at this point springs, it seems to me, not from
prudishness but from a sense of the numinous and also, no doubt
of what is aesthetically appropriate to his theme. [Marriage has
an important social aspect which belongs to the daylight world,
but its core is a complete uniting of souls and bodies that concerns none but the wedded couple. The darkness, the silence,
the 'sacred peace' of the night, conceal the lovers from the eyes
of men and should, if all goes well, withdraw from them all
consciousness of the outside world. But since night can have its
terrors, and according to popular superstition a newly-wedded
couple are particularly liable to attacks of evil influences, exorcism
was naturally included in the epithalamic tradition. The lovers
need protection as well as seclusion.]

The threats to bridal peace are both subjective and objective
and range from 'hidden feares' and 'deluding dreames' to the very
real annoyance of the croaking frogs. The 'evill sprights', witches,
hobgoblins, etc., may seem to occupy an intermediate position;
but, whatever Spenser's personal beliefs may have been, to many
of his contemporaries an evil spirit was as objectively existent as
a frog, and that is surely what we are meant to assume as we read
these lines. The Pouke is not an allegorical personification of evil,
he is a real source of it.

But what of the good influences that fill the bridal chamber?
Are the 'little winged loves' real spiritual presences, personifications of the emotions of the lovers or merely figures of speech,
derived from pictorial and literary tradition? These different

interpretations are not necessarily mutually exclusive. The Cupids
of classical and later art could be easily equated with the 'daemons
of Venus', for daemons, as Ficino tells us, 'mix agreeably and
eagerly in the government of lower things and especially of human
affairs'. If the 'sonnes of Venus' are daemons they are more akin
to the Pouke, the Hobgoblins, than to personifications such as
that of Silence or even to mythological figures such as the Muses
and the Hours, and in that case the correspondences and contrasts
between stanzas 19 and 20 and also the modification of the
refrain gain in significance.

[Since marriage is a natural and a social act, it is most fitting
that during daylight the woods should echo the sounds of
wedding mirth; but even at ordinary times men hurry home when
darkness falls and the newly-wed, who are so peculiarly vulner-
able, are even more eager to shut out the noises of the menacing
world outside. On the other hand, to return home at nightfall
may be a withdrawal into a sanctuary rather than retreat into a
fortress; and this is particularly true of the seclusion of the bridal
chamber.]Unlike the evil spirits and ill-omened birds, the dove-
like 'sonnes of Venus' can be as active as they like within; for no
echo of their sports will reach beyond the four walls of the bed-
room, nor will they even disturb the lovers themselves. But what
exactly does this mean? Is it just a pretty fancy without any
particular relevance to the human experience which is the main
theme of the poem? It is quite in accordance with the Neo-
Platonic outlook to hold that the independent reality of the
Venerean daemons, in no way prevents their close connection
with the emotions of the human occupants of the bridal bed.
Their presence is being felt, their activities described and in a
sense reproduced by the bridegroom himself, whom we may suppose to be watching the bride in her light and pleasing slumbers,
perhaps snatching a kiss now and then and embracing her in
moments of wakefulness. These pleasures are delightful, indeed,
but they are superficial and pass almost unnoticed because all
conscious thoughts and desires are focused on that complete
union, that 'paradise of joyes', which, as Spenser assures us in the
Amoretti and the *Hymne of Love*: is 'devoid of guilty shame'. This,
I believe, is the human experience implied by stanza 20, whether

the winged doves are Venerean daemons or poetic ornaments or both at once.

The Moon, whose appearance heralds the last section of *Epithalamion* has sometimes been identified with Queen Elizabeth. Elizabeth's dislike of the marriages of her courtiers was notorious and Professor Legouis suggests that Spenser is trying to rank himself with great noblemen such as Leicester, Raleigh, etc., by pretending that his marriage might excite the Queen's wrath.[1] This I find difficult to believe. It is true that Spenser did not scruple to insert into his poems passages of courtly flattery and even of self-advertisement. In *Daphnaida*, the mourning husband apologizes to the Queen for praising his dead wife:

Ne let *Elisa* royall Shepheardesse
The praises of my parted love envy,
For she hath praises in all plenteousnesse
Powr'd upon her like showers of *Castaly*
By her own Shepheard, *Colin*, her owne Shepherd,
That her with heavenly hymnes doth deifie,
Of rustick muse full hardly to be betterd.

In the *Fairie Queene* (Book VI, Canto X, Stanza 28), Colin Clout (i.e. Spenser) begs 'great Gloriana' to pardon him for praising her 'poore handmaid' and again in *Amoretti* (Sonnet 80) he asks permission to celebrate his love:

But let her prayses yet be low and meane,
fit for the handmayd of the Faery Queene.

It is, however, one thing to apologize for praising one's beloved, while fully acknowledging her inferiority to her royal mistress, and quite another to intimate that this same royal mistress will resent her handmaid's marriage. Since stanza 1 provides a particularly suitable context for a laudatory apology similar to those cited above, why should Spenser have inserted it in stanza 21 where it would not only spoil the poetry, but might well be taken as insulting rather than complimentary to the person addressed. Could anything have been less likely to please Elizabeth than the following suggestions: She is one of those outsiders against whose meddlesome curiosity the lovers sought the protection of the darkness (cf. ll. 319, 320, 360, 370), but her intelligence service is too efficient to be evaded; she will be jealous of Spenser's bride, for even if 'envy' means 'to be vexed', in the context both of the poem and of Elizabeth's notorious failing, the annoyance could only be caused by jealousy; she should remember that she herself has been in love and even has had a liaison with Endymion (Leicester?); she is an excellent midwife and notable for her encouragement of large families.

To identify Cynthia with Queen Elizabeth is not only to impute stupid tactlessness to the poet, it is to misunderstand the structure of the poem. [This structure, exclusive of the first prefatory stanza and the final envoy, can be divided into four parts, separated from one another by the appearances of Heavenly Bodies. The expectant dawn-song closes as the rising sun announces the wedding-day; the evening star ushers in the wedding night; the shining of the moon through the window before the approach of dawn, inaugurates a new and more farsighted phase of hopeful expectation.] [It was, as we have seen, part of the Epithalamic tradition that the farewell of friends and wedding-guests should include outspoken references to the pleasures of the coming night and the desirability of founding a family; Spenser adds beauty and solemnity to this theme, by transforming the good-wishes of the company into a private prayer made by the bridegroom as he and his wife look beyond themselves into the future.] The rising of the moon at this juncture has nothing to do with Queen Elizabeth, but, as Spenser himself informs us, very much to do with generation and 'wemen's labours', and surely, if Cynthia is to be connected with any mortal it is not with the poet's Queen but with his wife, who has already been likened to Phoebe (cf. l. 149) and from now on will be the active agent in bringing new life into the world.

Cynthia is invoked with other mythological figures concerned with marriage, but because she is both the moon who makes external things visible and the Moon-goddess who aids child-birth she has a more complex significance than her companions; for in several different ways she reverses the process of withdrawal that began for the lovers at sundown. By her concern for child-birth she breaks through the privacy of the lovers, for parenthood is a social function; as she shines through the window, darkness is dispelled and although silence is not broken its quality is changed for the cessation of the echo in ll. 388–9, 407–8 is not

the silencing of ill-omened sounds, or the muffling of private joys;
it is the creative silence in which the seed grows secretly.

The change of pronouns in the refrain is also significant. In
the first stanza, when Spenser is proposing to sing to himself
alone, the pronoun is naturally 'my'. After that the pronouns are
'your' or 'their' for the woods are echoing the sounds of birds,
nymphs, angels, human merrymakers and demonic spirits. With
the rising of the moon the pronoun changes to 'our', for the man
and woman are now one flesh and have almost lost the sense
of separate existence or present time in their creative joy and
anticipation.

The moon makes earth visible, but it makes it seem less solid
than the daylight world, less real than the brilliant starlit sky.
Unlike the lover of the first hymn, the Bridegroom does not
suggest that 'wretched earthly clods' can rival gods and angels,
nor does he mistake their earthly paradise for Heaven. His
desires have longer range. By begetting children he hopes not to
gain a kind of earthly immortality for himself and his wife, but
rather to increase the happy population both of this world and the
next.

As far as I can see, the last stanzas lend little support to Professor Hieatt's theory that 'the shimmering surface of Spenser's
marriage day', conceals a meditation on Mutability and on the
consoling thought that while time lasts the imperfection of
created things is compensated by 'cyclical return' and that 'the
individual, mortal life of is renewed in generation'.

Spenser was certainly deeply conscious of recurrence and
mutability and much of this poem depends on the intimate rela-
tions held between the bridal couple and their environment; but
the contrasts between light and darkness, sound and silence, the
changes in time and space are all parts of what Professor Hieatt
calls the surface and I prefer to call the body of the poem; the
vital heart of it is a human action which determines the quality
of the particular time and place in which it occurs and also has
eternal significance.

Spenser concludes *Epithalamion* with a kind of postscript sharply
separated from the main wedding-song and modelled on the
tornata, the traditional ending of the Italian *canzone.* In *Convivio*,[1]
Dante makes some interesting comments on the origin and use of

this particular form of 'envoy'. It was, he tells us, originally a
musical device, and was called the *tornata* because the poets who
first employed it did so, in order that when the Ode had been
sung they should return to it again with a certain part of the air.
He, on the other hand, uses a metre different from that of the
main poem in order to emphasize that his *tornata* serves an
intellectual purpose, for it conveys the author's comment on his
own work in a stanza addressed directly to the Ode itself, but
really intended for the reader. Spenser is obviously using the
same technique. Both in form and content his *Envoy* or *Tornata*
is sharply detached from the rest of the poem, and by addressing
his Song he is commenting on its occasion and purpose for the
benefit of his readers. The information, however, is not very
clearly conveyed and has given rise to much discussion.

The obscurity is partly due to loose syntax caused by over-
compression. If 'cutting off' stands for 'having been cut off' and
qualifies 'ornaments', the following interpretation seems plausible:
Something had happened to hasten on the marriage and consequently suitable gifts and ornaments could not be procured in
time for the wedding. The poet, therefore, dispatched his poem
earlier than he had intended in order to compensate his bride for
her disappointment. If 'cutting off' is taken as an action of the
personified Song, we must accept Professor Judson's suggestion
(*Spenser*, *Var*, *Life*, p. 172) that by 'ornaments' Spenser meant
poems and probably poems intended to supply a happy ending
to the temporary misunderstanding and separation recorded in the
last four sonnets of the *Amoretti*. His original intention was to
present his bride with an enlarged sonnet-sequence leading up to
the wedding-hymn, but an unexpected lack of time caused him
to change his plans. He proceeded at once to compose the
Epithalamion and dispatched it without delay as a not unworthy
offering even though shorn of the linking poems that should
have accompanied it. Since the Song is being exhorted to fulfil
its promise of recompensing the bride both for lack of 'ornaments' and for 'hasty accidents', it seems natural to suppose that
'short time' refers to the curtailment of the wedding preparations
rather than to the all too brief duration of the wedding-day. The
ambiguity, however, may be intentional.

The general meaning of the Envoy seems to me clear enough. The *Epithalamion* is intended as a personal gift to his bride, which will more than make up for any deficiencies in the actual wedding arrangements, for it is written in her honour and will 'immortalize' her and her wedding day. Its purpose is to frame the poem by recalling the first stanza and reminding us that the 'I' who speaks is a poet writing poetry about his wedding not a bridegroom actually experiencing it, but to do so in such a way that we are left with no excuse for doubting the genuineness of the poet's real feelings about his own real marriage. The abrupt descent from high contemplation to the everyday world of wedding presents and upset timetables, comes not as an anticlimax, but as a final affirmation of the authenticity of the experience described in the *Epithalamion.*

V. CONCLUSION

In *Epithalamion* and *Fowre Hymnes* Spenser presents love from three different and it would almost seem irreconcilable points of view. The Bridegroom of the *Epithalamion* and the wooer of the first two hymns agree in distinguishing love both from merely physical desire or a merely mental affinity, but they differ in their attitude to the outside world; the wooer's mind being wholly concentrated on the winning of his lady and on making a god of earthly love; the bridegroom even on the wedding-night seeing himself and his bride as part of a larger whole which includes both earth and heaven. It is interesting that both of these attitudes find expression in the *Amoretti*. In sonnet 22, the 'Ash Wednesday' sonnet, the as-yet unsuccessful suitor proposes to spend the 'holy season fit to fast and pray' in an idolatrous worship of his 'sweet saynt'; but in sonnet 68, the Easter-day sonnet, he can address himself with equal sincerity to his Risen Lord and his newly betrothed lady:

> So let us love, deare love, lyke as we ought,
> love is the lesson which the Lord us taught.

After his conversion, the lover of the hymns continues to differ from the bridegroom, but from the opposite point of view: for whereas the bridegroom regards his wedding as a *holy* event, pleasing to God and Man, the rejected suitor now seems to consider all earthly love to be incompatible with the love of God. Are we meant to agree with him? Is it then not only thwarted and idolatrous, but happy and lawful human love that must be renounced by the devotees of Divine Wisdom. Or should we rather conclude that a disillusioned person is apt to lose his sense of proportion? More difficulties arise when we remember that Spenser was a Protestant and that to an orthodox Protestant retirement from the world in order to enjoy the vision of God, could be as reprehensible as the desire to enjoy a mistress, since it could spring from spiritual pride and the desire for self enhancement. Yet Spenser evidently does not mean us to regard the love of Heavenly Beauty as a sin.

Some help in solving these problems may be gained by considering our poems in the context of Spenser's other works and particularly *The Fairie Queene*. To do so adequately would require a volume; here, it is only possible to offer a few tentative suggestions for further thought.

In Book III of *The Fairie Queene* Spenser makes it clear that Chastity is not a repudiation of human love but a manifestation of its purity. It can take different forms: Britomart, Belphoebe, Amoret and Florimel all exhibit pure and faithful love, but whereas Britomart and Belphoebe are self-reliant Amazons who actively assault vice; Amoret and Florimel are always on the defensive, protect their purity by passive resistance and flight and are constantly in need of help. Belphoebe, who attracts love but has chosen virginity, can terrorize her assailants; Amoret, who represents feminine sexuality which fulfils itself in marriage, has been abducted from her husband Scudamour (Shield-of-Love) and is constantly threatened by masculine lust, and saved by Britomart or Belphoebe. Amoret's passivity is innocent and feminine, but Scudamour's helplessness is unmanly and guilty and therefore his wife owes her release to the 'huge heroick magnanimity' of Britomart who passes unscathed through the flames which bar the entrance to Amoret's prison and drive back Scudamour 'all scorcht and pitifully brent'. It is significant that Scudamour's account of his winning and wooing of Amoret is composed in the court of love tradition and reminds one both of the *Hymne of Love* and of the *Amoretti* and moreover that the sonnets 72, 76, 77 and 84 imply a conflict between pure love and

carnal desire which has not been ended by the poet's betrothal.
Though Scudamour is a loving husband, he fails to live up to his
name, and his failure illustrates the distinction between love and
lust which is drawn in the first two hymns.

Do the successes of Britomart and Belphoebe, who have
transcended the limitations of sex, endorse the asceticism of the
fourth hymn? Does Belphoebe illustrate the superiority of
virginity to marriage and, if so, why is she described as the twin-
sister of Amoret, and why does the altercation between their
respective foster-mothers, Diana and Venus, end in a reconciliation brought about by the latter goddess?

In an interesting article entitled *Spenser's Accommodation of
Allegory to History in the Story of Timias and Belphoebe*, Mr. H. M.
English[1] maintains that Spenser's treatment of this episode is
governed by his desire to show that Raleigh's love for Elizabeth
Throckmorton was perfectly consistent with his devotion to
Queen Elizabeth. The historical allegory does not concern us,
but Mr. English's interpretation of the moral allegory is very
relevant to our subject.

According to Mr. English, Spenser regards virginity not as a
negative virtue of self-denial but as a positive virtue of singlemindedness which only involves renunciation of marriage because
sexual intercourse inevitably includes a measure of self-love and
therefore hinders that wholehearted devotion to an ideal which
leads to the disinterested service of one's fellow men. Virginity
is essentially the highest form of the New Testament 'Agape',
the love that descends to give and serve and comes from God and is
distinguishable from the Eros-love that ascends to get and enjoy
is founded on sexuality. Moreover, since the renunciation of
sexual love is the renunciation of something subject to time and
death, virginity frees us not only from self-love but also from
mutability and imparts an eternal quality even to our earthly
existence. But although virginity is the highest, it is not the only
form of chaste love and Belphoebe is over severe in her con-
demnation of Timias and insufficiently aware of her close relationship to Amoret; who, in her own way, achieves singlemindedness
and immortality. Amoret, who was reared in the fertile garden
of Adonis, represents the human form of that procreative love
by which all living things perpetuate their kinds and so are

assimilated into the order of Nature and made 'eterne in Mutabilitie'. (According to Professor Hieatt, Spenser expresses the same
idea in *Epithalamion* by an elaborate numerical symbolism.) Nor
is Amoret lacking in disinterestedness. Belphoebe serves an ideal,
Amoret serves a human being, but both sisters give themselves
unreservedly to the object of their love. As Mr. English puts it:
'For Spenser, as for Augustine before him, Eros is not one thing
and Agape quite another. The idea is rather that Eros contains
within itself the seeds that enable it to be transcended and sub-
sumed by Agape.'

If Mr. English's interpretation of the moral allegory of Books
III–IV is correct, it would seem reasonable to suppose that, like
Belphoebe, the lover of Sapience went too far in the depreciation
of earthly love, but was justified in valuing virginity as the best
way of life.

But did Spenser regard virginity as a more exalted state than
marriage? Admittedly there is something mysterious about Belphoebe who breaks suddenly into Book II like a visitant from
another world, a 'glorious mirrhour of celestiall grace, And
souveraine moniment of mortall vowes', nevertheless, the chief
heroine of Book III is Britomart, who, although she is still a
virgin, is doing her best to enter the holy estate of matrimony and
is therefore a more inclusive symbol of chaste love than either
Belphoebe or Amoret. This is borne out by the encomium which
opens the third Canto of Book III and praises Britomart as a
perfect exemplar of both Agape and Eros-love:

> Most sacred fire, that burnest mightily
> In liuing brests, ykindled first aboue,
> Emongst th'eternall spheres and lamping sky,
> And thence pourd into men, which men call Loue;
> Not that same, which doth base affections moue
> In brutish minds, and filthy lust inflame,
> But that sweet fit, that doth true beautie loue,
> And choseth vertue for his dearest Dame,
> Whence spring all noble deeds and neuer dying fame:
>
> Well did Antiquitie a God thee deeme,
> That ouer mortall minds has so great might,
> To order them, as best to thee doth seeme,

And all their actions to direct aright;
The fatall purpose of diuine foresight,
Thou doest effect in destined descents,
Through deepe impression of thy secret might,
And stirredst vp th' Heroes high intents,
Which the late world admyres for wondrous moniments.

But thy dread darts in none doe triumph more,
Ne brauer proofe in any, of thy powre
Shew'dst thou, then in this royall Maid of yore,
Making her seeke an vnknowne Paramoure,
From the worlds end, through many a bitter stowre;
From whose two loynes thou afterwards did rayse
Most famous fruits of matrimoniall bowre,
Which through the earth haue spred their liuing prayse,
That fame in trompe of gold eternally displays.

These verses do not suggest that virginity is an essential condition for the practice of the highest form of chaste love; on the
contrary they emphasize that the Divine Agape who stirred up
Britomart's 'high intents' and noble acts has also preordained
that her quest for Artegall should end in fruitful marriage.

A similar idea of love, I believe, underlies the plan for *The
Fairie Queene* outlined by Spenser in his much-discussed letter to
Sir Walter Raleigh. Gloriana dispatching from her court twelve
knights to perform twelve acts of mercy is surely illustrating
Agape-love, while Eros-love is equally plainly embodied in
Prince Arthur who has seen Gloriana in a vision and is now seeking her throughouth Fairyland. Spenser's statement of his intention has worried critics considerably, for his plan has seemed to
them to consist not of one plot but of two contradictory ones.
To Mrs. Josephine Bennet,[1] for instance, Gloriana's court and
Arthur's quest are two rival foci of the poem and set up a cross-
current in the action, Arthur being constantly deflected from his
movement towards the Queen, by bringing assistance to the
knights who are moving away from her. How Spenser would
have finally manipulated his narrative we cannot tell, but obviously
to him the theme of the Task did not seem incompatible with the
theme of the Quest or he would not have coupled them together
in his letter. In Book II, Canto VIII, he not only reconciles them
he almost identifies them; for Arthur, the central representative

G

of the questing Eros-love that seeks fulfilment, rescues the help-less, unconscious Guyon, as agent of the Grace of God Who sends out His angels 'to serve his wicked foe. . . . And all for loue, and nothing for reward: O why should heauenly God to men haue such regard?' I suspect that Spenser would have shown at the end of his poem, that, by aiding the Knights, Arthur was moving towards not away from the Fairy Queen, and certainly the conduct of the poem as it stands suggests that to try to separate Eros from Agape is about as sensible as to try and separate inhalation from exhalation in breathing. It also suggests that for Spenser love is not dual but trinal. Arthur's quest is obviously going to end in a marriage and a coronation. The purpose of the wooing gods Agape and Eros is to usher in Hymen, the god who neither descends nor ascends but unites, and by so doing brings joy and fulfilment.

Both *Epithalamion* and *The Fairie Queene* show that Spenser could have joined Leone Ebreo in saying: 'We define love as a desire to enjoy union, or let us say to become one with the object of love.' Could he also have joined him in applying this definition not only to our love for one another but to the reciprocal love of the Creator and the creature? Leone Ebreo sees that there is a difficulty. Paternal love, the love of the superior for the inferior is nobler than filial love since it is nobler to give than to get; but since love is evoked by worth the beloved must be worthier than the lover, and filial love nobler than paternal love because directed towards a nobler object. Is the Universe then nobler than God because God loves it? Leone Ebreo's answer is that God loves the Universe not for what it is in itself, but for what it becomes when perfected and united to Him by love. The difference between Neo-Platonism and Protestantism comes out clearly here. To an instructed Lutheran or Calvinist there was no problem for Leone Ebreo to solve. Certainly to give is nobler than to get; but it is not true that the beloved must be worthier than the lover; for, in that case all love would be egocentric and acquisitive. No creature can become worthy of God's love; but God may love it in spite of its unworthiness.

Where does Spenser stand? Are the lovers of Sapience and Gloriana's honour-seeking knights helping to perfect God's universe and to make it worthier of his love?

In *The Fairie Queene*, Spenser seems more aware of degeneration from a golden age in the past than of progress towards a future Utopia; nevertheless, even the fallen world is part of God's hierarchic Universe, and although the powers of evil have spoilt and obscured its beauty, they have not wholly destroyed its divinely planned structure, and it is the task of Gloriana's knights, of all heroic lovers, to restore and maintain the divine order in a sinful world. This means war, and war waged with no prospect of peace in sight. There are, indeed, lulls in the warfare, moments of victory when angelic music mingles with the secular rejoicings and Paradise seems almost regained. But such moments cannot last. The Blatant Beast remains at large; Artegall cannot stay with Britomart; Redcross must come down from the Hill of Contemplation and even leave Una in order to continue in the active service of the Fairy Queen. The perfect union between the Creator and his creation is postponed to the Day of Judgment and until that day, Love must remain on duty. For Spenser, therefore, Love is a militant virtue and one great distinction between love and lust is that the latter is slothful and short-sighted, while the former is a dynamic power that allows its followers no rest: 'It lets not scarse this Prince to breathe at all, But to his first poursuit him forward still doth call,' Acrasia's victim sees no further than his restful Bower of Bliss, the bridegroom of the *Epithalamion* sees beyond the bridal chamber even on his wedding-night.]

The action of *The Fairie Queene* could be cited in favour of Leone Ebreo's thesis, but it is not inconsistent with the Protestant doctrine that good works, though not in themselves meritorious, are the necessary product of the unmerited gift of grace, and it certainly endorses the familiar Protestant objections to monasticism. When Redcross leaves Una to resume his military duties, he is not mounting the Neo-Platonic ladder, but obeying the instructions of the Divine Agape. The actions of Belphoebe can be similarly interpreted: her virginity may, as Mr. English suggests, free her from worldly distractions; but it frees her for perilous adventure, not for mouldering 'in idle cell' or on top of the Hill of Contemplation. The lovers of Sapience live in her presence and reject worldly values; we are not told that they contract out of worldly duties.

Nevertheless, in spite of his insistence upon Grace, his belief in Predestination and approval of the active life, Spenser's conception of trinal love prevents him from excommunicating Eros or condemning as egocentric the desire for union with an object worthy of love. Arthur is not blamed for seeking Gloriana. Spenser could hardly have written *The Fairie Queene* had he believed in Total Depravity and the consequent worthlessness of all virtue and wisdom outside the Christian dispensation and most of the religiousness within it. It is true that Gloriana's knight-errants by fulfilling 'the fatall purpose of diuine foresight' are acting as *predestined* agents of that Divine-Agape-Love which is the theme of the third hymn, but the fourth hymn, which is concerned with the love of man for God contains no trace of the Lutheran distrust of mystical aspiration and both of the heavenly hymns appear to be based on the mediæval doctrine of 'caritas' rather than on the Protestant doctrine of 'salvation by faith alone'. The agape-love of Christ for men produces in them not only gratitude to Him and love for their fellow-sinners, it also stirs up a heavenly Eros-love, an insatiable desire for complete union with God, which can never be fully enjoyed in this life, though the accepted lovers of Sapience have a delightful foretaste of it and no worldly happiness can compensate for its absence.

Although Spenser praises love as an *active* virtue he does not value work for work's sake or believe that to travel hopefully is better than to arrive. On the contrary, he longs for 'that same time when no more *Change* shall be' and when, as Hooker puts it ' "the longing disposition of them that thirst is changed into the sweet affection of them that taste and are replenished". Whereas we now love the thing that is good, but good especially in respect of benefit unto us; we shall then love the thing that is good, only or principally for the goodness of beauty in itself. The soul being in this sort, as it is active, perfected by love of that infinite good, shall as it is receptive be also perfected with those supernatural passions of joy, peace, and delight. All this endless and ever-lasting.'[1]

But does not this imply self-love? In a sense it does; but unlike Luther and Calvin, Hooker supported the traditional scholastic view that Grace does not destroy Nature but perfects it; that there is a right as well as a wrong self-love, for to condemn every kind of self-love is to despise what God created.

Spenser has more in common with Hooker than with Ficino or Luther or Calvin, and the affinity is temperamental as well as doctrinal. Both the theologian and the poet have a deep sense of the holiness of beauty and the beauty of God and a firm conviction that the proper response to beauty is devotion and delight. Both men *feel* as well as think that natural life is good, but that men *naturally* desire a supernatural blessedness that only the Grace of God can grant them: 'For although the beauties, riches, honours, sciences, virtues, and perfections of all men living, were in the present possession of one; yet somewhat beyond and above all this there would still be sought and earnestly thirsted for. So that Nature even in this life doth plainly claim and call for a more divine perfection. . . .'[1]

Both the enjoyment of earthly beauty and the failure of earthly hopes can in their different ways intensify desire for the enjoyment of heavenly beauty in a world unspoilt by evil and unthreatened by time. As the bridegroom looks up at the starry sky, both he and his bride seem merely 'earthly clods', who, nevertheless, aspire to immortality. The lover of the fourth hymn need not be regarded as a deserter who refuses to come down from the Hill of Contemplation, because he seeks in God his own satisfaction and self-enhancement; but rather as a man who is learning a truth about the ultimate need of the human soul which is accessible to all men, but which in its fullness is perhaps more acceptable to the unsuccessful than to the successful lover of an earthly woman.

TO THE RIGHT HONORABLE AND MOST VERTUOUS LADIES
THE LADIE MARGARET COUNTESSE OF CUMBERLAND
AND THE LADIE MARIE
COUNTESSE OF WARWICKE[1]

HAVING in the greener times of my youth, composed these
former two Hymnes in the praise of Love and beautie, and finding
that the same too much pleased those of like age and disposition,
which being too vehemently caried with that kind of affection,
do rather sucke out poyson to their strong passion, then hony to
their honest delight, I was moved by the one of you two most
excellent Ladies, to call in the same. But being unable so to doe,
by reason that many copies thereof were formerly scattered
abroad, I resolved at least to amend, and by way of retractation
to reforme them, making in stead of those two Hymnes of earthly
or naturall love and beautie, two others of heavenly and celestiall.
The which I doe dedicate ioyntly unto you two honorable sisters,
as to the most excellent and rare ornaments of all true love and
beautie, both in the one & the other kinde, humbly beseeching
you to vouchsafe the patronage of them, and to accept this my
humble service, in lieu of the great graces and honourable favours
which ye dayly shew vnto me, vntill such time as I may by better
meanes yeeld you some more notable testimonie of my thankfull
mind and dutifull devotion.

And even so I pray for your happinesse.
Greenwich this first of September.
1596.

Yours Honors most bounden ever
in all humble service.
Ed. Sp.

FOWRE HYMNES

AN HYMNE IN
HONOUR OF
LOVE

Love,[1] that long since hast to thy mightie powre,
Perforce subdude my poore captived hart,
And raging now therein with restless stowre,[2]   *conflict*
Doest tyrannize in everie weaker part;
Faine would I seeke to ease my bitter smart,
By any service I might do to thee,
Or ought that else might to thee pleasing bee.

And now t'asswage the force of this new flame,[3]
And make thee more propitious in my need,
I meane to sing the praises of thy name,   10
And thy victorious conquests to areed;[4]   *proclaim*
By which thou madest many harts to bleed
Of mighty Victors, with wyde wounds embrewed,[5]
And by thy cruell darts to thee subdewed.

Onely I feare my wits enfeebled late,
Through the sharpe sorrowes, which thou hast me bred,
Should faint, and words should faile me, to relate
The wondrous triumphs of thy great godhed.
But if thou wouldst vouchsafe to overspred
Me with the shadow of thy gentle wing,   20
I should enabled be thy actes to sing.

Come then, ô come, thou mightie God of love,
Out of thy silver bowres and secret blisse,
Where thou doest sit in *Venus* lap[6] above,
Bathing thy wings in her ambrosiall kisse,
That sweeter farre then any Nectar is;
Come softly, and my feeble breast inspire
With gentle furie,[7] kindled of thy fire.

And ye sweet Muses,[1] which have often proved
The piercing points of his avengefull darts;   30
And ye faire Nimphs, which oftentimes have loved
The cruell worker of your kindly[2] smarts,
Prepare your selves, and open wide your harts,
For to receive the triumph of your glorie,[3]
That made you merie oft, when ye were sorie.

And ye faire blossomes of youths wanton breed,
Which in the conquests of your beautie bost,
Wherewith your lovers feeble eyes you feed,
But sterve their harts, that needeth nourture most,
Prepare your selves, to march amongst his host,   40
And all the way this sacred hymne do sing,
Made in the honor of your Soveraigne king.

GREAT GOD of might, that reignest in the mynd,
And all the bodie to thy hest doest frame,
Victor of gods, subduer of mankynd,
That doest the Lions and fell Tigers tame,
Making their cruell rage thy scornefull game,
And in their roring taking great delight;
Who can expresse the glorie of thy might?

Or who alive can perfectly declare,   50
The wondrous cradle of thine infancie?
When thy great mother *Venus* first thee bare,
Begot of Plentie and of Penurie,[4]
Though elder then thine owne nativitie;
And yet a chyld, renewing still thy yeares;
And yet the eldest of the heavenly Peares.[5]

For ere this worlds still moving mightie masse,[6]
Out of great *Chaos* ugly prison crept,
In which his goodly face long hidden was
From heavens view, and in deepe darkness kept,   60
Love, that had now long time securely slept
In *Venus* lap,[7] unarmed then and naked,
Gan reare his head, by *Clotho* being waked.

And taking to him wings of his owne heate,
Kindled at first from heavens life-giving fyre,
He gan to move out of his idle seate,
Weakely at first, but after with desyre
Lifted aloft, he gan to mount up hyre,
And like fresh Eagle, make his hardie flight
Through all that great wide wast, yet wanting light.   70   a).

Yet wanting light to guide his wandring way,
His owne faire mother,[1] for all creatures sake,
Did lend him light from her owne goodly ray: w)
Then through the world his way he gan to take,
The world that was not till he did it make;[2]
Whose sundrie parts[3] he from them selves did sever,
The which before had lyen confused ever.

The earth, the ayre, the water, and the fyre,
Then gan to raunge them selves in huge array,
And with contrary forces to conspyre   80
Each against other, by all meanes they may,
Threatning their owne confusion and decay:
Ayre hated earth, and water hated fyre,
Till Love relented their rebellious yre. ✳ note 149

He then them tooke, and tempering goodly well ✳ note 149
Their contrary dislikes with loved meanes,[4]
Did place them all in order, and compell
To keepe them selves within their sundrie raines,[5]
Together linkt with Adamantine chaines;
Yet so, as that in every living wight   90
They mixe themselves, and shew their kindly might.

So ever since they firmely have remained,
And duly well observed his beheast;
Through which now all these things that are contained
Within this goodly cope,[6] both most and least
Their being have, and dayly are increast,
Through secret sparks of his infused fyre,
Which in the barraine cold he doth inspyre.

Thereby they all do live, and moved are
To multiply the likenesse of their kynd,   100
Whilest they seeke onely, without further care,
To quench the flame, which they in burning fynd:
But man, that breathes a more immortall mynd,
Not for lusts sake, but for eternitie,
Seekes to enlarge his lasting progenie.[1]

For having yet in his deducted[2] spright,
Some sparks remaining of that heavenly fyre,
He is enlumind with that goodly light,
Unto like goodly semblant to aspyre:
Therefore in choice of love, he doth desyre   110
That seems on earth most heavenly, to embrace,
That same is Beautie, borne of heavenly race.

For sure of all, that in this mortall frame
Contained is, nought more divine doth seeme,
Or that resembleth more th'immortall flame
Of heavenly light, then Beauties glorious beame.
What wonder then, if with such rage extreme
Fraile men, whose eyes seek heavenly things to see,
At sight thereof so much enravisht bee?

Which well perceiving that imperious boy,[3]   120
Doth therwith tip his sharp empoisned darts;
Which glancing through the eyes with countenance coy,
Rest not, till they have pierst the trembling harts,
And kindled flame in all their inner parts,
Which suckes the blood, and drinketh up the lyfe
Of carefull wretches with consuming griefe.

Thenceforth they playne, & make ful piteous mone
Unto the author of their balefull bane;
The daies they waste, the nights they grieve and grone,
Their lives they loath, and heavens light disdaine;   130
No light but that, whose lampe doth yet remaine
Fresh burning in the image of their eye,
They deigne to see, and seeing it still dye.

The whylst thou tyrant Love doest laugh & scorne
At their complaints, making their paine thy play;
Whylest they lye languishing like thrals forlorne,
The whyles thou doest triumph in their decay,
And otherwhyles, their dying to delay,[1]
Thou doest emmarble the proud hart of her,
Whose love before their life they doe prefer.   140

So hast thou often done (ay me the more)
To me thy vassall, whose yet bleeding hart,
With thousand wounds thou mangled hast so sore
That whole remaines scarse any little part,
Yet to augment the anguish of my smart,
Thou hast enfrosen her disdainefull brest,
That no one drop of pitie there doth rest.

Why then do I this honor unto thee,
Thus to ennoble thy victorious name,
Since thou doest shew no favour unto mee,   150
Ne once move ruth in that rebellious Dame,
Somewhat to slacke the rigour of my flame?
Certes[2] small glory doest thou winne hereby,
To let her live thus free, and me to dy.

But if thou be indeede, as men thee call,
The worlds great Parent, the most kind preserver
Of living wights,[3] the soveraine Lord of all,
How falles it then, that with thy furious fervour,
Thou doest afflict as well the not deserver,[4]
As him that doeth thy lovely heasts despize,   160
And on thy subjects most doest tyrannize?

Yet herein eke[5] thy glory seemeth more,
By so hard handling those which best thee serve,
That ere thou doest them unto grace restore,
Thou mayest well trie if they will ever swerve,
And mayest them make it better to deserve,
And having got it, may it more esteeme,
For things hard gotten, men more dearely deeme.

So hard those heavenly beauties be enfyred,
As things divine, least passions doe impresse,   170
The more of stedfast mynds to be admyred,
The more they stayed be on stedfastnesse:[1]
But baseborne mynds such lamps regard the lesse,
Which at first blowing take not hastie fyre,
Such fancies feele no love, but loose desyre.

For love is Lord of truth and loialtie,
Lifting himselfe out of the lowly dust,
On golden plumes up to the purest skie,
Above the reach of loathly sinfull lust,
Whose base affect through cowardly distrust   180
Of his weake wings, dare not to heaven fly,
But like a moldwarpe[2] in the earth doth ly.

His dunghill thoughts, which do themselves enure[3]
To dirtie drosse, no higher dare aspyre,
Ne can his feeble earthly eyes endure
The flaming light of that celestiall fyre,
Which kindleth love in generous[4] desyre,
And makes him mount above the native might
Of heavie earth, up to the heavens hight.

Such is the powre of that sweet passion,   190
That it all sordid basenesse doth expell,
And the refyned mynd doth newly fashion
Unto a fairer forme, which now doth dwell
In his high thought, that would it selfe excell;
Which he beholding still with constant sight,
Admires the mirrour of so heavenly light.[5]

Whose image printing in his deepest wit,
He thereon feeds his hungrie fantasy,
Still full, yet never satisfyde with it,
Like *Tantale*,[6] that in store doth sterved ly: 200
So doth he pine in most satiety,
For nought may quench his infinite desyre,
Once kindled through that first conceived fyre.

Thereon his mynd affixed wholly is,
Ne thinks on ought, but how it to attaine;
His care, his joy, his hope is all on this,
That seemes in it all blisses to containe,
In sight whereof, all other blisse seemes vaine.
Thrise happie man, might he the same possesse;
He faines[1] himselfe, and doth his fortune blesse.   210

And though he do not win his wish to end,
Yet thus farre happie he him selfe doth weene,
That heavens such happie grace did to him lend,
As thing on earth so heavenly, to have seene,
His harts enshrined saint, his heavens queene,
Fairer then fairest, in his fayning eye,
Whose sole aspect he counts felicitye.

Then forth he casts in his unquiet thought,
What he may do, her favour to obtaine;
What brave exploit, what perill hardly wrought,   220
What puissant conquest, what adventurous paine,
May please her best, and grace unto him gaine:
He dreads no danger, nor misfortune feares,
His faith, his fortune, in his breast he beares.

Thou art his god, thou art his mightie guyde,
Thou being blind, letst him not see his feares,
But cariest him to that which he hath eyde,
Through seas, through flames, through thousand swords and
     speares:
Ne ought so strong that may his force withstand,
With which thou armest his resistlesse hand.   230

Witnesse *Leander*, in the Euxine waves,
And stout *Æneas* in the Trojane fyre,
Achilles preassing through the Phyrgian glaives,
And *Orpheus* daring to provoke the yre
Of damned fiends, to get his love retyre:
For both through heaven and hell thou makest way,
To win them worship which to thee obay.[2]

And if by all these perils and these paynes,
He may but purchase lyking in her eye,
What heavens of joy, then to himselfe he faynes,   240
Eftsoones he wypes quite out of memory,
What ever ill before he did aby,[1]
Had it bene death, yet would he die againe,
To live thus happie as her grace to gaine.

Yet when he hath found favour to his will,
He nathemore can so contented rest,
But forceth further on, and striveth still
T'approch more neare, till in her inmost brest,
He may embosomd bee, and loved best;
And yet not best, but to be lov'd alone,   250
For love can not endure a Paragone.[2]

The feare whereof, ô how doth it torment
His troubled mynd with more then hellish paine!
And to his fayning fansie represent
Sights never seene, and thousand shadowes vaine,
To breake his sleepe, and waste his ydle braine;
Thou that hast never lov'd canst not beleeve,
Least part of th'evils which poore lovers greeve.

The gnawing envie, the hart-fretting feare,
The vaine surmizes, the distrustfull showes,   260
The false reports that flying tales doe beare,
The doubts, the daungers, the delayes, the woes,
The fayned friends, the unassured foes,
With thousands more then any tongue can tell,
Doe make a lovers life a wretches hell.

Yet is there one more cursed then they all,
That cancker worme, that monster Gelosie,
Which eates the hart, and feedes upon the gall,
Turning all loves delight to miserie,
Through feare of loosing his felicitie.   270
Ah Gods, that ever ye that monster placed
In gentle love, that all his joyes defaced.

By these, ô Love, thou doest thy entrance make,
Unto thy heaven, and doest the more endeere,
Thy pleasures unto those which them partake,
As after stormes when clouds begin to cleare,
The Sunne more bright and glorious doth appeare;
So thou thy folke, through paines of Purgatorie,
Dost beare unto thy blisse, and heavens glorie.

There thou them placest in a Paradize   280
Of all delight, and joyous happie rest,
Where they doe feede on Nectar heavenly wize,
With *Hercules* and *Hebe*,[1] and the rest
Of *Venus* dearlings, through her bountie blest,
And lie like Gods in yvorie beds arayd,
With rose and lillies over them displayd.

There with thy daughter *Pleasure* they doe play
Their hurtlesse sports, without rebuke or blame,
And in her snowy bosome boldly lay
Their quiet heads, devoyd of guilty shame,   290
After full joyance of their gentle game,
Then her they crowne their Goddesse and their Queene,
And decke with floures thy altars well beseene.

Ay me, deare Lord, that ever I might hope,
For all the paines and woes that I endure,
To come at length unto the wished scope
Of my desire, or might my selfe assure,
That happie port for ever to recure.[2]
Then would I thinke these paines no paines at all,
And all my woes to be but penance small.   300

Then would I sing of thine immortall praise
An heavenly Hymne, such as the Angels sing,
And thy triumphant name then would I raise
Bove all the gods, thee onely honoring,
My guide, my God, my victor, and my king;
Till then, dread Lord, vouchsafe to take of me
This simple song, thus fram'd in praise of thee.

FINIS

AN HYMNE IN
HONOUR OF
BEAUTIE

AH whither, Love, wilt thou now carrie mee?
What wontlesse[1] fury dost thou now inspire
Into my feeble breast, too full of thee?
Whylest seeking to aslake thy raging fyre,
Thou in me kindlest much more great desyre,
And up aloft above my strength doest rayse
The wondrous matter of my fyre[2] to prayse.

That as I earst in praise of thine owne name,
So now in honour of thy Mother deare,
An honourable Hymne I eke should frame,   10
And with the brightnesse of her beautie cleare,
The ravisht harts of gazefull men might reare,
To admiration of that heavenly light,
From whence proceeds such soule enchaunting might.

Therto do thou great Goddesse, queene of Beauty,
Mother of love, and of all worlds delight,
Without whose soverayne grace and kindly dewty,[3]
Nothing on earth seemes fayre to fleshly sight,
Doe thou vouchsafe with thy love-kindling light,
T'illuminate my dim and dulled eyne,   20
And beautifie this sacred hymne of thyne.

That both to thee, to whom I meane it most,
And eke[4] to her, whose faire immortall beame,
Hath darted fyre into my feeble ghost,
That now it wasted is with woes extreame,
It may so please that she at length will streame
Some deaw of grace, into my withered hart,
After long sorrow and consuming smart.

WHAT time this worlds great workmaister[1] did cast
To make al things, such as we now behold,   30
It seemes that he before his eyes had plast
A goodly Paterne to whose perfect mould,
He fashioned them as comely as he could,
That now so faire and seemely they appeare,
As nought may be amended any wheare.

That wondrous Paterne[2] wheresoere it bee,
Whether in earth layd up in secret store,
Or else in heaven, that no man may it see
With sinfull eyes, for feare it to deflore,
Is perfect Beautie which all men adore,   40
Whose face and feature doth so much excell
All mortal sence, that none the same may tell.

Thereof as every earthly thing partakes,
Or more or lesse by influence divine,
So it more faire accordingly it makes,
And the grosse matter of this earthly myne,
Which clotheth it, thereafter doth refyne,
Doing away the drosse which dims the light
Of that faire beame, which therein is empight.[3]

For through infusion of celestiall powre,   50
The duller earth it quickneth with delight,
And life-full spirits[4] privily doth powre
Through all the parts, that to the lookers sight
They seeme to please. That is thy soveraine might,
O *Cyprian* Queene, which flowing from the beame
Of thy bright starre, thou into them doest streame.

That is the thing which giveth pleasant grace
To all things faire, that kindleth lively fyre,
Light of thy lampe, which shyning in the face,
Thence to the soule darts amorous desyre,   60
And robs the harts of those which it admyre,
Therewith thou pointest thy Sons poysned arrow,
That wounds the life, and wastes the inmost marrow.

H

How vainely then doe ydle wits invent,
That beautie is nought else, but mixture made
Of colours faire, and goodly temp'rament
Of pure complexions,[1] that shall quickly fade
And passe away, like to a sommers shade,
Or that it is but comely composition
Of parts well measurd, with meet disposition.   70

Hath white and red in it such wondrous powre,
That it can pierce through th'eyes unto the hart,
And therein stirre such rage and restlesse stowre,
As nought but death can stint his dolours smart?
Or can proportion of the outward part,
Move such affection in the inward mynd,
That it can rob both sense and reason blynd?

Why doe not then the blossomes of the field,
Which are arayd with much more orient hew,
And to the sense most daintie odours yield,   80
Worke like impression in the lookers vew?
Or why doe not faire pictures like powre shew,
In which oftimes, we Nature see of Art
Exceld, in perfect limming every part.

But ah, beleeve me, there is more then so
That workes such wonders in the minds of men.
I that have often prov'd, too well it know;
And who so list the like assayes to ken,
Shall find by tryall, and confesse it then,
That Beautie is not, as fond men misdeeme,   90
An outward shew of things, that onely seeme.

For that same goodly hew of white and red,
With which the cheekes are sprinckled, shal decay,
And those sweete rosy leaves so fairely spred
Upon the lips, shall fade and fall away
To that they were, even to corrupted clay.
That golden wyre, those sparckling stars so bright
Shall turne to dust, and loose their goodly light.

But that faire lampe,[1] from whose celestiall ray
That light proceedes, which kindleth lovers fire, 100
Shall never be extinguisht nor decay,
But when the vitall spirits doe expyre,
Unto her native planet shall retyre,
For it is heavenly borne and can not die,
Being a parcell of the purest skie.

For when the soule, the which derived was
At first, out of that great immortall Spright,[2]
By whom all live to love, whilome did pas
Downe from the top of purest heavens hight,
To be embodied here, it then tooke light 110
And lively spirits from that fayrest starre,[3]
Which lights the world forth from his firie carre.

Which powre retayning still or more or lesse,
When she in fleshly seede is eft[4] enraced,
Through every part she doth the same impresse,
According as the heavens have her graced,
And frames her house, in which she will be placed,
Fit for her selfe, adorning it with spoyle
Of th'heavenly riches, which she robd[5] erewhyle.

Therof it comes, that these faire soules, which have 120
The most resemblance of that heavenly light,
Frame to themselves most beautifull and brave
Their fleshly bowre, most fit for their delight,
And the grosse matter by a soveraine might
Tempers so trim, that it may well be seene,
A pallace fit for such a virgin Queene.[6]

So every spirit, as it is most pure,
And hath in it the more of heavenly light,
So it the fairer bodie doth procure
To habit in, and it more fairely dight 130
With chearefull grace and amiable sight.
For of the soule the bodie forme doth take:
For soule is forme, and doth the bodie make.[7]

Therefore where ever that thou doest behold
A comely corpse,[1] with beautie faire endewed,
Know this for certaine, that the same doth hold
A beauteous soule, with faire conditions thewed,
Fit to receive the seede of vertue strewed.
For all that faire is, is by nature good;
That is a signe to know the gentle blood.   140

Yet oft it falles, that many a gentle mynd
Dwels in deformed tabernacle drownd,
Either by chaunce, against the course of kynd,
Or through unaptnesse in the substance fownd,
Which it assumed of some stubborne grownd,
That will not yield unto her formes direction,
But is perform'd[2] with some foule imperfection.

And oft it falles (ay me the more to rew)
That goodly beautie, albe heavenly borne,
Is foule abusd, and that celestiall hew,[3]   150
Which doth the world with her delight adorne,
Made but the bait of sinne, and sinners scorne;[4]
Whilest every one doth seeke and sew to have it,
But every one doth seeke, but to deprave it.

Yet nathemore is that faire beauties blame,
But theirs that do abuse it unto ill:
Nothing so good, but that through guilty shame
May be corrupt, and wrested unto will.[5]
Nathelesse the soule is faire and beauteous still,
How ever fleshes fault it filthy make: 160
For things immortall no corruption take.[6]

But ye faire Dames, the worlds deare ornaments,
And lively images of heavens light,
Let not your beames with such disparagements
Be dimd, and your bright glorie darkned quight:
But mindfull still of your first countries sight,
Doe still preserve your first informed grace,[7]
Whose shadow yet shynes in your beauteous face.

Loath that foule blot, that hellish fierbrand,
Disloiall lust, faire beauties foulest blame,   170
That base affections, which your ears would bland,[1]
Commend to you by loves abused name;
But is indeed the bondslave of defame,
Which will the garland of your glorie marre,
And quench the light of your bright shyning starre.

But gentle Love, that loiall is and trew,
Will more illumine your resplendent ray,
And adde more brightnesse to your goodly hew,
From light of his pure fire, which by like way
Kindled of yours, your likenesse doth display,   180
Like as two mirrours by opposed reflexion,
Doe both expresse the faces first impression.[2]

Therefore to make your beautie more appeare,
It you behoves to love, and forth to lay
That heavenly riches, which in you ye beare,
That men the more admyre their fountaine may,
For else what booteth that celestiall ray,
If it in darknesse be enshrined ever,
That it of loving eyes be vewed never?

But in your choice of Loves, this well advize,   190
That likest to your selves ye them select,
The which your forms first sourse may sympathize,
And with like beauties parts be inly deckt:
For if you loosely love without respect,
It is no love, but a discordant warre,
Whose unlike parts amongst themselves do jarre.

For Love is a celestiall harmonie,
Of likely harts composd of starres concent,
Which joyne together in sweete sympathie,
To worke ech others joy and true content,   200
Which they have harbourd since their first descent
Out of their heavenly bowres, where they did see
And know ech other here belov'd to bee.

Then wrong it were that any other twaine
Should in loves gentle band combyned bee,
But those whom heaven did at first ordaine,
And made out of one mould the more t'agree:
For all that like the beautie which they see,
Streight do not love: for love is not so light,
As streight to burne at first beholders sight.   210

But they which love indeede, looke otherwise,
With pure regard and spotlesse true intent,
Drawing out of the object of their eyes,
A more refyned forme, which they present
Unto their mind, voide of all blemishment;
Which it reducing to her first perfection,
Beholdeth free from fleshes frayle infection.

And then conforming it unto the light,
Which in it selfe it hath remaining still
Of that first Sunne, yet sparckling in his sight,   220
Thereof he fashions in his higher skill,
An heavenly beautie to his fancies will,
And it embracing in his mind entyre,
The mirrour of his owne thought doth admyre.

Which seeing now so inly faire to be,
As outward it appeareth to the eye,
And with his spirits proportion to agree,
He thereon fixeth all his fantasie,
And fully setteth his felicitie,
Counting it fairer, then it is indeede,   230
And yet indeede her fairenesse doth exceede.

For lovers eyes more sharply sighted bee
Then other mens, and in deare loves delight
See more then any other eyes can see,
Through mutuall receipt of beames bright,
Which carrie privie message to the spright,
And to their eyes that inmost faire display,
As plaine as light discovers dawning day.[1]

Therein they see through amorous eye-glaunces,
Armies of loves still flying too and fro,   240
Which dart at them their little fierie launces,
Whom having wounded, backe againe they go,
Carrying compassion to their lovely foe;
Who seeing her faire eyes so sharpe effect,
Cures all their sorrowes with one sweete aspect.

In which how many wonders doe they reede
To their conceipt, that others never see,
Now of her smiles, with which their soules they feede,
Like Gods with Nectar in their bankets free,
Now of her lookes, which like to Cordials bee;   250
But when her words embassade forth she sends,
Lord how sweete musicke that unto them lends.

Sometimes upon her forhead they behold
A thousand Graces masking[1] in delight,
Sometimes within her eye-lids they unfold
Ten thousand sweet belgards,[2] which to their sight
Doe seeme like twinckling starres in frostie night:
But on her lips like rosy buds in May,
So many millions of chaste pleasures play.

All those, ô *Cytherea*,[3] and thousands more   260
Thy handmaides be, which do on thee attend
To decke thy beautie with their dainties store,
That may it more to mortall eyes commend,
And make it more admyr'd of foe and frend;
That in mens harts thou mayst thy throne enstall,
And spred thy lovely kingdome over all.

Then *Iö tryumph*, ô great beauties Queene,
Advance the banner of thy conquest hie,
That all this world, the which thy vassals beene,
May draw to thee, and with dew fealtie,   270
Adore the powre of thy great Majestie,
Singing this Hymne in honour of thy name,
Compyld by me, which thy poore liegeman am.

In lieu whereof graunt, ô great Soveraine,
That she whose conquering beautie doth captive
My trembling hart in her eternall chaine,
One drop of grace at length will to me give,
That I her bounden thrall by her may live,
And this same life, which first fro me she reaved,
May owe to her, of whom I it receaved.   280

And you faire *Venus* dearling, my deare dread,
Fresh flowre of grace, great Goddesse of my life,
When your faire eyes these fearefull lines shal read,
Deigne to let fall one drop of dew reliefe,
That may recure my harts long pyning griefe,
And shew what wondrous powre your beauty hath,
That can restore a damned wight from death.

FINIS

AN HYMNE OF
HEAVENLY
LOVE

LOVE, lift me up upon thy golden wings,
From this base world unto thy heavens hight,
Where I may see those admirable things,
Which there thou workest by thy soveraine might,
Farre above feeble reach of earthly sight,
That I thereof an heavenly Hymne may sing
Unto the god of Love, high heavens king.[1]

Many lewd layes (ah woe is me the more)
In praise of that mad fit, which fooles call love,
I have in th'heat of youth made heretofore,   10
That in light wits did loose affection move.
But all those follies now I do reprove,
And turned have the tenor of my string,[2]
The heavenly prayses of true love to sing.

And ye that wont with greedy vaine desire
To reade my fault, and wondring at my flame,
To warme your selves at my wide sparckling fire,
Sith now that heat is quenched, quench my blame,
And in her ashes shrowd my dying shame:
For who my passed follies now pursewes,   20
Beginnes his owne, and my old fault renewes.

BEFORE this worlds great frame, in which al things
Are now containd, found any being place,
Ere flitting Time could wag his eyas wings
About that mightie bound, which doth embrace
The rolling Spheres, and parts their houres by space,[1]
That high eternall powre,[2] which now doth move
In all these things, mov'd in it selfe by love.

It lov'd it selfe, because it selfe was faire;
(For faire is lov'd;) and of it selfe begot   30
Like to it selfe his eldest sonne and heire,
Eternall, pure, and voide of sinfull blot,
The firstling of his joy, in whom no jot
Of loves dislike, or pride was to be found,
Whom he therefore with equall honour crownd.

With him he raignd, before all time prescribed,
In endlesse glorie and immortall might,
Together with that third from them derived,
Most wise, most holy, most almightie Spright,
Whose kingdomes throne no thought of earthly wight   40
Can comprehend, much lesse my trembling verse
With equall words can hope it to reherse.

Yet ô most blessed Spirit,[3] pure lampe of light,
Eternall spring of grace and wisedome trew,
Vouchsafe to shed into my barren spright,
Some little drop of thy celestiall dew,
That may my rymes with sweet infuse[4] embrew,
And give me words equall unto my thought,
To tell the marveiles by thy mercie wrought.

Yet being pregnant still with powrefull grace,   50
And full of fruitfull love, that loves to get
Things like himselfe, and to enlarge his race,
His second brood[1] though not in powre so great,
Yet full of beautie, next he did beget
An infinite increase of Angels bright,
All glistring glorious in their Makers light.

To them the heavens illimitable hight,
Not this round heaven, which we from hence behold,
Adornd with thousand lamps of burning light,
And with ten thousand gemmes of shyning gold,   60
He gave as their inheritance to hold,[2]
That they might serve him in eternall blis,
And be partakers of those joyes of his.

There they in their trinall triplicities[3]
About him wait, and on his will depend,
Either with nimble wings to cut the skies,
When he them on his messages doth send,
Or on his owne dread presence to attend,
Where they behold the glorie of his light,
And caroll Hymnes of love both day and night.   70

Both day and night is unto them all one,
For he his beames doth still to them extend,
That darknesse there appeareth never none,
Ne hath their day, ne hath their blisse an end,
But there their termelesse time in pleasure spend,
Ne ever should their happinesse decay,
Had not they dar'd their Lord to disobay.

But pride impatient of long resting peace,
Did puffe them up with greedy bold ambition,
That they gan cast their state how to increase   80
Above the fortune of their first condition,
And sit in Gods owne seat without commission:
The brightest Angell,[4] even the Child of light
Drew millions more against their God to fight.

Th'Almighty seeing their so bold assay,
Kindled the flame of his consuming yre,
And with his onely breath them blew away
From heavens hight, to which they did aspyre,
To deepest hell, and lake of damned fyre;
Where they in darknesse and dread horror dwell,   90
Hating the happie light from which they fell.

So that next off-spring of the Makers love,
Next to himselfe in glorious degree,
Degendering[1] to hate fell from above
Through pride; (for pride and love may ill agree)
And now of sinne to all ensample bee:
How then can sinfull flesh it selfe assure,
Sith purest Angels fell to be impure?

But that eternall fount of love and grace,
Still flowing forth his goodnesse unto all,   100
Now seeing left a waste and emptie place
In his wyde Pallace, through those Angels fall,
Cast[2] to supply the same, and to enstall
A new unknowen Colony therein,
Whose root from earths base groundworke shold begin.

Therefore of clay, base, vile, and next to nought,
Yet form'd by wondrous skill, and by his might:
According to an heavenly patterne wrought,
Which he had fashiond in his wise foresight,
He man did make, and breathd a living spright   110
Into his face most beautifull and fayre,[3]
Endewd with wisedomes riches, heavenly, rare.

Such he him made, that he resemble might
Himselfe, as mortall thing immortall could;
Him to be Lord of every living wight,
He made by love out of his owne like mould,
In whom he might his mightie selfe behould:
For love doth love the thing belov'd to see,
That like it selfe in lovely shape may bee.

But man forgetfull of his makers grace,   120
No lesse then Angels, whom he did ensew,[1]
Fell from the hope of promist heavenly place,
Into the mouth of death to sinners dew,
And all his off-spring into thraldome threw:
Where they for ever should in bonds remaine,
Of never dead, yet ever dying paine.

Till that great Lord of Love, which him at first
Made of meere love, and after liked well,
Seeing him lie like creature long accurst,
In that deepe horror of despeyred hell,   130
Him wretch in doole[2] would let no lenger dwell,
But cast out of that bondage to redeeme,
And pay the price, all were his debt extreeme.

Out of the bosome of eternall blisse,
In which he reigned with his glorious syre,
He downe descended, like a most demisse[3]
And abject thrall, in fleshes fraile attyre,
That he for him might pay sinnes deadly hyre,
And him restore unto that happie state,
In which he stood before his haplesse fate.   140

In flesh at first the guilt committed was,
Therefore in flesh it must be satisfyde:
Nor spirit, nor Angell, though they man surpas,
Could make amends to God for mans misguyde,
But onely man himselfe, who selfe did slyde.
So taking flesh of sacred virgins wombe,
For mans deare sake he did a man become.

And that most blessed bodie, which was borne
Without all blemish or reprochfull blame,
He freely gave to be both rent and torne   150
Of cruell hands, who with despightfull shame
Revyling him, that them most vile became,[4]
At length him nayled on a gallow tree,
And slew the just, by most unjust decree.

O huge and most unspeakeable impression
Of loves deepe wound, that pierst the piteous hart
Of that deare Lord with so entyre affection,
And sharply launching[1] every inner part,
Dolours of death into his soule did dart;
Doing him die, that never it deserved,   160
To free his foes, that from his heast had swerved.

What hart can feele least touch of so sore launch,
Or thought can think the depth of so deare wound?
Whose bleeding sourse their streames yet never staunch,
But stil do flow, and freshly stil redound,
To heale the sores of sinfull soules unsound,
And clense the guilt of that infected[2] cryme,
Which was enrooted in all fleshly slyme.

O blessed well of love, ô floure of grace,
O glorious Morning starre, ô lampe of light,   170
Most lively image of thy fathers face,
Eternall King of glorie, Lord of might,
Meeke lambe of God before all worlds behight,
How can we thee requite for all this good?
Or what can prize that thy most precious blood?

Yet nought thou ask'st in lieu of all this love,
But love of us for guerdon of thy paine.
Ay me; what can us lesse then that behove?
Had he required life of us againe,
Had it beene wrong to aske his owne with gaine?   180
He gave us life, he it restored lost;
Then life were least, that us so litle cost.

But he our life hath left unto us free,
Free that was thrall, and blessed that was band;[3]
Ne ought demaunds, but that we loving bee,
As he himselfe hath lov'd us afore hand,
And bound therto with an eternall band,
Him first to love, that us so dearely bought,
And next, our brethren to his image wrought.

Him first to love, great right and reason is,   190
Who first to us our life and being gave;
And after when we fared had amisse,
Us wretches from the second death did save;
And last the food of life, which now we have,
Even himselfe in his deare sacrament,
To feede our hungry soules unto us lent.

Then next to love our brethren, that were made
Of that selfe mould, and that selfe makers hand,
That we, and to the same againe shall fade,
Where they shall have like heritage of land,   200
How ever here on higher steps we stand;
Which also were with selfe same price redeemed
That we, how ever of us light esteemed.[1]

And were they not, yet since that loving Lord
Commaunded us to love them for his sake,
Even for his sake, and for his sacred word,
Which in his last bequest he to us spake,
We should them love, and with their needs partake;
Knowing that whatsoere to them we give,
We give to him, by whom we all doe live.   210

Such mercy he by his most holy reede[2]
Unto us taught, and to approve it trew,
Ensampled[3] it by his most righteous deede,
Shewing us mercie, miserable crew,
That we the like should to the wretches shew,
And love our brethren; thereby to approve,
How much himselfe that loved us, we love.

Then rouze thy selfe, ô earth, out of thy soyle,[4]
In which thou wallowest like to filthy swyne,
And doest thy mynd in durty pleasures moyle,[5]   220
Unmindfull of that dearest Lord of thyne;
Lift up to him thy heavie clouded eyne,
That thou his soveraine bountie mayst behold,
And read through love his mercies manifold.

Beginne from first, where he encradled was
In simple cratch,[1] wrapt in a wad of hay,
Betweene the toylefull Oxe and humble Asse,
And in what rags, and in how base aray,
The glory of our heavenly riches lay,
When him the silly[2] Shepheards came to see,   230
Whom greatest Princes sought on lowest knee.

From thence reade on the storie of his life,
His humble carriage, his unfaulty wayes,
His cancred foes, his fights, his toyle, his strife,
His paines, his pouertie, his sharpe assayes,
Through which he past his miserable dayes,
Offending none, and doing good to all,
Yet being malist[3] both of great and small.

And looke at last how of most wretched wights,
He taken was, betrayd, and false accused,   240
How with most scornefull taunts, and fell despights
He was revyld, disgrast, and foule abused,
How scourgd, how crownd, how buffeted, how brused;
And lastly how twixt robbers crucifyde,
With bitter wounds through hands, through feet and syde.

Then let thy flinty hart that feeles no paine,
Empierced be with pittifull remorse,
And let thy bowels bleede in every vaine,
At sight of his most sacred heavenly corse,
So torne and mangled with malicious forse,   250
And let thy soule, whose sins his sorrows wrought,
Melt into teares, and grone in grieved thought.

With sence whereof whilest so thy softened spirit
Is inly toucht, and humbled with meeke zeale,
Through meditation of his endlesse merit,
Lift up thy mind to th'author of thy weale,
And to his soveraine mercie doe appeale;
Learne him to love, that loved thee so deare,
And in thy brest his blessed image beare.

With all thy hart, with all thy soule and mind,   260
Thou must him love, and his beheasts embrace,
All other loves, with which the world doth blind
Weake fancies, and stirre up affections base,
Thou must renounce, and utterly displace,
And give thy selfe unto him full and free,
That full and freely gave himselfe to thee.

Then shalt thou feele thy spirit so possest,
And ravisht with devouring great desire
Of his deare selfe, that shall thy feeble brest
Inflame with love, and set thee all on fire   270
With burning zeale, through every part entire,
That in no earthly thing thou shalt delight,
But in his sweet and amiable sight.

Thenceforth all worlds desire will in thee dye,
And all earthes glorie on which men do gaze,
Seeme durt and drosse in thy pure sighted eye,
Compar'd to that celestiall beauties blaze,
Whose glorious beames all fleshly sense doth daze
With admiration of their passing light,[1]
Blinding the eyes and lumining the spright.   280

Then shall thy ravisht soule inspired bee
With heavenly thoughts, farre above humane skil,
And thy bright radiant eyes shall plainely see
Th'Idee of his pure glorie[2] present still
Before thy face, that all thy spirits shall fill
With sweete enragement of celestiall love,
Kindled through sight of those faire things above.

FINIS

AN HYMNE OF
HEAVENLY
BEAUTIE

Rapt with the rage[1] of mine own ravisht thought,
Through contemplation of those goodly sights,
And glorious images in heaven wrought,
Whose wondrous beauty breathing sweet delights,
Do kindle love in high conceipted sprights:
I faine[2] to tell the things that I behold,
But feel my wits to faile, and tongue to fold.

Vouchsafe then, ô thou most almightie Spright,
From whom all guifts of wit and knowledge flow,
To shed into my breast some sparkling light   10
Of thine eternall Truth, that I may show
Some litle beames to mortall eyes below,
Of that immortall beautie, there with thee,
Which in my weake distraughted mynd I see.

That with the glorie of so goodly sight,
The hearts of men, which fondly here admyre
Faire seeming shewes, and feed on vaine delight,
Transported with celestiall desyre
Of those faire formes, may lift themselves up hyer,
And learne to love with zealous humble dewty   20
Th'eternall fountaine of that heavenly beauty.

Beginning then below, with th'easie vew
Of this base world, subject to fleshly eye,
From thence to mount aloft by order dew,
To contemplation of th'immortall sky,
Of the soare[3] faulcon so I learne to fly,
That flags awhile her fluttering wings beneath,
Till she her selfe for stronger flight can breath.

I

Then looke who list,[1] thy gazefull eyes to feed
With sight of that is faire, looke on the frame   30
Of this wyde *universe*, and therein reed
The endlesse kinds of creatures, which by name
Thou canst not count, much lesse their natures aime:
All which are made with wondrous wise respect,
And all with admirable beautie deckt.

First th'Earth,[2] on adamantine pillers founded,
Amid the Sea engirt with brasen bands;
Then th'Aire still flitting, but yet firmely bounded
On everie side, with pyles of flaming brands,
Never consum'd nor quencht with mortall hands;   40
And last, that mightie shining christall wall,
Wherewith he hath encompassed this All.

By view whereof, it plainly may appeare,
That still as every thing doth upward tend,
And further is from earth, so still more cleare
And faire it growes, till to his perfect end
Of purest beautie, it at last ascend:
Ayre more then water, fire much more then ayre,
And heaven then fire appeares more pure and fayre.

Looke thou no further, but affixe thine eye,   50
On that bright shynie round still moving Masse,
The house of blessed Gods, which men call *Skye*,
All sowd with glistring stars more thicke then grasse,
Whereof each other doth in brightnesse passe;
But those two most, which ruling night and day,
As King and Queene, the heavens Empire sway.

And tell me then, what hast thou ever seene,
That to their beautie may compared bee,
Or can the sight that is most sharpe and keene,
Endure their Captains flaming head to see?   60
How much lesse those, much higher in degree,
And so much fairer, and much more then these,
As these are fairer then the land and seas?

For farre above these heavens which here we see,
Be others farre exceeding these in light,
Not bounded, not corrupt, as these same bee,
But infinite in largenesse and in hight,
Unmoving, uncorrupt, and spotlesse bright,
That need no Sunne t'illuminate their spheres,
But their owne native light farre passing theirs.   70

And as these heavens still by degrees arize,
Untill they come to their first Movers bound,
That in his mightie compasse doth comprize,
And carrie all the rest with him around,
So those likewise doe by degrees redound,
And rise more faire, till they at last arive
To the most faire, whereto they all do strive.

Faire is the heaven, where happie soules have place,
In full enjoyment of felicitie,
Whence they doe still behold, the glorious face,   80
Of the divine eternall Majestie;
More faire is that, where those *Idees* on hie,
Enraunged be, which *Plato* so admyred,
And pure *Intelligences* from God inspyred.

Yet fairer is that heaven, in which doe raine
The soveraine *Powres* and mightie *Potentates*,
Which in their high protections doe containe
All mortall Princes, and imperiall States;
And fayrer yet, whereas the royall Seates
And heavenly *Dominations* are set,   90
From whom all earthly governance is fet.

Yet farre more faire be those bright *Cherubins*,
Which all with golden wings are overdight,
And those eternall burning *Seraphins*,
Which from their faces dart out fierie light;
Yet fairer then they both, and much more bright
Be th'Angels and Archangels, which attend
On Gods owne person, without rest or end.

These thus in faire each other farre excelling,
As to the Highest they approch more neare,   100
Yet is that Highest farre beyond all telling,
Fairer then all the rest which there appeare,
Though all their beauties joynd together were:
How then can mortall tongue hope to expresse,
The image of such endlesse perfectnesse?

Cease then my tongue,[1] and lend unto my mynd
Leave to bethinke how great that beautie is,
Whose utmost parts so beautifull I fynd,
How much more those essentiall parts of his,
His truth, his love, his wisedome, and his blis,   110
His grace, his doome,[2] his mercy and his might,
By which he lends us of himselfe a sight.

Those unto all he daily doth display,
And shew himselfe in th'image of his grace,
As in a looking glasse, through which he may
Be seene, of all his creatures vile and base,
That are unable else to see his face,
His glorious face which glistereth else so bright,
That th'Angels selves can not endure his sight.

But we fraile wights, whose sight cannot sustaine   120
The Suns bright beames, when he on us doth shyne,
But that their points rebutted backe againe
Are duld, how can we see with feeble eyne,
The glory of that Majestie divine,
In sight of whom both Sun and Moone are darke,
Compared to his least resplendent sparke?

The meanes therefore which unto us is lent,
Him to behold, is on his workes to looke,
Which he hath made in beauty excellent,
And in the same, as in a brasen booke,[3]   130
To reade enregistred in every nooke
His goodnesse, which his beautie doth declare,
For all thats good, is beautifull and faire.

Thence gathering plumes of perfect speculation,[1]
To impe[2] the wings of thy high flying mynd,
Mount up aloft through heavenly contemplation,
From this darke world, whose damps the soule do blynd,
And like the native brood of Eagles kynd,
On that bright Sunne of glorie fixe thine eyes,
Clear'd from grosse mists of fraile infirmities.   140

Humbled with feare and awfull reverence,
Before the footestoole of his Majestie,
Throw thy selfe downe with trembling innocence,
Ne dare looke up with corruptible eye,
On the dred face of that great *Deity*,
For feare, lest if he chaunce to looke on thee,
Thou turne to nought, and quite confounded be.

But lowly fall before his mercie seate,
Close covered with the Lambes integrity,[3]
From the just wrath of his avengefull threate,   150
That sits upon the righteous throne on hy:
His throne is built upon Eternity,
More firme and durable then steele or brasse,
Or the hard diamond, which them both doth passe.

His scepter is the rod of Righteousnesse,
With which he bruseth all his foes to dust,
And the great Dragon[4] strongly doth represse,
Under the rigour of his judgement just;
His seate is Truth, to which the faithfull trust;
From whence proceed her beames so pure and bright,   160
That all about him sheddeth glorious light.

Light farre exceeding that bright blazing sparke,
Which darted is from *Titans*[5] flaming head,
That with his beames enlumineth the darke
And dampish aire, wherby al things are red:
Whose nature yet so much is marvelled
Of mortall wits, that it doth much amaze
The greatest wisards,[6] which thereon do gaze.

But that immortall light which there doth shine,
Is many thousand times more bright, more cleare,   170
More excellent, more glorious, more divine,
Through which to God all mortall actions here,
And even the thoughts of men, do plaine appeare:
For from th'eternall Truth it doth proceed,
Through heavenly vertue, which her beames doe breed.

With the great glorie of that wondrous light,
His throne is all encompassed around,
And hid in his owne brightnesse from the sight
Of all that looke thereon with eyes unsound:
And underneath his feet are to be found,   180
Thunder, and lightning, and tempestuous fyre,
The instruments of his avenging yre.

There in his bosome *Sapience* doth sit,[1]
The soveraine dearling of the *Deity*,
Clad like a Queene in royall robes, most fit
For so great powre and peerelesse majesty.
And all with gemmes and jewels gorgeously
Adornd, that brighter then the starres appeare,
And make her native brightnes seeme more cleare.

And on her head a crowne of purest gold   190
Is set, in signe of highest soveraignty,
And in her hand a scepter she doth hold,
With which she rules the house of God on hy,
And menageth the ever-moving sky,
And in the same these lower creatures all,
Subjected to her powre imperiall.

Both heaven and earth obey unto her will,
And all the creatures which they both containe:
For of her fulnesse which the world doth fill,
They all partake, and do in state remaine,   200
As their great Maker did at first ordaine,
Through observation of her high beheast,
By which they first were made, and still increast.

The fairenesse of her face no tongue can tell,
For she the daughters of all wemens race,
And Angels eke, in beautie doth excell,
Sparkled on her from Gods owne glorious face,
And more increast by her owne goodly grace,[1]
That it doth farre exceed all humane thought,
Ne can on earth compared be to ought.   210

Ne could that Painter[2] (had he lived yet)
Which pictured *Venus* with so curious quill,
That all posteritie admyred it,
Have purtrayd this, for all his maistring skill;
Ne she her selfe, had she remained still,
And were as faire, as fabling wits do fayne,
Could once come neare this beauty soverayne.

But had those wits the wonders of their dayes,
Or that sweete *Teian* Poet which did spend
His plenteous vaine in setting forth her prayse,   220
Seene but a glims of this, which I pretend,
How wondrously would he her face commend,
Above that Idole of his fayning thought,
That all the world shold with his rimes be fraught?[3]

How then dare I, the novice of his Art,
Presume to picture so divine a wight,
Or hope t'expresse her least perfections part,
Whose beautie filles the heavens with her light,
And darkes the earth with shadow of her sight?
Ah gentle Muse[4] thou art too weake and faint,   230
The pourtraict of so heavenly hew to paint.

Let Angels which her goodly face behold
And see at will, her soveraigne praises sing,
And those most sacred mysteries unfold,
Of that faire love of mightie heavens king.
Enough is me t'admyre so heavenly thing,
And being thus with her huge love possest,
In th'only wonder of her selfe to rest.

But who so may, thrise happie man him hold,
Of all on earth, whom God so much doth grace,   240
And lets his owne Beloved to behold:
For in the view of her celestiall face,
All joy, all blisse, all happinesse have place,
Ne ought on earth can want unto the wight,
Who of her selfe can win the wishfull sight.

For she out of her secret threasury,
Plentie of riches forth on him will powre,
Even heavenly riches, which there hidden ly
Within the closet of her chastest bowre,
Th'eternall portion of her precious dowre,   250
Which mighty God hath given to her free,
And to all those which thereof worthy bee.

None thereof worthy be, but those whom shee
Vouchsafeth to her presence to receave,[1]
And letteth them her lovely face to see,
Wherof such wondrous pleasures they conceave,
And sweete contentment, that it doth bereave
Their soule of sense, through infinite delight,
And them transport from flesh into the spright.

In which they see such admirable things,   260
As carries them into an extasy,
And heare such heavenly notes, and carolings
Of Gods high praise, that filles the brasen sky,
And feele such joy and pleasure inwardly,
That maketh them all worldly cares forget,
And onely thinke on that before them set.

Ne from thenceforth doth any fleshly sense,
Or idle thought of earthly things remaine,
But all that earst seemd sweet, seemes now offense,
And all that pleased earst, now seemes to paine,   270
Their joy, their comfort, their desire, their gaine,
Is fixed all on that which now they see,
All other sights but fayned shadowes bee.

beauty of women

And that faire lampe,[1] which useth to enflame
The hearts of men with selfe consuming fyre,
Thenceforth seemes fowle, and full of sinfull blame;
And all that pompe, to which proud minds aspyre
By name of honor, and so much desyre,
Seemes to them basenesse, and all riches drosse,
And all mirth sadnesse, and all lucre losse.   280

So full their eyes are of that glorious sight,
And senses fraught with such satietie,
That in nought else on earth they can delight,
But in th'aspect of that felicitie,
Which they have written in their inward ey;
On which they feed, and in their fastened mynd
All happie joy and full contentment fynd.

Ah then my hungry soule, which long hast fed
On idle fancies of thy foolish thought,
And with false beauties flattring bait misled,   290
Hast after vaine deceiptfull shadowes sought,
Which all are fled, and now have left thee nought,
But late repentance through thy follies prief;[2]
Ah ceasse to gaze on matter of thy grief.

And looke at last up to that soveraine light,
From whose pure beams al perfect beauty springs,
That kindleth love in every godly spright,
Even the love of God, which loathing brings
Of this vile world, and these gay seeming things;
With whose sweete pleasures being so possest,   300
Thy straying thoughts henceforth for ever rest.

EPITHALAMION

YE learned sisters[1] which have oftentimes
beene to me ayding, others to adorne:
Whom ye thought worthy of your gracefull rymes,
That even the greatest did not greatly scorne
To heare theyr names sung in your simple layes,
But joyed in theyr prayse.
And when ye list your owne mishaps to mourne,[2]
Which death, or love, or fortunes wreck did rayse,
Your string could soone to sadder tenor turne,
And teach the woods and waters to lament   10
Your dolefull dreriment.
Now lay those sorrowfull complaints aside,
And having all your heads with girland crownd,
Helpe me mine owne loves prayses to resound,
Ne let the same of any be envide,
So Orpheus did for his owne bride,[3]
So I unto my selfe alone will sing,
The woods shall to me answer and my Eccho ring.

EARLY before the worlds light giving lampe,
His golden beame upon the hils doth spred,   20
Having disperst the nights unchearefull dampe,
Doe ye awake, and with fresh lusty hed,
Go to the bowre of my beloved love,
My truest turtle dove
Bid her awake; for Hymen is awake,[4]
And long since ready forth his maske to move,
With his bright Tead that flames with many a flake,[5]
And many a bachelor to waite on him,
In theyr fresh garments trim.
Bid her awake therefore and soone her dight,   30
For lo the wished day is come at last,
That shall for al the paynes and sorrowes past,
Pay to her usury of long delight,[6]
And whylest she doth her dight,

Invokes Muses, nymphs, Mulla & Diana to sing & deck b.
build-up of verse

Doe ye to her of joy and solace sing,
That all the woods may answer and your eccho ring.

(3) BRING with you all the Nymphes that you can heare[1]
both of the rivers and the forrests greene:
and of the sea that neighbours to her neare,[2]
Al with gay girlands goodly wel beseene.[3]   40
And let them also with them bring in hand,
Another gay girland
For my fayre love of lillyes and of roses,
Bound truelove wize with a blew silke riband.

19 And let them make great store of bridale poses,
And let them eeke bring store of other flowers
To deck the bridale bowers.
And let the ground whereas her foot shall tread,
For feare the stones her tender foot should wrong
Be strewed with fragrant flowers all along,   50
And diapred lyke the discolored mead.[4] *multicoloured*
Which done, doe at her chamber dore awayt,   *timing*
For she will waken strayt,
The whiles doe ye this song unto her sing,
The woods shall to you answer and your Eccho ring.

River.

(4) YE Nymphes of Mulla[5] which with carefull heed,
The silver scaly trouts doe tend full well,
and greedy pikes which use therein to feed,
(Those trouts and pikes all others doo excell)
And ye likewise which keepe the rushy lake,   60
Where none doo fishes take,
18 Bynd up the locks the which hang scatterd light,
And in his waters which your mirror make,
Behold your faces as the christall bright,
That when you come whereas my love doth lie,
No blemish she may spie.
And eke ye lightfoot mayds which keep the dere,
That on the hoary mountayne use to towre,[6]
And the wylde wolves which seeke them to devoure,
With your steele darts doo chace from comming neer   70
Be also present heere,

To helpe to decke her and to help to sing,
That all the woods may answer and your eccho ring.

WAKE now my love, awake; for it is time,
The Rosy Morne long since left Tithones bed,[1]
All ready to her silver coche to clyme,
And Phœbus[2] gins to shew his glorious hed.
Hark how the cheerefull birds do chaunt theyr laies
And carroll of loves praise.
The merry Larke hir mattins sings aloft,   80
The thrush replyes, the Mavis descant playes,
The Ouzell shrills, the Ruddock warbles soft,
So goodly all agree with sweet consent,
To this dayes merriment.
Ah my deere love why doe ye sleepe thus long,
When meeter were that ye should now awake,
T'awayt the comming of your joyous make,
And hearken to the birds lovelearned song,
The deawy leaves among.
For they of joy and pleasance to you sing,   90
That all the woods them answer & theyr eccho ring.

MY love is now awake out of her dreames,
and her fayre eyes like stars that dimmed were
With darksome cloud, now shew theyr goodly beams
More bright then Hesperus[3] his head doth rere.
Come now ye damzels, daughters of delight,[4]
Helpe quickly her to dight,
But first come ye fayre houres which were begot
In Joves sweet paradice, of Day and Night,
Which doe the seasons of the yeare allot,   100
And al that ever in this world is fayre
Doe make and still repayre.[5]
And ye three handmayds of the Cyprian Queene,[6]
The which doe still adorne her beauties pride,
Helpe to addorne my beautifullest bride:
And as ye her array, still throw betweene
Some graces to be seene,
And as ye use to Venus, to her sing,
The whiles the woods shal answer & your eccho ring.

Now is my love all ready forth to come, 110
Let all the virgins therefore well awayt,
And ye fresh boyes that tend upon her groome
Prepare your selves; for he is comming strayt.
Set all your things in seemely good aray
Fit for so joyfull day,
The joyfulst day that ever sunne did see.
Faire Sun, shew forth thy favourable ray,
And let thy lifull heat not fervent be
For feare of burning her sunshyny face,
Her beauty to disgrace. 120
O fayrest Phœbus, father of the Muse,[1]
If ever I did honour thee aright,
Or sing the thing, that mote thy mind delight,
Doe not thy servants simple boone[2] refuse,
But let this day, let this one day be myne,
Let all the rest be thine.
Then I thy soverayne prayses loud wil sing,
That all the woods shal answer and theyr eccho ring.

HARKE how the Minstrels gin to shrill aloud,
Their merry Musick that resounds from far, 130
The pipe, the tabor, and the trembling Croud,
That well agree withouten breach or jar.
But most of all the Damzels doe delite,
When they their tymbrels smyte,[3]
And thereunto doe daunce and carrol sweet,
That all the sences they doe ravish quite,[3]
The whyles the boyes run up and downe the street,
Crying aloud with strong confused noyce,
As if it were one voyce.
Hymen io Hymen, Hymen they do shout,[4] 140
That even to the heavens theyr shouting shrill
Doth reach, and all the firmament doth fill,
To which the people standing all about,
As in approvance doe thereto applaud
And loud advaunce her laud,
And evermore they Hymen Hymen sing,
that al the woods them answer and theyr eccho ring.

Loe where she comes along with portly[1] pace,
Lyke Phoebe[2] from her chamber of the East,
Arysing forth to run her mighty race,   150
Clad all in white, that seemes a virgin best.
So well it her beseemes that ye would weene
Some angell she had beene.
Her long loose yellow locks lyke golden wyre,
Sprinckled with perle, and perling[3] flowres a tweene,
Doe lyke a golden mantle her attyre,
And being crowned with a girland greene,
Seeme lyke some mayden Queene.[4]
Her modest eyes abashed to behold
So many gazers, as on her do stare,   160
Upon the lowly ground affixed are.
Ne dare lift up her countenance too bold,
But blush to heare her prayses sung so loud,
So farre from being proud.
Nathlesse doe ye still loud her prayses sing.
That all the woods may answer and your eccho ring.

Tell me ye merchants daughters did ye see
So fayre a creature in your towne before,
So sweet, so lovely, and so mild as she,
Adornd with beautyes grace and vertues store,   170
Her goodly eyes lyke Saphyres shining bright,
Her forehead yvory white,
Her cheekes lyke apples which the sun hath rudded,[5]
Her lips lyke cherryes charming men to byte,
Her brest like to a bowle of creame uncrudded,[6]
Her paps lyke lyllies budded,
Her snowie necke lyke to a marble towre,
And all her body like a pallace fayre,
Ascending uppe with many a stately stayre,
To honors seat and chastities sweet bowre.   180
Why stand ye still ye virgins in amaze,
Upon her so to gaze,
Whiles ye forget your former lay to sing,
To which the woods did answer and your eccho ring.

But if ye saw that which no eyes can see,
The inward beauty of her lively spright,
Garnisht with heavenly guifts of high degree,
Much more then would ye wonder at that sight,
And stand astonisht lyke to those which red
Medusaes mazefull hed.[1]   190
There dwels sweet love and constant chastity,
Unspotted fayth and comely womanhead,
Regard of honour and mild modesty,
There vertue raynes as Queene in royal throne,
And giveth lawes alone.
The which the base affections doe obay,
And yeeld theyr services unto her will,
Ne thought of thing uncomely ever may
Thereto approch to tempt her mind to ill.
Had ye once seene these her celestial threasures,   200
And unrevealed pleasures,
Then would ye wonder and her prayses sing,
That al the woods should answer and your echo ring.

Open the temple gates unto my love,
Open them wide that she may enter in,
And all the postes adorne as doth behove,
And all the pillours deck with girlands trim,
For to recyue this Saynt with honour dew,
That commeth in to you,
With trembling steps and humble reverence,   210
She commeth in, before th'almighties vew,
Of her ye virgins learne obedience,
When so ye come into those holy places,
To humble your proud faces.
Bring her up to th'high altar, that she may,
The sacred ceremonies there partake,
The which do endlesse matrimony make;
And let the roring Organs loudly play,
The praises of the Lord in lively notes,
The whiles with hollow throates,   220
The Choristers the joyous Antheme sing,
That al the woods may answere and their eccho ring.

BEHOLD whiles she before the altar stands
Hearing the holy priest that to her speakes
And blesseth her with his two happy hands,
How the red roses flush up in her cheekes,
And the pure snow with goodly vermill stayne,
Like crimsin dyde in grayne,[1]
That even th'Angels which continually,
About the sacred Altare doe remaine,   230
Forget their service and about her fly,[2]
Ofte peeping in her face that seemes more fayre,
The more they on it stare.
But her sad eyes still fastened on the ground,
Are governed with goodly modesty,
That suffers not one looke to glaunce awry,
Which may let in a little thought unsownd,
Why blush ye love to give to me your hand,
The pledge of all our band,
Sing ye sweet Angels, Alleluya sing,[3]
That all the woods may answere and your eccho ring.   240

Now al is done; bring home the bride againe,
bring home the triumph of our victory,[4]
Bring home with you the glory of her gaine,
With joyance bring her and with jollity.
Never had man more joyfull day then this,
Whom heaven would heape with blis.
Make feast therefore now all this live long day,
This day for ever to me holy is,
Poure out the wine without restraint or stay,   250
Poure not by cups, but by the belly full,
Poure out to all that wull,
And sprinkle all the postes and wals with wine,[5]
That they may sweat, and drunken be withall.
Crowne ye God Bacchus with a coronall,
And Hymen also crowne with wreathes of vine,
And let the Graces daunce unto the rest;
For they can doo it best:
The whiles the maydens doe theyr carroll sing,
To which the woods shal answer & theyr eccho ring.   260

RING ye the bels, ye yong men of the towne,
And leave your wonted labors for this day:
This day is holy; doe ye write it downe,
that ye for ever it remember may.
This day the sunne is in his chiefest hight,
With Barnaby the bright,[1]
From whence declining daily by degrees,
He somewhat loseth of his heat and light,
When once the Crab behind his back he sees.
But for this time it ill ordained was,   270
To chose the longest day in all the yeare,
And shortest night, when longest fitter weare:
Yet never day so long, but late would passe.
Ring ye the bels, to make it weare away,
And bonefiers make all day,
And daunce about them, and about them sing:
that all the woods may answer, and your eccho ring.

AH when will this long weary day have end,
And lende me leave to come unto my love?
How slowly do the houres theyr numbers spend?   280
How slowly does sad Time his feathers move?
Hast thee O fayrest Planet[2] to thy home
Within the Westerne fome:
Thy tyred steedes long since have need of rest.
Long though it be, at last I see it gloome,
And the bright evening star with golden creast
Appeare out of the East.
Fayre childe of beauty, glorious lampe of love
That all the host of heaven in rankes doost lead,
And guydest lovers through the nightes dread,[3]   290
How chearefully thou lookest from above,
And seemst to laugh atweene thy twinkling light
As joying in the sight
Of these glad many which for joy doe sing,
That all the woods them answer and their echo ring.

Now ceasse ye damsels[4] your delights forepast;
Enough is it, that all the day was youres:

K

Now day is doen, and night is nighing fast:
Now bring the Bryde into the brydall boures.
Now night is come, now soone her disaray,   300
And in her bed her lay;
Lay her in lillies and in violets,
And silken courteins over her display,
And odourd sheetes, and Arras coverlets.
Behold how goodly my faire love does ly
In proud humility;
Like unto Maia,[1] when as Jove her tooke,
In Tempe, lying on the flowry gras,
Twixt sleepe and wake, after she weary was,
With bathing in the Acidalian brooke.   310
Now it is night, ye damsels may be gon,
And leave my love alone,
And leave likewise your former lay to sing:
The woods no more shal answere, nor your echo ring.

Now welcome night, thou night so long expected,
that long daies labour doest at last defray,
And all my cares, which cruell love collected,
Hast sumd in one, and cancelled for aye:[2]
Spread thy broad wing over my love and me,
that no man may us see,   320
And in thy sable mantle us enwrap,
From feare of perrill and foule horror free.
Let no false treason seeke us to entrap,
Nor any dread disquiet once annoy
the safety of our joy:
But let the night be calme and quietsome,
Without tempestuous storms or sad afray:
Lyke as when Jove with fayre Alcmena lay,
When he begot the great Tirynthian groome:[3]
Or lyke as when he with thy selfe did lie,   330
And begot Majesty.[4]
And let the mayds and yongmen cease to sing:
Ne let the woods them answer, nor theyr eccho ring.

Let no lamenting cryes, nor dolefull teares,
Be heard all night within nor yet without:
Ne let false whispers, breeding hidden feares,
Breake gentle sleepe with misconceived dout.
Let no deluding dreames, nor dreadful sights
Make sudden sad affrights;
Ne let housefyres, nor lightnings helpelesse harmes,   340
Ne let the Pouke,[1] nor other evill sprights,
Ne let mischivous witches with theyr charmes,
Ne let hob Goblins, names whose sence we see not,
Fray us with things that be not.
Let not the shriech Oule, nor the Storke be heard:[2]
Nor the night Raven that still deadly yels,
Nor damned ghosts cald up with mighty spels,
Nor griesly vultures make us once affeard:
Ne let th'unpleasant Quyre of Frogs still croking
Make us to wish theyr choking.   350
Let none of these theyr drery accents sing;
Ne let the woods them answer, nor theyr eccho ring.

But let stil Silence trew night watches keepe,
That sacred peace may in assurance rayne,
And tymely sleep, when it is tyme to sleepe,
May poure his limbs forth on your pleasant playne,[3]
The whiles an hundred little winged loves,[4]
Like divers fethered doves,
Shall fly and flutter round about your bed,
And in the secret darke, that none reproves,   360
Their prety stealthes shal worke, & snares shal spread
To filch away sweet snatches of delight,
Conceald through covert night.
Ye sonnes of Venus, play your sports at will,
For greedy pleasure, carelesse of your toyes,
Thinks more upon her paradise of joyes,
Then what ye do, albe it good or ill.
All night therefore attend your merry play,
For it will soone be day:
Now none doth hinder you, that say or sing,   370
Ne will the woods now answer, nor your Eccho ring.

WHO is the same, which at my window peepes?
Or whose is that faire face, that shines so bright,
Is it not Cinthia,[1] she that never sleepes,
But walkes about high heaven al the night?
O fayrest goddesse, do thou not envy
My love with me to spy:
For thou likewise didst love, though now unthought,
And for a fleece of woll, which privily,
The Latmian shephard once unto thee brought,   380
His pleasures with thee wrought.
Therefore to us be favorable now;
And sith of wemens labours thou hast charge,
And generation goodly dost enlarge,
Encline thy will t'effect our wishfull vow,
And the chast wombe informe with timely seed,
That may our comfort breed:
Till which we cease our hopefull hap to sing,
Ne let the woods us answere, nor our Eccho ring.

AND thou great Juno,[2] which with awful might   390
the lawes of wedlock still dost patronize,
And the religion of the faith first plight
With sacred rites hast taught to solemnize:
And eeke for comfort often called art
Of women in their smart,
Eternally bind thou this lovely band,
And all thy blessings unto us impart.
And thou glad Genius,[3] in whose gentle hand,
The bridale bowre and geniall bed remaine,
Without blemish or staine,   400
And the sweet pleasures of theyr loves delight
With secret ayde doest succour and supply,
Till they bring forth the fruitfull progeny,
Send us the timely fruit[4] of this same night.
And thou fayre Hebe, and thou Hymen free,[5]
Grant that it may so be.
Til which we cease your further prayse to sing,
Ne any woods shal answer, nor your Eccho ring.

And ye high heavens, the temple of the gods,[1]
In which a thousand torches flaming bright   410
Doe burne, that to us wretched earthly clods:
In dreadful darknesse lend desired light;
And all ye powers which in the same remayne,
More then we men can fayne,
Poure out your blessing on us plentiously,
And happy influence upon us raine,
That we may raise a large posterity,
Which from the earth, which they may long possesse,
With lasting happinesse,
Up to your haughty pallaces may mount,   420
And for the guerdon of theyr glorious merit
May heavenly tabernacles there inherit,
Of blessed Saints for to increase the count.
So let us rest, sweet love, in hope of this,
And cease till then our tymely joyes to sing,[2]
The woods no more us answer, nor our eccho ring.

Song made in lieu of many ornaments,
With which my love should duly have bene dect,
Which cutting off through hasty accidents,
Ye would not stay your dew time to expect,   430
But promist both to recompens,
Be unto her a goodly ornament,
And for short time an endlesse moniment.[3]

FINIS

NOTES

When not given in the note, particulars of the exact title and of the edition used will be found under the appropriate heading in the *Bibliography*, and the author's name will be printed in italics.

INTRODUCTION

p. 3, 1. *Tillyard*, p. 2.

p. 4, 1. In her fascinating and learned study of Giordano Bruno, Frances Yates shows that to the Italian Neo-Platonists Hermes Trismegistus was an almost more important source of inspiration than Plato; for they regarded him as a real Egyptian priest and prophet of remote antiquity, who had foretold the coming of Christianity and anticipated some of its doctrines. In *Fowre Hymnes*, however, Spencer is not concerned with Hermetic magic and mysticism but with the Platonic doctrine of love. See also *Wind*, ch. I, 'Poetical Theology'.

p. 5, 1. *Ficino, De Amore*, Speech VI, Ch. 1–8. For full title, text and translation by S. P. Jayne, see *Ficino*.

p. 5, 2. For a reprint of the first edition published in 1667, see *History of the Royal Society*, by Thomas Sprat, edit. Jackson, I. Cope and H. W. Jones, Routledge and Kegan Paul, 1959.

p. 7, 1. References to *Timaeus* are to Professor Cornford's translation. See *Cornford*. References to other dialogues of Plato are to the edition of his works, with texts and translations in The Loeb Classical Library. *Timaeus* is in Vol. VII of this edition.

p. 8, 1. *Plato*, Vol. I, D 26, p. 473.

p. 8, 2. *Plato*, Vol. V.

p. 10, 1. *Plato*, Vol. V, p. 206.

p. 10, 2. In classical Greek the verb ἐράω means 'to long for', 'to desire passionately'; whereas ἀγαπάω is a vaguer, more colourless term, referring to the will rather than to the emotions and meaning, 'to esteem', 'to show goodwill', 'to like', etc. The noun ἀγάπη occurs very rarely, if at all, in classical Greek. In the Septuagint, ἀγαπάω, ἀγάπη are almost always used to translate Hebrew words denoting love, even the love between man and woman described in Hosea and The Song of Solomon. In the New Testament ἐράω, ἔρως do not occur at all; ἀγαπάω, ἀγάπη, are the usual words employed to denote: (1) love within the eternal, triune life of God; (2) the love of God for men; (3) the love of men for God; (4) love between human beings. It is supposed that the term 'Eros' was avoided on account of its pagan and sexual associations. See s.v. *love* in *A Theological Word Book of the Bible*, ed. Alan Richardson (S.C.M. Press), and ἀγαπάω in G. Abbott-Smith, *A Manual Greek Lexicon of the New Testament*. (T. T. Clark, Edinburgh.) Nygren carries to an extreme the view that the essential quality of Christian Agape-love is selflessness and that it is therefore incompatible with Eros-love which is evoked by the desirability of its object, and, in its highest form, by the supreme desirability of God. He maintains that in Christian thought and devotion Agape-love has been partially contaminated by Eros-love, and that the Protestant Reformation was largely an attempt to purify it. Nygren's views have been influential, but have not gained universal assent. See *Nygren* and for a different view *D'Arcy S.J.*

p. 10, 3. 1 Jn. 4. 19 and also vv. 10 and 11.

p. 11, 1. See *Plotinus*; *Armstrong*, Ch. 16, 17; William Nelson (see *Nelson*) thinks it likely that Spenser had direct knowledge of Plotinus; but since all the Neo-Platonic passages in *Fowre Hymnes* could have been equally well drawn from later sources, I have not thought it necessary to go into the question.

p. 13, 1. *Lewis, Allegory of Love*, pp. 2 ff.

p. 13, 2. For St. Paul's views on marriage see 1 Corinthians, Ch. 7 and Ephesians, Ch. 5, vv. 22–33. Peter Lombard (*c.* 1100–64) counted matrimony as one of the seven sacraments. Protestants only acknowledged two sacraments (as generally necessary to Salvation', Baptism and Holy Communion; but the Puritans objected that the Anglican wedding service contained vestiges of sacramental belief. 'As for matrimonie, that also hath corruptions to [*sic*] many. It was wonte to be compted a sacramente and therefore they yet use a sacramental signe, to whiche they attribute the vertue of wedlocke. I mean the wedding ring, . . .' (*An Admonition to the Parliament* in *Puritan Manifestoes*, ed. W. H. Frere and C. E. Douglas, London S.P.C.K., 1954, p. 27.) In the twenty-fifth of the *Articles of Religion* in *The Book of Common Prayer*, it is stated that marriage is not to be counted for one of the 'sacraments of the Gospel', but in one of the *Homilies*, authorized to be read in Church, it is compared with the Sacrament of Baptism: 'By like holy promise the Sacrament of matrimony knitteth man and wife in perpetual love, that they desire not to be separated for any displeasure or adversity that shall after happen.' *Homilies*, A Sermon against Swearing and Perjury: Pt. I, p. 64. O.U.P., 1844.
See also Arts, *Marriage (Christian)* in *Encyclopaedia of Religion and Ethics*, ed. James Hastings and Art. *Matrimony* in *The Oxford Dictionary of the Christian Church*.

p. 13, 3. *Lewis*, p. 14.

p. 14, 1.   'Dir li potro': tenea d'angel sembianza
                              che fosse del tu' regno;
                              non mi fu fallo, s'eo li posi amanza.'

    Rime di Guido Guinizelli, v, ll. 58–60 in *di Benedetto*, p. 9. For a verse translation see *Rossetti*, pp. 21–2.

p. 14, 2. For commentary, text and translation see *Shaw*, also for text *di Benedetto*, pp. 25–7.

p. 15, 1. For translation see *Rossetti, The New Life*, pp. 137–207.

p. 15, 2. *Rossetti*, p. 167.

p. 16, 1. *Dante: A Translation of the Latin Works of Dante Alighieri*, Epistle X, p. 361.

p. 16, 2. *Dante: Purgatorio XXX*, 22–145.

p. 16, 3. *Rossetti*, p. 197.

p. 16, 4. *Rossetti*, p. 202.

p. 16, 5. *Dante: Convivio.*

p. 16, 6. *Rossetti*, p. 202.

p. 16, 7. *Dante: Convivio*, Treatise II, Ch. 2, p. 68.

p. 17, 1. *Dante: Convivio*, pp. 4, 5.

p. 17, 2. *Petrarch, Secret*, Dialogue 3, pp. 109–65.

p. 18, 1. *Petrarch, Sonnets*, tr. Cayley, Sonnet CCCXII, p. 453.

        'Omai son stanco, e mia vita reprendo
        Di tanto error, che di vertute il seme
        Ha quasi spento; e le mie parti estreme,
        Alto Dio, a te devotamente rendo,
        Pentito e tristo de' miei si spesi anni,
        Che spender si deveano in miglior uso, . . .

             Petrarch, *Le Rime*, Sonnet CCCLXIV [CCCLX], p. 509.

p. 19, 1. *Ficino*, Speech I, Ch. 3, p. 127.

p. 19, 2. *Ficino*, Speech V, Ch. 10, p. 178.

p. 20, 1. *Ficino*, Speech VI, Ch. 7, p. 190.

p. 20, 2. Plotinus expounds the Platonic myth in the third *Ennead*, Tractate 5, see *Spenser*: Studies; William Nelson, p. 217.

p. 21, 1. *Ficino*, Speech VI, Ch. 7, p. 191.

p. 21, 2. *Ficino*, Speech V, Ch. 3, p. 168; Ch. 4, p. 169; Speech VI, Ch. 17, p. 212, Ch. 18, p. 215.

p. 22, 1. See *Pico*, Bk. 3, Ch. 10, commenting on stanza 6. Thomas Stanley's translation of this passage is unusually close to the original.

p. 23, 1. *Bembo*, p. 189.

p. 24, 1. *Castiglione*, p. 322.

p. 25, 1. *Ficino*, Speech 2, Ch. 7, p. 143.

p. 25, 2. *Ficino*, Speech 1, Ch. 4, p. 130.

p. 26, 1. *Leone Ebreo*, p. 55.

p. 26, 2. *Leone Ebreo*, p. 181-2

p. 27, 1. *Bruno*, French translation, p. 198, English translation vol. 2, p. 89. The French translation is more accurate than the English one, which is at times very poor.

p. 27, 2. *Bruno*, Fr. tr., p. 90.

p. 27, 3. *Bruno*, Fr. tr., p. 180; Eng. tr., vol. 1, p. 73.

p. 28, 1. *Bruno*, Fr. tr., p. 172; Eng. tr., vol. 1, pp. 67, 68.

p. 28, 2. *Bruno*, Fr. tr., pp. 177, 178.

p. 28, 3. *Bruno*, Fr. tr., pp. 204-8; Eng. tr., vol. 1, pp. 90-4.

p. 30, 1. *Ruysbroeck*, Bk. 1, ch. 1, pp. 6-9.

p. 31, 1. See Matthew Arnold, *Culture and Anarchy*, Ch. 4.

p. 32, 1. See *Augustine, City of God* (Vol. II), Bk. 14, Ch. 26, 27; Bk. 15, Ch. 3, 21; *Augustine Synth*. XII, Nos. 623-5, pp. 345, 346, Nos. 630, 631, pp. 348, 349; No. 643, pp. 353-4.

p. 33, 1. *Aquinas, Gilby*, p. 31, No. 84. See also *Aquinas, Pégis*, Vol. I, Summa Th. Pt. I, Q 1, Art 1, pp. 5, 6, Q, 2 Arts 1, 2, pp. 18-24, Q 12, Arts 12, 13, pp. 109, 111; Vol. II, Summa Th. First part of Part 2, Q 109, Arts. 1-4, pp. 979 ff.

p. 33, 2. William Perkins, Works I, pp. 109-11 quoted by *H. C. Porter*, p. 309.

p. 33, 3. *Luther, The Bondage of the Will*, p. 209.

p. 34, 1. *Luther, The Bondage of the Will*, p. 101: see also pp. 232-3.

p. 34, 2. *Luther, Reform, Writings*, pp. 183-5.

p. 34, 3. For the violence of the dispute in Elizabethan Cambridge see *Porter*, especially Part III.

p. 34, 4. Walton's 'Life of Hooker in *Hooker*', Vol. I, p. 41.

p. 34, 5. 'Mr. Hooker's Answer' in *Hooker*, Vol. II, pp. 691-2.

p. 35, 1. *Hooker*, Vol. I, Bk. II, Ch. II, pp. 148-52.

p. 36, 1. *Hooker*, Vol. I, Bk. III, Ch. VIII, par. 9, p. 305.

p. 36, 2. See *Spenser*, F.Q. Bk. I, Canto IX, Stanzas 6, 7, 53; Canto X, Stanza I; Bk. III, Canto 3, Stanza 2; H.H.B. ll. 250-4.

p. 37, 1. For an account of the ancient Hymn, see *Daremberg et Saglio* s.v. *Hymnus*. See also *Smyth*.

p. 38, 1. Ronsard wrote a number of lengthy hymns, but Spenser's hymns show no trace of their influence.

p. 39, 1. See *infra*. pp. 144, 156.

p. 46, 1. *Ficino*, Speech VI, Ch. VI, pp. 188 ff. and Speech VI, Ch. XVIII, p. 213. See also *Pico*, Bk. III, Ch. X, pp. 68 ff.

p. 48, 1. *Ellrodt*, p. 134.

p. 53, 1. These interpretations have been conveniently listed by *Ellrodt*, Ch. IX, p. 164; see also Ch. XI, pp. 183 ff., and *infra* pp. 170-1, H.H.B., l. 183, and note.

p. 54, 1. Ecclesiasticus I. 4-9.

p. 54, 2. Jn. 3; 16.

p. 54, 3. Rom. 1. 20.

p. 56, 1. *Ellrodt*, p. 163.

p. 57, 1. *Hooker*, Vol. I, Bk. I, Ch. II, 6, 5, pp. 151, 152.

p. 58, 1. *Hooker*, Vol. I, Bk. I, Ch. XI, par. 2, 3, pp. 200, 201.

p. 58, 2. *Hooker*, Vol. I, Bk. I, Ch. XVI, par. 8, p. 228.

p. 60, 1. W. K. Wimsatt, *The Verbal Icon*, University of Kentucky Press, 1954, Preface, xv, p. 5.

p. 60, 2. *Ellrodt*, p. 122.

p. 63, 1. *Spenser, Var. Minor Poems*, Vol. II, pp. 631-8, 647-52.

p. 63, 2. *Spenser, Renwick*, pp. 192–6.

p. 64, 1. *Spenser, Var. Minor Poems*, Vol. II, p. 650.

p. 64, 2. Homer, *Iliad*, XVIII, ll. 491–6, text and translation by A. T. Murray, in Loeb Classical Library, Vol. II, 1925 : see also 'The Shield of Herakles' in *Hesiod*, tr. A. W. Mair, Oxford, Clarendon Press, 1908, p. 78.

p. 65, 1. For text and translation see *The Greek Bucolic Poets*, tr. J. M. Edmonds in the Loeb Classical Library, Heinemann, 1919, pp. 224–31.

p. 66, 1. Claudite ostia, virgines:
lusimus satis, at, boni
conjuges, bene vivete et
munere assiduo valentem
exercete juventam. *Catullus* Carmen 61.

p. 66, 2. *Statius*, Vol. I, *Sylvae*, I, 2, pp. 14–37.

p. 66, 3. *Claudian*, Vol. I, pp. 230–67, Vol. II, pp. 204–15.

p. 67, 1. Scaliger, *Poetices Libriseptem*, Bk. III, Ch. 101.

p. 68, 1. *Ronsard*, Vol. I, pp. 9–16.

p. 68, 2. *Belleau*, Vol. II, pp. 88–98.

p. 68, 3. *du Bellay*, Vol. V, pp. 199–226.

p. 68, 4. *de Buttet*, pp. 363–84.

p. 69, 1. *Spenser, Epith. Studies, McPeek*, also *Spenser, Var. Minor Poems*, Vol. II. p. 653.

p. 69, 2. *Case Eng. Epith.*, pp. 1–3 and *The Complete Works of Sir Philip Sidney*, edit. A. Feuillerat, C.U.P., 1922, Vol. II, p. 63. In this version Lalus is re-named Thyrsis. The original *Arcadia* was published by Feuillerat, op. cit., Vol. IV, 1926. Dychus' Song is on pp. 229 ff. Republished as *Prose Works of Sir Philip Sidney*, 4 vols. C.U.P. 1963–1965.

p. 70, 1. *Case Eng Epith.*, pp. 4–6 and *La Diana Enamorada*, Cinco Libros. Que prosiguen los siete de Jorge de Montemayor por Gaspar Gil Polo, Madrid, 1802, pp. 468–70.

p. 71, 1. 'Hic fuit illes dies: noctem canat ipse maritus', *Statius*, Vol. I, *Sylvae*, I, 2, l. 241, pp. 34, 35.

p. 73, 1. *Claudian*, Vol. I, pp. 232–5.

p. 73, 2. *Legouis, Spenser*, pp. 94, 95, quoted in *Spenser, Var. Minor Poems*, Vol. II, p. 646.

p. 74, 1. *du Bellay*, vol. V, pp. 217, 218; see also note *Epith*, ll. 189–90 and note 198.

p. 79, 1. 'Il est trop certain qu'il demande à Elizabeth pardon de son mariage comme d'une trahison'—Legouis in Revue de Litterature Comparée, l. 413, n. 3. See also Legouis, *Spenser*, p. 93, quoted in *Spenser, Var. Minor Poems*, Vol. II, pp. 488, 489.

p. 81, 1. *Dante, Convivio*, Treatise II, Ch. XII, pp. 108 ff.

p. 85, 1. JEGP 59, 1960, pp. 417–29.

p. 87, 1. *The Evolution of 'The Fairie Queene'*, Univ. of Chicago Press, Chicago, Illinois, 1942, pp. 28–9.

p. 90, 1. *Hooker*, Bk. I, Ch. XI, 31.

p. 91, 1. *Hooker*, Bk. I, Ch. XI, 4.

AN HYMNE IN HONOUR OF LOVE

p. 92, 1. *To the Right Honorable . . . Warwicke*. Lady Margaret was a daughter of Francis Russell, Earl of Bedford, and wife of George Clifford, Earl of Cumberland. Samuel Daniel, who was tutor to her daughter Anne, addressed a poem to her. She died in 1616. Her sister whose name was Anne, not Marie, was the wife of Leicester's brother, Ambrose Dudley, Earl of Warwick. She died in 1604.

p. 93, 1, ll. 1–21. *Love . . . actes to sing*: cf. Benivieni, *Canzona della Amore*, stanza I:

Amor, dalle cui man sospes'el freno
Del mio cor pende, et nel cui sacro regno
Nutrir non hebbe ad sdegno
La fiamma che per lui già in quel fu accessa,
Muove la lingua mia, sforza l'ingegno
Ad dir di lui quel che l'ardente seno
Chiude; ma il cor vien meno,
Et la lingua repugna, a tanta impresa,
Ne quel ch'en me può, dir ne far difesa;
Et pur convien che'l mio concetto esprima:
Forza contro ad maggior forza non vale.
Ma perchè al pigro ingegno amor quell'ale
Promesso ha, con le qual nel cor mio in prima
Discese, benchè in cima,
Credo per mai partir, dalle sue piume
Fa nido, quanto el lume
Del suo vivo splendor fia al cor mio scorta
Spero aprir quel che di lui asscoso hor porta.

[Love, suspended from whose hands hangs the bridle of my heart and who in his sacred dominion does not disdain to nourish the flame, which he long ago kindled within me, moves my tongue and compels my wit to speak of him that which my burning breast contains: but the heart fails and the tongue falters before so great an enterprise, nor is there anything within me which can speak in my defence; nevertheless, I am constrained to express my thought; force can avail nothing against greater force. But because Love has promised to my sluggish wit those wings with which he first descended into my heart (although on its summit he has made a feathered nest whence, I believe, he will never more depart), therefore, as far as the light of his living splendour guides me, I hope to disclose that knowledge of him which is now hidden within me.] English verse translations are by Thomas Stanley (see *Pico*) and by J. B. Fletcher in an article in *MP* 8 (1911), 545 ff.

p. 93, 2, l. 3. *stowre*: tumult, conflict.

p. 93, 3, l. 8. *new flame*. The poet does not pretend that this is his first love affair, but the hymns are not necessarily autobiographical.

p. 93, 4, l. 11. *areed*: to proclaim, make known.

p. 93, 5, l. 13. *embrewed*: stained. Love has manifested his overwhelming power by conquering even great military conquerors, the kind of people, we are obviously meant to infer, who are more accustomed to shedding the blood of others than to being wounded themselves.

p. 93, 6, l. 24. *Venus lap*. Throughout the two hymns Venus is regarded as the goddess of Beauty and parent of Love, and the picture suggested here is that of a happy child fondled by his mother. It also suggests a heavenly condition for Love is sitting 'above' and ambrosia and nectar are the food and drink of immortal gods. This heavenly state, however, is not necessarily devoid of sensuous delight, for Love's 'silver bowers' described in this stanza appear to be identical with the lovers' paradise described in ll. 280–93. The poet's object is to persuade Love that his true nature is to cause not sorrow but delight. This idea can be interpreted in a spiritual or in an earthly sense or in both. According to Ficino the Divine Beauty is a continuous attraction moving in a circle which is identified by three names: 'Inasmuch as it begins in God and attracts to Him, it is Beauty; inasmuch as going across into the world it captivates the world we call it Love; and inasmuch as it returns to its source and with Him joins its labours then we call it Pleasure.' Pico's account of the origin of Beauty differs from that of Ficino, for in Bk. II, ch. vi he says that according to the most general and usual definition Beauty occurs whenever several diverse things concur in a third, and since no simple thing can be beautiful, God who is simple cannot be beautiful, but beauty begins *after* Him with the creation. Pico and Benivieni, though not always consistent, usually call beauty Venus. Like Pico and Benivieni, Spenser calls beauty Venus but his conception of beauty is undoubtedly that of Ficino.

p. 93, 7, l. 28. *furie*: here refers to the 'furor poeticus', the divine madness with which poets were sometimes supposed to be possessed.

p. 94, 1, l. 29. *And ye sweet Muses*. The Muses seem to have been originally regarded as virgins, but later stories mention their love affairs and their children. For instance, the Sirens were daughters of Melpomene, Muse of Tragedy and the river-god Achelous. (See also *infra* pp. 172–3, *Epith*. l. 1 and note.)

p. 94, 2, l. 32. *kindly*: in the sixteenth century could mean either 'natural' or 'kind' and Spenser probably means us to take the word in both senses, but with special stress on the latter one.

p. 94, 3, ll. 33–4. *Prepare your selves ... glorie*. Prepare yourselves to give a heartfelt welcome to the triumphal procession of Love, who is your glory (cf. *Epith*. ll. 243–4). Here and in the following stanza Spenser may be recalling the closing words of Agathon's eulogy in Plato's *Symposium*, where Eros is praised as '... the fairest and best of leaders whom every man should follow, singing beautifully and joining in the song wherewith he enchants the minds of gods and men'.

p. 94, 4, ll. 50–3. *Or who alive ... Penurie*. These lines have been severely criticized. How can Love have one mother and two fathers? The confusion is ultimately due to the desire to reconcile the account of Love's birth given in the *Symposium* (see *supra* pp. 9, 10) with the tradition that Cupid was the son of Venus. Plato says that: 'Love from the beginning has been attendant and minister to Aphrodite, since he was begotten on the day of her birth'; according to *Comes* (4. 14. p. 404) his constant attendance on her led to the belief that he was her son.

Ficino's interpretation of the Platonic allegory though subtle is intelligible, for he does not confuse Plato's account of Love's parentage by bringing Venus into the picture (cf. *supra*, pp. 20, 21). Pico and Benivieni follow Ficino in translating Porus as Plenty and in making the birth of Love within the Angelic Mind. According to Pico (Bk. II, ch. xi) Love's birth was made possible by the existence in the Angelic Mind of the archetypal ideas in an *imperfect* form, for 'if the lover were wholly deprived of the thing beloved there would be no similitude between them, which [i.e. similitude] is the cause of Love. Therefore this Love is born when Poro who signifies Abundance, that is to say the affluence of the ideas, mixes with that unformed Nature [which is] called Penia because it is poor and mendicant, being deprived of all being and all act; nor is Penia the real essence of unformed Nature but the indigence and imperfection of it'.

On the face of it this seems consistent with Ficino's account of the matter. Benivieni, however, creates some confusion by translating Penia and Porus by two feminine nouns *Inopia* and *Richezza*, thus apparently giving Love two mothers. Pico notes this, attributes it to poetic elegance and tries to explain it. His explanation, which is not without its own obscurities, depends upon his previous distinction between the efficient cause of our actions, which since it originates in our soul is primary, superior and masculine; and the material cause of these same actions which since it consists in the objects of our actions, the matters with which our actions are concerned, is secondary, inferior and feminine. Venus, he says, 'is not a power of the soul, but she is the beauty of which Love is generated, and therefore Venus is well called the Mother of Love, not as the productive principle [i.e. the masculine efficient cause] but as the object [i.e. the material feminine cause] of the act of loving' (Bk. II, chap. ix, pp. 23–4). In other words, the efficient cause of Love is in the will of the lover who desires beauty, the material cause of Love is the beauty which the lover desires and apart from which love would have no function. This is all very well but it does not explain why Beauty the Mother of Love should be called Penia or why Porus should have to change his sex. Benivieni, says Pico, turned both Poverty and Riches into feminine nouns because 'to be in one way in possession of the beloved object and in another way deprived of it is not the principle and efficient cause of Love, which we have said above is signified by the father, but they are that kind of cause which is said by philosophers to be that without which the effect cannot follow', the kind of cause which must be classified as a material cause on account of its secondary and inferior character;

and that, concludes Pico, was why Benivieni gave 'a feminine name to both the one and the other' (Bk. III, ch. vii, pp. 54–5). Pico's interpretation implies that in Benivieni's poem Plenty and Penury are not to be regarded as separate entities representing the two parents of Love, but rather are to be conjoined into one allegorical female personage signifying that state of partial possession and partial deprivation of beauty, which is the mother or material cause of love. But unfortunately Pico, as we have seen, has elsewhere assured us that the mother of love is Venus or Beauty, and Benivieni appears to hold the same opinion, for having told us in the last lines of stanza 3 that Love was born of Inopia and Richezza on the birthday of Venus he tells us in the opening lines of stanza 4 that Love was born at first of the beautiful Cyprian, i.e. Venus; so either we must identify Porus plus Penia with Venus or we must endow Love with two mothers and apparently no father.

Allegory is notoriously shifty but does this make sense? If love by definition desires beauty he can hardly desire to perpetuate a state of partial deprivation of it, but must rather desire to possess it wholely, and surely the conjunction of Riches and Poverty (whether they personify one or two parents) must be constituents of the lover's soul and so be the efficient masculine cause of the activities of love. Indeed, Pico himself seems to be making this very point (*loc. cit.*, II, xi, p. 25) when he says that love would be impossible if the *lover* were *wholely* deprived of the thing beloved.

At any rate that is surely what Spenser meant in lines 51–3. Like Benivieni he couples Penury and Plenty together as one allegorical pair but very wisely changes the sex from feminine to masculine. The possession of Plenty and Penury constitute a state of soul and thus linked together personify the father or efficient cause of the love of which Venus is the material cause or mother. This makes good sense, whether it makes good poetry is another matter.

p. 94, 5, ll. 54–6. *Though elder . . . Peares.* In *De Amore* V 10, Ficino explains the paradox that 'Love is the beginning and the end, the first and last of the gods' (cf. *supra*, p. 19). *Peares* could mean both 'equals' and 'noblemen' and probably Spenser has both meanings in mind. Love is the elder and the younger and (since he belongs to their own rank) the equal of the gods.

p. 94, 6, ll. 57–91. *For ere this worlds . . . kindly might.* Having declared the wonders of Love's birth the poet goes on to describe the first of his mighty acts, namely the transformation of chaos into cosmos. 'This worlds still moving mightie masse' is neither just our earth nor the whole Creation, for the Angelic Mind is immobile and the World-Soul is incorporeal; but it refers specifically to the World-Body, which exists potentially in primeval chaos; but when actualized and liberated by Love, manifests itself as a huge nest of concentric spheres in perpetual circular motion.

p. 94, 7, ll. 61–70. *Love, that had now long time . . . yet wanting light.*
Both here and in l. 24 Love in Venus' lap represents Love in close
contact with Beauty and therefore satisfied; but there is a difference
between the two pictures which calls for explanation. In line 24 Love
is enjoying himself; here he is safely asleep; in line 24 he is called down
from above, but here he is roused to mount up from his 'idle sleep'.
The explanation is to be found in the role of Clotho. Clotho was
one of the three Fates and was supposed to spin the thread of life
and preside over the moment of birth. According to Hesiod the
Fates were daughters of Night, hence Comes makes them the off-
spring of Chaos (cf. *infra* p. 184). Ficino (speech V, xi, pp. 179–80)
discusses the relationship between Love and Necessity: '. . . if it is
spoken of absolutely the rule of Love is older than that of Necessity,
since the power of Love begins in God and the power of Necessity
begins in created things. But if we speak of it with reference to the
things created by God, the reign of the tyrant Necessity preceded
that of Love, since things themselves are produced by Necessity and
in proceeding degenerate until they are turned towards their father by
Love.' This discussion is a continuation of a discussion of Love's age,
and is really another way of making the same subtle and paradoxical
point. Love we have to remember inherits the characteristics of his
father Porus-and-Penia, Plenty-and-Penury. Porus, the power of
Love, has its source in God, and there it is in full possession of the
beauty it requires for in Heaven desire exists only as the consciousness
of its perpetual fulfilment. Love on Venus' lap therefore is Love fully
satisfied, it needs no armour for it has no opposition to fear. The
position of Penia, the desire for beauty, is very different. Penia has
her source in Chaos and would remain there as a mere hopeless
emptiness were it not for the intervention of Porus, for the infusion
of a spark of the power of Love which kindles lack into desire, desire
into will and will into action. Action is required because the *created*
universe being distinct from the creator is *necessarily* imperfect and
liable to degeneration. So Clotho, who is both daughter of Chaos and
is also the Fate who presides over birth, has to wake Love up and
furnish him with arms. Love as the offspring of Porus-and-Penia is
Love at work in the universe and from that point of view the 'lap of
Venus' may well be described as an 'idle seate', and the same could be
said of Penia's position in Chaos before being quickened by Porus at
the call of Clotho.

p. 95, 1, l. 72. *His owne faire mother* is Venus, goddess of beauty. According to Ficino (cf. Speech VI, x, pp. 198–9) '. . . the light of beauty, which
is both Plenty and the father of Love, has this virtue, that it is directed
back to that whence it has come and with it draws anyone who loves it.
It descends first from God; going across into the Angelic Mind and
the World Soul as if through glass; and from the Soul going easily out
into the Body. . . .' Ficino and Spenser personify beauty differently;

but they agree in identifying it with light. 'Do you think beauty is anything else but light?' asks Ficino (Speech VI, xvii p. 211). Benivieni (*op. cit.*, stanza 4) says that Love always follows the light of Venus because he was originally born in her arms.

p. 95 2, l. 75. *The world that was not till he did it make*, may mean in a general way the whole World-Body, but Spenser is now particularly concerned with our earth and the sublunar spheres of the four elements, the primary forms of matter which in various combinations compose all material bodies. In chaos the four elements are mixed together in disorderly confusion; so Love like Plato's Demiurge (cf. *Timaeus* 53B; Cornford p. 198) begins by separating and defining them and then when 'otherness' leads to hostility, like the heavenly Eros of Eryximachus (cf. *Symposium* 188; Loeb, pp. 129–37), he reconciles them and makes them co-operative and productive. Spenser's description of this process is not altogether easy to grasp, but then neither are the theories on which it is based. Each element was supposed to have a natural tendency to move towards its own sphere in a straight line, fire and air moving upwards and earth water and downwards; but, for reasons which fortunately do not concern us here, they never sort themselves out completely into their respective spheres but are perpetually combining in different ways and being transformed into one another and by their permutations making mundane existence possible. This notion seems to lie behind the apparent contradictions of lines 85–91 in which it is asserted that the elements are compelled to keep within their own separate bounds and yet enabled to mix themselves 'in every living wight'. Perhaps the solution is that although certain particles of water may turn into certain particles of air the essential natures of air and water remain unchanged and distinct from one another.

p. 95, 3, ll. 76–84. *Whose sundrie parts ... rebellious yre.* According to Pico (Bk. II, ch. vi) there is a sense in which every created body can be called beautiful because it is composite; for beauty is a 'harmony resulting from several things proportionately concurrent to constitute a third'. Everything is generated by discord and concord together but the concord must control the discord otherwise everything would dissolve into its component parts. The poets say that Venus loves Mars because beauty needs contrariety, but that Venus dominates Mars because the 'temperament' (*Ital.* 'temperamento', tempering, mixing, softening) mitigates, bridles and blunts the strife and hate between contrary natures ('. . . quel têperamêto mitiga, rafrena, & retunde la pugna & l'odio che e fra quelle nature contrarie').

p. 95, 4, l. 86. *loued meanes.* 'Meanes' here does not, as in line 81, signify ways, methods; but *media*, intermediaries, midway positions, and may be roughly equivalent to Pico's 'temperamento'. For instance, on the principle that love depends on similitude love cannot exist between contraries such as heat and cold which, when unmitigated, are mutually destructive; but when heat is cooled or cold heated, both of them can 'love' the warmth produced by their combination. Spenser may also have been thinking of a passage from the *Timaeus* (31 B–32 C; Cornford, p. 44) where Plato explains how the Demiurge constructed the World Body of the four elements. In order to make it visible and tangible he began by constructing it of fire and earth. 'But two things alone cannot be satisfactorily united without a third; for there must be some bond between them drawing them together;' and in this case one such bond was not sufficient for 'the world was to be solid in form, and solids are always conjoined, not by one mean, but by two. Accordingly the god set water and air between fire and earth, and made them so far as was possible proportional to one another, so that as fire is to air, so is air to water, and as air is to water, so is water to earth, and thus he bound together the frame of a world visible and tangible. For these reasons and from such constituents, four in number, the body of the universe was brought into being, coming into concord by means of proportion, and from these it acquired Amity, so that coming into unity with itself it became indissoluble by any other save him who bound it together.' This passage makes no mention of tempering the 'contrary dislikes' of lines 85–6 but it helps us to interpret the rest of the stanza.

p. 95, 5, l. 88. *raines* means rules, dominions, and refers to the elemental spheres which are linked together in an unchangeable order. This universal order was sometimes pictured as a chain stretching from the throne of God to the lowest of inanimate creatures and identified with the golden chain which according to Homer was let down from heaven by Zeus. Jean de Meung (quoted Ellrodt, p. 126) speaks of 'the beautiful golden chain which links the four elements'. (See also *Tillyard*, pp. 23 ff.) Spenser uses the adjective 'adamantine' to emphasize the unbreakable, enduring quality of the bond.

p. 95, 6, l. 95. *cope*: (Med. Lat. *Copa*) a long cloak, a cape; *fig.*, anything resembling a canopy, a vault. According to Ptolemaic theory the Universe was spherical.

p. 96, 1, ll. 99–105. *Thereby they all do live . . . progenie.* Although Love causes the lower creatures to reproduce their kind, their only conscious purpose is the satisfaction of their sexual instincts, whereas man deliberately begets children 'not for lusts sake, but for eternitie'. What does this mean? According to Plato, Ficino and many others the desire for procreation is the desire to achieve an earthly immortality, and Renwick (p. 215) thinks that Spenser went no further than this. A comparison with *Epith.* 417–23, suggests that he is speaking as an orthodox Christian. Human beings desire to populate not only the earth but Heaven.

p. 96, 2, l. 106. *deducted*: is used here in its original Latin sense of 'drawn down'. The descent is not the Christian fall into sin, but the

Platonic fall into matter and the sight of beauty awakens desire for
the heavenly things that have never been wholly forgotten. This is,
of course, a Platonic commonplace, but Spenser handles it in a very
un-Platonic way. The Platonist treats human love as a starting-point
for the heavenly quest; Spenser here treats heavenly desires as an
explanation of the violence of human love.

p. 96, 3, l. 120. *Which well perceiving, that imperious boy.* This is a
turning point in the poem. The creation culminates in man, and when
Love reaches humanity, he is transformed into Cupid, the god of
lovers, the god who is at the moment tormenting the poet and causing
him to ask why he should be so tormented. Then again (cf. 11, 156 ff.)
the mood changes. Cupid once more increases in stature and appears
as 'the world's great Parent', etc.; but now his power is seen not in
his organizing of the cosmos but in his uplifting of the human spirit.

In the Quarto the occurrence of the comma after 'boy' is probably
a mistake of the compositor and is emended in the folios, F1 and F3
placing a comma after 'perceiving' and 'boy', F2 after 'perceiving'
only.

p. 97, 1, l. 138. ... *their dying to delay*: 'to prolong their death
throes'.

p. 97, 2, l. 153. *Certes*: certainly.

p. 97, 3, l. 157. *wights*: creatures, persons.

p. 97, 4, l. 159. *the not deserver*: the innocent, the man who does not
deserve punishment.

p. 97, 5, l. 162. *eke*: moreover.

p. 98 1, ll. 169–72. *So hard ... stedfastnesse.* As divine things are
least influenced by passions, so those heavenly beauties (i.e. the
marble-hearted ladies of whom Spenser's beloved is one) are not easily
inflamed and the more steadfast they are, the more they are to be
admired by steadfast minds. The general sense is clear enough, but in
this and the preceding stanza the syntax is awkward, the style too
compressed to be clear or even grammatical, and the effect of the over-
frequent use of inversion spoils the music of the verse. This is one of
Spenser's recurrent faults.

p. 98, 2, l. 182. *moldwarpe*: mole, *lit.* earth-thrower.

p. 98, 3, l. 183. *themselves enure*: habituate themselves, accustom
themselves.

p. 98, 4, l. 187. *generous*: noble-minded.

p. 98, 5, ll. 190–6. *Such is the powre ... heavenly light.* There is
ambiguity here. Is the lover admiring his mental image of his lady's
appearance because it mirrors the heavenly light behind her beauty
more perfectly than her outward form can do; or is he admiring his
mental image of his lady's outward form, because that outward form
is a mirror of the heavenly light? In some contexts these distinctions
would be important, but here they make no great difference for
Spenser's meaning is pretty clear. His lover's position is that of the

L

Neo-Platonist on the second rung of his ladder (cf. *supra*, p. 22), but Spenser is more concerned with the contrast between two different types of love, than between two different images of heavenly beauty, or between different stages of the lover's progress. As usual, he is using Neo-Platonic ideas in his own individual way. The lustful man is concerned only with the lady's outward appearance because he dare not expose himself to the spiritual beauty of which it is the expression. True love, on the contrary, so purifies and refines the lover's mind that it becomes ever more conformable to the spiritual beauty of the lady and so capable of mirroring it in a fairer form than that which the bodily eye perceives. It seems to be implied that the refining process is reciprocal. The lady's inward beauty refines and elevates her lover's mind and he then is able to mirror her inward beauty in a mental image which is even lovelier than her actual bodily form. But this does not lead to any repudiation of sexual love; if anything it intensifies it.

p. 98, 6, l. 200. *Tantale*: Tantalus, was a son of Zeus and the ancestor of the tragic Argive Kings, grandfather of Atreus and Thyestes, great-grandfather of Agamemnon and Aegisthus. He committed a great crime (accounts of it differ) and was punished in Hell with an insatiable hunger and thirst. He stands in a pool of water that reaches up to his chin but flows away when he tries to drink it, and overhead hangs a bough of fruit which is blown away as soon as he tries to pick it.

p. 99, 1, l. 209–10. *Thrise happie man . . . fortune blesse*: Here as in line 240 'faines', i.e. 'feigns' probably means imagines rather than pretends. We may compare lines 216–17 where the lover's 'fayning eye' is conjuring up a *mental* and perhaps an idealized, but not a wholly false image of his lady's beauty. Lines 209–10 are too compressed and elliptic to be easily construed. They could mean either: 'He imagines what a thrice-happy man he would be if only he might gain possession of his love; and then, as in imagination he achieves this object, he blesses his good fortune'; or: 'He imagines . . . possession of his love, and then, as he thinks in this way, he blesses his good fortune for giving him such a love to pursue.' According to the first interpretation he exults in an *anticipated success* in love; according to the second, he exults in a *present experience* of loving. The next stanza tells in favour of the latter interpretation, but in that case the punctuation should be altered so that the comma is placed after 'possesse' and the semi-colon after 'himself'.

p. 99, 2, ll. 231–7. *Witnesse Leander . . . obay*. Leander of Abydos swam the Hellespont in order to spend his nights with Hero, priestess of Venus, who guided him with a torch from her high tower at Sestos. One night he was drowned and on seeing his dead body Hero threw herself into the sea. The story is not mentioned in classical Greek literature. It is the theme of Ovid, *Heroides* 18, 19. Marlowe's *Hero and Leander* was founded on a late Greek poem which George Chapman (who translated it) called 'the incomparable Love-Poem of the world'. Its author, Musaeus (*c.* late fifth century A.D.), was mistakenly identified with a mythical poet Musaeus, a supposed contemporary of the legendary Orpheus. Aeneas returned through the burning streets of Troy in order to rescue his family. He bore away on his back his aged father, Anchises (cf. Vergil *Aeneid* II, 634 ff). Achilles was so angered with Agamemnon, the Greek general, that he refused to leave his tent until his grief for his friend Patroclus drove him into battle, in order to avenge his death upon his slayer Hector (cf. *Iliad* Bks. 18–22). For *Orpheus* see *Epith.* l. 16, and note.

p. 100, 1, l. 242. *aby*: buy, purchase, suffer, pay the penalty.

p. 100, 2, l. 251. *Paragone*. Here has not its usual meaning of 'a pattern of' but is used in the now obsolete sense of 'rival'.

p. 101, 1, l. 283. *Hercules and Hebe*. After a life spent in ridding the world of monsters, Hercules was poisoned by his wife, Dejanira, who thought she was giving him a love potion. In order to escape from agony, he burnt himself to death on a funeral pyre; but Zeus with the approval of the Olympian gods raised him up to Heaven and Hera gave to him in marriage their daughter Hebe, the goddess of Youth, who acted as cup-bearer to the gods.

p. 102, 2, ll. 297–8. *or might ... to recure*. If recure means 'to recover', 'regain', the phrase must mean 'or might assure myself of regaining that happy haven forever'. Better sense and better rhythm is gained by placing the comma after 'port' instead of after 'assure' and taking 'recure' as 'regain health'. The meaning then would be: '... or that I might assure myself of that happy haven and so regain my health forever.'

AN HYMNE IN HONOUR OF BEAUTIE

p. 102, 1, l. 2. *wontlesse*: unaccustomed, strange.

p. 102, 2, l. 7. *matter of my fyre*: Venus, goddess of beauty and mother of Cupid. (Cf. *supra* pp. 145–7, H.L. ll. 50–3 and note).

p. 102, 3, l. 17. *kindly dewty*. Winstanley (*The Fowre Hymnes*, p. 53) explains as 'natural power' and suggests that the exigencies of rhyme led to this strained use of the word. But 'dewty' cannot mean power. In Spenser's day it could mean homage, debt, one's due, as well as duty. It was part of the cosmic order that the higher should give of itself to the lower; so that Beauty might be said to be under a kind of obligation to irradiate the world. Duty like Grace may here imply something given, granted. But, no doubt, it was difficult to find a rhyme to beauty.

p. 102, 4, ll. 10, 23. *eke*: 'also'.

p. 103, 1, ll. 29–35. *What time this worlds great workmaister . . . any wheare.* This is derived directly or indirectly from Plato's *Timqeus* 29, C: '. . . we must go back to this question about the world: After which of the two models did its builder [ὁ τεκταινόμενος] frame it—after that which is always in the same unchanging state, or after that which has come to be? Now if this world is good and its maker [Δημιουργὸς] is good, clearly he looked to the eternal; . . . for the world is the best of things that have become, and he is the best of causes.' (W. Cornford, pp. 22–3.) On pp. 40–1 Cornford points out that the Model contemplated by the Demiurge is not the Form of the Good contemplated by the Philosopher in the *Republic*, nor the Absolute Beauty contemplated by the Lover in the *Symposium*, but the Form of the Perfect Living Creature. The Florentine Neo-Platonists found no difficulty in equating it with the orderly pattern of ideas in the Angelic Mind. The phrase 'as comely as he could' accords better with the Platonic notion that the Demiurge, the great Work-Master, was hampered by the material he had to use than with the account of the Creation given in the first chapter of Genesis.

p. 103, 2, ll. 36–42. *That wondrous Paterne . . . the same may tell.* Ellrodt's ironical comments on this stanza (p. 127) seem to me undeserved. Readers of Plato and of his commentators ancient and modern, may well sympathise with Spenser's uncertainty as to the location of this 'wondrous Paterne'. Christian Neo-Platonists were probably deviating from Plato when they placed the Form or forms *within* the Divine Mind. According to St. Augustine (who influenced Ficino) God created the Universe by one single direct act; but this act included the planting of formative principles in chaotic matter, and these forms, like seeds, remained latent in matter until they ordained time for their emergence and maturity had arrived; for the Cosmos was created by God not *in* but *together with* time. Spenser expresses himself somewhat naively, and 'earth' is an inaccurate word in this context, nevertheless these lines do suggest the recurrent dispute as to whether the Forms (including, of course, the Form of Beauty) transcend the cosmos or are immanent within it.

p. 103, 3, ll. 43–9. *Thereof as every earthly thing . . . empight.* 'Empight', implanted. Ficino in *de Amore* has a short chapter headed 'The Divine Beauty Shines through Everything and is Loved in Everything'. See also a passage from his *Opera Omnia* quoted by *Kristeller*, p. 79.

'The divine mind gives to the lower bodies only life like warmth; to the higher ones, also sense perception like light; to the highest ones also intellect like lightness. . . . Thus that divine ray that penetrates all things exists in the stones without living, lives in the plants without shining, shines in the animals without being reflected in itself and without returning to its source. But in men it exists, lives, shines, and is reflected in itself.'

A mine being a dark and concealed source of material which becomes valuable when it is cut away from its surroundings and brought up into the light, is an appropriate image for that matter which is never experienced in its chaotic state, but which underlies all the forms of the physical world. Spenser expresses the same idea in his famous description of the gardens of Adonis: FQ. III, vi, 36:

> For in the wide wombe of the world there lyes,
> In hatefull darknesse and in deepe horrore,
> An huge eternal *Chaos*, which supplyes
> The substances of natures fruitfull progenyes.

p. 103, 4, l. 52. *life-full spirits*: the cosmic equivalent of the 'vital spirits' which played such an important part in mediæval and Renaissance physiology. 'So strong is the power of light that it connects celestial things easily and in one moment with earthly things from which they are otherwise far removed beyond all proportion. Not only does it transport the forces of the stars to the following things, but it brings the sun and the stars themselves to the lower beings, just as our spirit brings the forces of the Soul and the Soul itself to the humours and members. And as in us the spirit is the bond (connecting link) of Soul and body, so the light is the bond of the universe (*vinculum universi*)' (Ficino, quoted, *Kristeller*, p. 116).

On the mediating function of the vital spirits Ficino has much to say: 'The Soul . . . is most pure, therefore it cannot be united to this thick earthly body, which is far away from it, except by a most subtle and light-bearing body, which we call "spirit" and which is generated by the warmth of the heart out of the finest part of the blood and spread from there throughout the whole body'. (Quoted Kristeller, p. 372.) In *de Amore*, Speech 6, ch. vi, 188–9, Ficino gives a lengthy account of the 'spirit', explaining how it receives the powers of the soul and transfers them to the body, at the same time receiving through the senses the images of external things and displays them to the soul which 'being present to the spirit, in every part, easily sees the images of bodies shining in it as though in a mirror, and through them it judges bodies and this cognition is called by the Platonists sense perception. See also HB ll. 99–147 and note.

p. 104, 1, ll. 66–7. *goodly temp'rament of pure complexions*. Temperament and complexion had originally much the same meaning, i.e. a combination of elements, humours or qualities in a certain proportion. In Spenser's day 'temperament', like the Italian 'temperamento', could mean either moderating, mixing, mitigating or the result of the process. Probably it is used here in the first sense. In the second sense temperament like complexion could be manifested in outward appearance and by the sixteenth century the latter word was also used to denote the texture or colour of the skin, especially of the face. Spenser is using 'complexions' in the latter sense.

p. 105, 1, ll. 99–147. *But that faire lampe . . . foule imperfection*. In these stanzas Spenser is following his Neo-Platonic models very closely and some of his lines read like a paraphrase of Benivieni's *Canzone*, stanza 6:

> Quando formata in pria dal divin volto,
> Per descendere qua giù lalma si parte,
> Dalla più eccelsa parte
> Ch' alberghi el sol nel cor human s'imprime;
> Dov' esprimendo con mirabil arte
> Quel valor poi che da sua stella ha tolto,
> Et che nel grembo accolto
> Vive di sua celeste spoglie prime,—
> Quanto nel seme human posson sue lime,
> Forma suo albergo; in quel fabrica et stampa,
> C'hor più, hor men, repugna al divin culto.

[When the soul, which was originally formed in the Divine Image, departs in order to descend here below, she leaves the highest regions that house the sun and penetrates the human heart; there expressing with marvellous skill that excellence which she has now brought away from her star and which lives garnered up in the bosom of her former heavenly booty; she forms, as best she may with her implements, a house for herself in human clay (*lit.* seed) and constructs and moulds that which is more or less repugnant to divine cultivation.]

This obscure verse becomes more intelligible when read in the light of Pico's commentary on it (Bk. III, ch. x) and of Ficino (Speech VI, chs. iii and iv). Having explained in chapter iii the difference between the souls of the spheres and the stars, who are called 'gods', and the subordinate daemons, Ficino explains in chapter iv how God distributes gifts to men through mediating 'daemons'. These gifts are qualities or capacities such as the power of contemplation, the ability to govern, etc., each of which is specially connected with one of the planets. 'God first contains the capacity for these gifts in Himself. Then to the seven gods who move the seven planets and whom we call Angels, He distributes the power of these gifts so that each of the gods takes one in preference to the other. They in turn grant them to the seven kinds of subservient daemons, each one specially to his own [i.e. each "god" possesses his own bunch of daemons], and these then hand them on to men.' That, however, is not the end of the matter, for as soon as they have been born from God and endowed with their appropriate gifts, 'the souls slipping down out of the Milky Way through Cancer into a body, are draped in a certain heavenly and clear wrap, clothed in which they are then enclosed in earthly bodies. For the order of nature requires that the perfectly pure soul cannot descend into this more impure body until it receives a certain median and pure garment, which since it is baser than the Soul, but purer and finer than this body, is judged by the Platonists to be the most fitting copula of the soul with the earthly body.'

This 'heavenly wrap' seems to be the equivalent of the 'celestial vehicle' described by Pico in terms which remind one of the 'astral body' of spiritualistic theory. According to the Platonists, he explains, we have two bodies: one, called the celestial vehicle, is directly animated by the rational soul and is incorruptible; the other is the visible body, compounded of the four elements and is corruptible (Bk. I, ch. xi).

Pico interprets Benivieni's stanza 6 in the light of this theory. Platonists affirm, he says, that the conformity of individual souls, with individual planets, is caused by God himself, who, according to Plato: ' "Soweth and scattereth souls, some in the moon, others in other planets and stars." . . . Many imagine the Rational Soul descending from her Star in her "Vehiculum Caelesti", of herself forms the Body, to which by that Medium she is united. Our Author upon these grounds supposeth, that into the "vehiculum" of the Soul, by her endued with Power to form the Body, is infused from her Star a particular formative vertue, distinct according to that Star; thus the aspect of one is Saturnine, of another Jovial, etc. In their looks we reade the nature of their Souls. But because inferiour Matter is not ever obedient to the Stamp, the vertue of the Soul is not always equally expressed in the visible Effigies; hence it happens that two of the same Nature are unlike; the Matter whereof the one consists, being lesse disposed to receive that Figure than the other; what, in that is compleat is in this imperfect; our Author infers, that the figures of two Bodies being formed by vertue of the same Star, this Conformity begets Love' (Pico, Bk. III, ch. x, tr. Stanley pp. 74–75).

It is difficult to determine the relationship between the vital spirits of physiological theory 'generated by the warmth of the heart out of the finest part of the blood' and the 'heavenly and clear wrap' in which the soul descends to earth for both are sometimes called vehicles and said to act as mediating links between the human soul and its earthly body. In the passages quoted above Pico and Benivieni seem to be identifying them. According to Kristeller (*op. cit.*, pp. 371–3), Ficino distinguished them, but they are easily confused and Neo-Platonists held various opinions on the subject.

What is Spenser's position? I believe 'that faire lampe' is best interpreted as the ethereal body which contains the lady's soul and through whose translucent matter her heavenly beauty shines. Although her physical body dies when the 'vital spirits' cease to link it with her soul, her ethereal body being 'a parcel of the purest skie' does not die and she is drawn back in it to her native planet. Why not to heaven? Perhaps for Spenser as for Dante, location in a planet symbolizes our rank in heaven. In the final paragraph of *De Amore*, Speech 4, ch. vi, Ficino praises love because 'he leads us back to heaven' and there 'he arranges us in our places and makes us all content with that distribution'. If this is the correct interpretation, the 'vital spirits' which are syntactically distinguished from the 'lampe' must be the spirits of physiological theory and cannot easily be identified with 'the lively spirits' of line 111 which seem to be the equivalent of the celestial vehicle and therefore in some sense also with the 'lampe'. Possibly the 'lampe' image emphasizes the ethereal embodiment of the soul, while the 'spirits' image emphasizes the formative mediating power which the embodied soul retains from its heavenly source. If, however, the 'lampe' is the lady's soul, both the 'vital' and the 'lively spirits' are more easily identified with the celestial vehicle or ethereal body; but the difficulty here is that it is the ethereal body rather than the disembodied soul that can be suitably described as 'a parcell of the purest skie'. The word 'expire' (l. 102) here means exhale rather than die, and could therefore possibly be applied either to the vital spirits or the ethereal body.

However, these distinctions matter very little for the underlying ideas are much the same in either case and may be summarized as follows: The Creator supplies each soul He has created with a spark of His own creative love by means of which it will be enabled to form a body for itself and then He allots it to a particular star whence it will derive its own particular characteristics and the capacity to mould its body into a shape that can fittingly express them. Thus equipped the soul starts on its downward journey and in order—as it were—to break its fall it is first given the ether to work upon, and out of this ethereal matter it forms for itself a heavenly wrap or celestial vehicle which is not subject to decay or death. Enwrapped in this pure body of ether the soul descends to earth and is incorporated into the human race ('enraced') by being begotten of a physical father. Since in the womb it still retains some flickers of the divine light, it begins to mould out of sublunar matter composed of the four elements a physical, mortal body for itself which shall be as far as possible a visible expression of its invisible excellence. The soul's success in this artistic effort, however, depends partly upon where it lands, for even a good and beautiful soul may be unlucky enough to find that the only available material is too faulty to be modelled into a speaking likeness of its inner nature. Nevertheless, a kindred soul descended from the same star and consequently possessed of similar spiritual qualities may recognize even an unlovely body as an image of a familiar ideal and consequently see and love in it the spiritual beauty which the beloved soul has tried to reproduce rather than the actual physical product of its efforts.

p. 105, 2, l. 107. *that great immortall Spright* is Spenser's equivalent of Benivieni's 'divin volte', divine countenance, i.e. God. Pico comments that according to Catholics the Soul was created directly, according to Platonists indirectly by God.

p. 105, 3, l. 111. *that fayrest starre* is the sun, the source of light and life. In the Neo-Platonic system, *Sol* was one of the planets, with its own particular gifts and daemons; but Spenser's account of the soul's descent suggests that the sun is the native planet of all human beings, a notion inconsistent with the belief that only those souls who hail from the same planet should love one another. Perhaps Spenser thought that by 'the highest part that harbours the sun', Benivieni meant the sun's sphere, whereas according to Pico, he meant the Tropic of Cancer: the fourth Sign of the Zodiac.

p. 105, 4, l. 114. *eft*: afterwards.

p. 105, 5, l. 119. *robd*: robbed. Spenser is following Benivieni very closely. Neither poet means to imply that the soul's action was lawless, but rather that the soul forms its own body by communicating to it a beauty which belongs to the spiritual rather than to the earthly realm.

p. 105, 6, l. 126. *a virgin Queene*: a soul. Spenser was particularly fond of this phrase, no doubt because it usually implied a direct or indirect compliment to Queen Elizabeth, though it has no such reference here. Mediæval spiritual writers frequently used the phrase in reference to the individual soul.

p. 105, 7, ll. 132–3. *For of the soule ... bodie make*. Aristotle disagreed with Plato's view that the body was a temporary and not very satisfactory habitation of the soul and defined the soul as the form [i.e. the formative life-principle] of the body. Spenser is following Benivieni in regarding the soul as a separate entity which fashions the body it is to inhabit.

p. 106, 1, l. 135. *corpse*: Lat. corpus, a body, not necessarily a dead one.

p. 106, 2, l. 147. *perform'd*: in the obsolete sense of constructed, completed, made.

p. 106, 3, l. 150. *hew*: Hue, form, appearance (not merely colour).

p. 106, 4, l. 152. *sinners scorne*: means, not that beauty is scorned by sinners, but that sinners turn it into a thing of scorn by treating it as a purely physical attraction which temps to lust.

p. 106, 5, l. 158. *will*: was sometimes used as equivalent to self-will, evil-will.

p. 106, 6, ll. 159–61. *Nathelesse the soule ... corruption take*. The belief that evil originates in the flesh and cannot corrupt the soul is heretical, for according to Christian doctrine sin originates in the will. It is, however, just possible to give Spenser's line an orthodox interpretation, if we remember that 'the flesh' when used in a pejorative sense (by St. Paul, for instance) often means not the physical body by itself, but the whole human personality wrongly directed, and that there was also a tradition that the *essence*, the highest and most inward part of our spiritual being is made in the image of God and can never be totally in every sense severed from Him, for if it were it would fall into nothingness. The point is made with great clarity by the mediæval mystic Ruysbrock: 'This is that nobleness which we possess by nature in the essential unity of our spirit, where it is united with God according to nature. This neither makes us holy, nor blessed, for all men, whether good or evil, possess it within themselves; but it is certainly the first cause of all holiness and blessedness.' . . . 'The essential being of the spirit is so noble, that even the damned cannot will their own annihilation. But sin builds up a barrier, and gives rise to such darkness . . . that the spirit cannot be united with its proper essence' (*Adornment of the Spiritual Marriage*, Bk. 2, chs. lvii and lx, pp. 127, 130–1.

p. 106, 7, ll. 166–7. *But mindfull still . . . informed grace.* This refers to the soul's heavenly origin. 'Informed', p. part. of 'inform' in the sense of impress, instil, be the formative principle of.

p. 107, 1, ll. 169–71. *Loath that foule blot . . . bland.* Spenser is using 'bland' for 'blandish'. He is exhorting 'faire Dames' to loath the 'disloiall lust' that men of 'base affections' who seek to cajole them, commend to them under the false name of love.

p. 107, 2, ll. 176–82. *But gentle Love . . . first impression.* This warning against confusing lust with love brings Spenser to the main point of his hymn. So far he has been trying to please his lady by praising beauty; now he wants to persuade her that women can enhance their loveliness by returning the affection of their true lovers. The general purport of this stanza is clear enough: unlike lust, faithful love, especially when reciprocated, enhances beauty and reveals its true nature. To construe these lines in detail, however, is difficult, and to arrive at their exact meaning it is necessary to interpret them in the light both of Neo-Platonic thought in general and of Spenser's particular exposition of it in H.L. ll. 176–96 and H.B. ll. 211–38. Spenser is here applying to hetero-sexual love the Platonic notion that the beloved sees himself in his lover as in a mirror (*Phaedrus*, 36 D, in *Loeb* I, p. 501) and is combining it with the Neo-Platonic commonplace that the beloved is more beautiful as mirrored in the lover's mind than he or she is in physical—though not in spiritual—reality. In H.L. ll. 190–203 this process of idealization is described from the point of view of a lover whose affection is not as yet fully reciprocated and it only increases his desire for the physical presence of his beloved. In this poem the idealization is considered from the lady's point of view and is commended to her as a process that redounds to her honour, is partly at least dependent on her readiness to return love for love and should culminate in 'a celestiall harmonie of likely harts'. I am not sure of the precise meaning of the phrase 'which by like way kindled of yours', but I think that it must refer to the lady's fire of love and imply that her suitor's loving vision of her is caused by her love for him as well as by her beauty. C. S. Lewis (*Sixteenth-Century Literature*, p. 375) says: 'In the lady the lover sees his potential and more beautiful self. But Spenser sadly bungles the idea by likening the two lovers to two mirrors which face one another. Surely the results would be very uninteresting.' But ll. 176–90 only make sense on the assumption that the lover sees the image, not of his potential self, but of the true inner beauty of his lady; and that the lady—who can only appreciate her own *inner* beauty by its effect on others—sees her beauty idealized in her lover's mind. So far from bungling his ideas, Spenser is surely expressing them with considerable exactitude. The originating image is the lady's beauty; this is reflected in a mental image in her lover's mind, which is the first mirror; the lady, whose mind is the second mirror, gains a fresh idea of her own beauty by seeing it, as it were, through her lover's eyes. We need not, I think, carry the image any further, but when Lewis speaks of its 'uninteresting result' he is, I imagine, thinking of the indefinite multiplication and diminution of images in confronting mirrors. I am not at all sure that Spenser meant us to consider this; but if he did, he may have been thinking of mutual love as a proliferating force. In *De Amore*, Speech II, ch. viii, pp. 144–45, there is a long account of the effect of mutual love, which is very relevant here, though Ficino is apparently speaking of love or friendship between men rather than between man and woman. 'Here, surely, is a remarkable circumstance that whenever two people are brought together in mutual affection, one lives in the other and the other in him? In this way they mutually exchange identities. . . . When you love me you contemplate me, and as I love you, I find myself in your contemplation of me. . . . In fact, there is only one death in mutual love, but there are two resurrections, for a lover dies within himself the moment he forgets about himself, but he returns to life immediately in his loved one as soon as the loved one embraces him in loving contemplation. He is resurrected once more when he finally recognizes himself in his beloved and no longer doubts that he is loved. O happy death, which is followed by two lives. O wondrous exchange in which each gives himself up for the other, yet does not cease to have himself . . . when two so become one, that each of the two, instead of one alone, becomes two, and as though doubled. . . .' It may be remarked in passing that some of the verses in Donne's *Ecstasy* are strongly reminiscent of this passage:

> But as all severall Soules containe
> Mixture of things, they know not what,
> Love, there mixed soules doth mixe againe,
> And makes both one, each this and that.
> A single violet transplant,
> The strength, the colour and the size,
> (All which before was poore and scant),
> Redoubles still and multiplies.

It is also interesting that Donne, unlike Ficino, but like Spenser, is not content with a purely spiritual union:

> But, O alas, so long, so farre,
> Our bodies why do we forbear
> They are ours, they are not we. . . .

p. 108, 1, ll. 211–38. *But they which love indeede . . . dawning day.* These four stanzas deal once more with the lover's idealization of the lady's physical beauty, but the emphasis is somewhat different. In H.L. ll. 190 ff., Spenser shows how true love refines the lover's mind and makes it capable of creating an adequate image of the lady's inner beauty. In H.B. 176 ff., Spenser, as we have seen, encourages the lady to facilitate this idealization by responding sympathetically to her lover; in the lines now under discussion, Spenser assumes that love is reciprocated and describes the idealizing process in more detail. In line 224, the lover does seem for once to be admiring his own creativity; though possibly the line means that he admires the heavenly beauty as it is mirrored in his thoughts; not that he admires his mind for its power of mirroring heavenly beauty. However, that may be, the poet makes haste to explain that the image in his mind is, after all, a true one, for the lady's inner beauty really does exceed the beauty of her outward form.

p. 109, 1, l. 254. *masking*: here evidently means to take part in a masquing entertainment not to hide the face under a face-mask.

p. 109, 2, l. 256. *belgards*: from Ital. *bel guardo*, a loving look.

p. 109, 3, l. 260. *Cytherea*: a title of Aphrodite, who was born of the sea-foam and blown by the breeze to the isle of Cythera.

AN HYMNE OF HEAVENLY LOVE

p. 110, 1, ll. 1–7. *Love . . . high heavens king.* See H.L. ll. 301–5 and Introduction, p. 64.

p. 110, 2, l. 13. *And turned have . . . string*: the equivalent of our phrase 'have changed my tune'. 'Tenor' here means quality of tone, pitch. The string is the string of the harp, the traditional instrument of the poet. Spenser may have used the word 'turn' because he was thinking of the turning of the wooden pegs by which harpists altered the pitch.

p. 111, 1, ll. 22–6. *Before this worlds . . . by space*: (cf. H.H.B. ll. 36–105 and notes). The 'mightie bound' is the *Primum Mobile*, the cosmic sphere which revolves in twenty-four hours round the fixed central earth, containing and carrying with it the sphere of the fixed stars and also the spheres of the planets which have their own individual movements. This outermost sphere is divided into twenty-four spatial divisions, demarcated by imaginary lines drawn from the north to the south celestial pole and called Hours, presumably because as they move round with the sphere of the fixed stars they define the periods within which the heavenly bodies rise and set. When personified the Hours may be imagined as stationed round the Celestial Sphere at equal distances from each other in order that they may preside over these sidereal comings and goings. Hieatt holds that Spenser has these sidereal hours in mind, not only here and in the *Mutability* cantos cp. FQ. VII, vii, stanza 45), but also in *Epith*. ll. 98–102. *eyas*: an unfledged or untrained hawk, derived from Lat. *nidus*, nest. The spelling is influenced by M.E. *ey*: egg.

p. 111, 2, ll. 27–42. *That high eternall powre . . . reherse*. Spenser is here trying to state in poetry the paradoxical doctrine of the Holy Trinity. 'That high eternall powre' is the Godhead, who being Eternal Love is not a bare Unit, but Unity, Three Persons in One God. In l. 29 'It' refers both to the Triune Godhead and also (more specifically) to the Father, for as St. Augustine says (*De Trin.*, IV. 20): 'The Father is the Principle of the whole Deity', and as Aquinas explains: '. . . although we attribute to the Father something of authority by reason of His being the principle, still we do not attribute any kind of subjection or inferiority to the Son, or to the Holy Ghost . . .' for the term 'principle' . . . 'does not signify priority but origin.' (*Aquinas, Summa Theologica*, Pt. I, Q. 33, Art. I, in *Pégis*, vol. I, p. 325). Spenser, like Ficino, finds Absolute Beauty in God where, of course, it is inseparable from Eternal Love.

p. 111, 1, l. 43. *Yet O most blessed Spirit*. See H.L. 22–9. Spenser here invokes the Holy Spirit to inspire his poem because the Holy Spirit is particularly associated with love and especially with the love which unites the persons of the Holy Trinity. 'The Name of the Holy Ghost: Love.' Under this heading, Aquinas answers in the affirmative the question: 'Whether *Love* is the proper name of the Holy Ghost?' and explains that this in no way contradicts the truth that Love is characteristic of the Trinity as a whole. 'When the term *to love* is taken in a notional sense, it means nothing else than *to spirate* [i.e. breathe forth] *loue*; just as *to speak* is to produce a word, and to flower is to produce flowers, . . . so do we say that by the Word, or the Son, the Father speaks Himself and His creatures and that the Father and the Son love each other and us by the Holy Ghost, or by Love proceeding' (cf. *Summa Theologica*, Pt. I, Q. 37, Art. 2, in *Pégis*, vol. I, p. 357).

The first two Hymns are inspired by human Eros-Love; the last two Hymns are inspired by divine Agape-Love; but Trinitarian doctrine introduces a complication for the love of God for man is manifested both by the Incarnate Christ and by the Holy Spirit, though in different ways. The Holy Spirit acts as an inspiring, invisible influence, perpetually recalling, interpreting, rendering effective the works performed by the visible Christ, living and dying in historic time (cf. St. John 16. 13–15). Eros-Love is both the inspiration and theme of the first Hymn; the Incarnate Christ is the theme of the *Hymne of Heavenly Love*; the Holy Spirit is the inspiration both of this and of the *Hymne of Heavenly Beautie*, and Spenser speaks of Him as the 'lampe of light', the source of grace, wisdom, knowledge, truth.

p. 111, 4, l. 47. *infuse*: infusion.

p. 111, 2, l. 53. *His second brood*. The description of the angels as the second brood begotten by the high Eternal Power is certainly heretical, if taken literally to imply a first brood; but ll. 22–39 show that Spenser held the orthodox doctrine of the Trinity (cf. Introduction, pp. 49–51); for, of course, God the Father did not *create* the Son, or the Holy Spirit.

p. 112, 2, ll. 57–61. *To them the heavens . . . to hold*. The angels do not inhabit the sphere of the fixed stars, nor the crystalline sphere of the Primum Mobile but the Empyrean Heaven which is outside space and time.

p. 112, 3, l. 64. *trinall triplicities*. Aquinas, *Summa Theologica*, Pt. I, Q. 108, Arts. 1, 2, and *Pégis*, vol. I, pp. 995 ff.) grades the angels into three hierarchies, each hierarchy being divided into three Orders. He does this on the authority of the so-called Pseudo-Dionysius, a writer of unknown date whose works are mentioned in the sixth century and who was wrongly identified with Dionysius the Areopagite, converted by St. Paul (cf. Acts 17. 34). From the sixth century onwards the works of Dionysius had considerable influences on Christian thought and were still much studied from the thirteenth century into the Renaissance.

p. 112, 4, l. 83. *The brightest Angell*. Lucifer, the highest of the Archangels, who rebelled against God through pride and became the Devil.

p. 113, 1, l. 94. *Degendering*: degenerating.

p. 113, 2, l. 103. *Cast*: planned.

p. 113, 3, ll. 106–11. *Therefore of clay . . . and fayre*. Compare H.B. 159–61 and note. But this stanza is unquestionably orthodox and is based on Genesis 1. 27: 'So God created man in his own image', and Genesis 2. 7: 'And the Lord God formed man of the dust of the ground, and breathed into his nostrils the breath of life; and man became a living soul'.

p. 114, 1, l. 121. *ensew*: ensue, follow.

p. 114, 2, l. 131. *doole*: misery.

p. 114, 3, l. 136. *demisse*: abandoned, humiliated.

p. 114, 4, l. 152. *that them most vile became*: an action that ill became them, that did not redound to their credit.

p. 115, 1, l. 158. *launching*: lancing, piercing.

p. 115, 2, l. 167. *infected*: infixed, infused.

p. 115, 3, ll. 176–84. *Yet nought . . . that was band. Lieu* (l. 176): reward, return; *Band* (l. 184): banned, condemned, damned. The style in these lines especially in ll. 181–2, is elliptical but the meaning is fairly clear: In return for all this love all you ask is our love as a return for

your pain and that is the very least that we can give you. Would it
have been wrong for Him to require our lives in return; for had he
not every right to expect us to repay our debt to him with interest.
He gave us life in the first place and when we had lost it He restored
it to us; consequently the life that cost us so little was the very least
He could claim from us. But instead of doing this, He has freed our
lives from slavery and damnation, and demanded nothing but our love
in return.

p. 116, 1, ll. 197–203. *Then next to love . . . light esteemed.* Spenser's
style is at its most elliptical. The words 'were made of' should be
understood after 'that we' in line 199, and 'were redeemed with' after
'that we' in line 203. For this unusual use of *that*: as, see *N.E.D.* s.
that, *rel. and pron.* 4. We may then paraphrase the lines as follows:
We ought to love our brethren who were made out of the same dust
and by the same Maker as we were; and although here and now we
may occupy a higher position, nevertheless when we and they return
to dust we shall all inherit the same amount of land, and however
lightly we may esteem them, their redemption was just as costly as
our own.

p. 116, 2, l. 211. *reede*: counsel.

p. 116, 3, l. 213. *Ensampled*: exemplified.

p. 116, 4, l. 218. *soyle*: could be used for manure, dirt, a muddy
place, a pool used as a last refuge by a hunted animal.

p. 116, 5, l. 220. *moyle*: to toil, drudge, make oneself muddy.

p. 117, 1, l. 226. *cratch*: a manger.

p. 117, 2, l. 230. *silly*: (from O.E. seelig) innocent, blessed.

p. 117, 3, l. 238. *malist*: regarded with malice.

p. 118, 1, l. 279. *passing*: surpassing.

p. 118, 2, l. 284. *Th' Idee of his pure glorie, present still. . . .* I cannot
agree with Professor Renwick's view (pp. 221–2) that the use of the
Platonic term Idea is incongruous and does nothing to elucidate
Spenser's meaning. It is *structurally* important because it corresponds
to H.L. ll. 190 ff. and H.B. ll. 210 ff., where the poet enlarges on the Neo-
Platonic commonplace that the lover's mental image of his lady is more
beautiful than its physical counterpart. The historic Christ is, of course,
present to Spenser's mind, not to his sense-perceptions; but, since he
believed in the historical accuracy of the New Testament, there is an
analogy, though an imperfect one, between the two cases: meditation
on the Incarnate Lord corresponds to his physical sight of the lady,
meditation on the exalted Christ corresponds to the mental image
which exceeded her physical but not her spiritual beauty. The 'idea',
the essence of the glory of the ascended Christ, is the beauty of the
Godhead and can only begin to be discerned by the soul whose love
has been kindled by the incarnate Christ. The punctuation of the
Folio which places the comma after 'glorie' is more logical than that
of the Quarto which places it after 'still'.

AN HYMNE OF HEAVENLY BEAUTIE

p. 119, 1, ll. 1–14. *Rapt with the rage . . . I see.* These first two stanzas show the influence of Benivieni; cf. H.L. ll. 1–21 and note; and for the reference to the Holy Spirit (cf. H.H.L. l. 43 and note).

p. 119, 2, l. 6. *faine*: am fain, desire.

p. 119, 3, l. 26. *soare*: sore. A term in falconry applied to a hawk who is not yet moulted and still has red plumage.

p. 120, 1, ll. 29, 30. *Then looke . . . the frame.* The sense would be improved were a comma inserted after 'looke' and omitted after 'list'.

p. 120, 2, ll. 36–105. *First th' Earth . . . endlesse perfectnesse.* That the glory of God is manifested in His Creation is a commonplace of Christian thought and there is nothing specifically Calvinistic in these stanzas (but see F. M. Padelford, 'Spenser and the Theology of Calvin' in *M.P.* XII (1914), 1–18. They do, however, bear a striking resemblance to an episode in *Asolani*, where the Hermit having reminded Lavinello of the unsatisfactory nature of earthly love, advises him to contemplate the Ptolemaic Universe and then to contemplate the unseen world beyond it which increases in beauty as it draws nearer and nearer to God (cf. *supra*, pp. 22, 23, and *Bembo*, Bk. 3, pp. 187 ff.). Spenser's account of the universe is based on the Ptolemaic system as understood and modified by Arabian and mediaeval scholars. At the central and lowest point of the cosmos rests the small spherical earth; its foundation on 'adamantine pillars' and its enclosure by brazen boundary walls being a metaphorical description of its firmness and fixity. Above the earth and below the moon rise the spheres of water, air and fire in an ascending scale of purity, clarity and beauty. Mediæval philosophers recognized that there were fiery and airy exhalations and a mingling of elements in the sublunar regions and found considerable difficulty in explaining why the earth appears above the sphere of water; nevertheless, they held that each element had its own proper sphere towards which it tended. Having considered the elements, Spenser passes over all the planetary spheres and arrives at the outermost bound of the corporeal universe. The 'christall wall' (l. 41) is not the sphere of the fixed stars, but the *primum mobile*, the ninth sphere (added by the Arabs to the Ptolemaic eight), to which no star is affixed, but which encloses the whole temporal and spatial cosmos and communicates to it motion originating from the *Prime Mover*. It is sometimes difficult to be sure whether a writer is referring to the *primum mobile* or to the Heaven of the fixed stars, but since the movement of the latter is caused directly by that of the former, this usually does not matter very much. It should be borne in mind that Spenser is not intending to provide a versified primer of astronomy, but rather to call attention to the variety and order of the cosmos and particularly to the way in which created things increase in clarity and beauty as they rise higher and higher above the earth. Even in our sublunary sphere we can discern the grading of the four elements; but even fire, the highest of them, is less pure than that fifth element— variously called ether or quintessence, of which all the heavenly bodies are composed, but which attains its highest degree of purity in that crystalline wall that bounds our cosmos and is too translucent to be visible.

Since Spenser was writing for educated readers, there was no need to trace in detail all the cosmic circlings; nevertheless, he does not ignore the regions above the moon, but invites contemplation of the incomparable beauty of the Sun and Moon and Stars, adorning 'The house of blessed Gods, which men call *Skye*'. It may seem strange that in this Christian hymn Spenser should describe the heavenly bodies as 'blessed Gods', but the phrase cannot be dismissed as mere poetic diction. The notion was derived from Plato, who regarded the stars and planets as the first set of living beings or embodied souls produced by the Demiurge to inhabit the upper regions of the cosmos and used by him to produce lower sets of living beings to inhabit the lower regions of air, water and earth. Plato seems to have equated the gods venerated by the Greeks with the souls of the Heavenly Bodies and in Book XII of *The Laws* he uses their movements as an argument against atheism. In the *Metaphysics* (Bk. Λ 1074 b) Aristotle suggests a similar interpretation of traditional mythology, though his account of celestial movement is different from that of Plato.

In a passage in *Convivio*, Treatise 2, ch. v, Dante discusses whether 'the Intelligences which are vulgarly called Angels' corresponds in number to the 'circulatings in the heaven', which admittedly they control. This, says Dante, was the opinion expressed by Aristotle in his *Metaphysics*. 'Others were there such as Plato, a man of supreme excellence, who laid down not only as many Intelligences as there are movements of heaven, but just as many as there are kinds of things . . . Plato calls them Ideas, which is as much as to say Forms and Universals. The Gentiles called them gods and goddesses, though they did not conceive them so philosophically as did Plato; and they adored images of them, and made most magnificent temples for them; for Juno, for example, whom they called the goddess of power; . . . no one neither philosopher, nor Gentile, nor Jew, nor Christian, nor any sect—doubts that either all of them, or the greater part, are full of all blessedness, or doubts that these blessed ones are in the most perfect state.'

The classical gods played a considerable part in sixteenth-century Neo-Platonism. In *De Amore*, Speech I, ch. iii, Cavalcanti explains how 'God, who is omnipotent, created in the Angelic Mind . . . the forms of all things to be created' and their prototypes are the Ideas: 'The Form or Idea of the heavens we call the god Uranus, the form of the first planet we call the god Saturn, of the second Jove and so on with all the rest of the planets. . . .' In Speech VI, chapter iii, we are told that

M

'the ten higher spheres of the universe, because of their sublimity are peopled with rational creatures only . . . the souls of the twelve spheres and of the stars, the Platonists call worldly gods, the foot-followers, as it were, of the Angelic Mind and of God'. Ficino distinguishes between the 'Gods' who are immortal and impassible and the daemons who are immortal but passible, and explains that the souls of the spheres and the stars and also of the good daemons are all called Angels by Dionysius (cf. Kristeller, pp. 385–9).

Spenser's account in lines 64–98 of the spheres of the Empyrean Heaven beyond the *primum mobile* is neither as original, nor as confused, nor as heretical as Renwick suggests (p. 222): much the same idea is expressed in *Asolani* and it corresponds fairly closely with certain passages in Dante's *Convivio*, Treatise 2, chapter iv. 'But beyond all these the Catholics assert the empyrean heaven, which is as much to say the heaven of flame, or the luminous heaven; and they assert it to be immovable. . . . This is the place of the blessed spirits, according as holy Church, which may not lie, will have it. . . . This is the sovran edifice of the world, wherein all the world is included, and outside of which there is nought; and it is not itself in space but was formed only in the primal mind. . . .' In chapter vi, Treatise 2, of the same work, Dante explains that we now know from the teaching of Holy Church that the angels are innumerable and are divided into nine Hierarchies corresponding to the nine moving spheres: the revolving heavens, which are nine, declare the numbers, the orders and the hierarchies; and the tenth proclaimeth the very oneness and stability of God. In Canto IV of the *Paradiso*, when Dante has reached the sphere of the moon and encountered the blessed souls who inhabit it; he is surprised to find that Plato's heretical view that souls return to their stars is true after all, but Beatrice explains that all good spirits and angels are in the Empyrean sphere: 'All make beautiful the first circle [from our point of view, of course, the tenth] and share sweet life, with difference, by feeling more and less the eternal breath.' When the blessed spirits, who were inconstant in their earthly life, appear to Dante as located in the lunar sphere, this is simply an illustration of the comparatively lowly spiritual state and is a concession to the limitation of Dante's human understanding. His powers of intellectual vision, however, increase as he ascends, and when he reaches the Empyrean Heaven itself, he sees there all the varied hierarchies of souls forming the petals of a vast white rose, and as he gazes into the divine light he sees ingathered within its depths 'bound by love in one volume, the scattered leaves of all the universe' and finally the mysterious circling of the Blessed Trinity 'the Love that moves the sun and other stars'.

The difficulty that the Angels in the Empyrean are identical with the Intelligences who move the cosmic spheres is met by Aquinas in *Summa Theologica*, Pt. I, Q. 110, Art. 3, replying to Objection 3,

Pegis, I, p. 1022, where he explains that the angels' power is not as limited as that of the human soul. 'An angel's power is not limited to any body, and hence it can move locally bodies not joined to it.' I am not suggesting that Spenser was concerned with these niceties which were irrelevant to his purpose. In l. 71, 'these heavens' are, of course, the corporeal spheres to which the Empyrean spheres correspond, and it seems that ll. 64–7 are susceptible of Dante's kind of exegesis; but even if Spenser does mean us to take the Empyrean spheres literally, he, nevertheless, emphasizes the difference in quality between them and their cosmic counterparts.

Spenser's account of the inhabitants of the Empyrean is more open to criticism. If Spenser knew Dante's *Convivio*, the identification of angels, Platonic ideas and Aristotelian intelligences may well have confused him and the complexities of the Neo-Platonic cosmos were not calculated to clear the mind. The insertion of the Intelligences and Ideas into the angelic hierarchies is more excusable than the exalting of the Angels and Archangels above the Cherubim and Seraphim. Again, *if* he knew the *Convivio*, he might have been misled by an over-hasty reading or imperfect recollection of Treatise 2, chapter vi. 'And each hierarchy has three orders, so that the Church holds and affirms nine orders of spiritual creatures. The first is that of the Angels, the second of the Archangels, the third of the Thrones and these three orders make the first hierarchy, not first in order of nobility, nor in order of creation, for the others are more noble and all were created at once, but first in the order of our ascent to their loftiness.'

p. 122, 1, l. 106. *Cease then my tongue....* This is a turning point. So far Spenser has been describing the beauty of the universe, but as he approaches God, he realizes that he is approaching what can neither be imagined nor described. So he begins to reflect, and, his first reflection is that if God's 'utmost parts' (i.e. the creation) are beautiful, his 'essentiall parts' (i.e. the attributes, the qualities that are part of his own nature) must be even more so. His attributes of truth, love, etc., are displayed to his sinful creatures in his gracious dealings with them, and we can get some glimpses of his goodness, by studying the beauty of the creation, for goodness and beauty are inseparable.

p. 122, 2, l. 111. *doome*: justice.

p. 122, 3, l. 130. *brasen book*: an indestructible book, strong as brass.

p. 123, 1, l. 134. *speculation*: used here in its original but now obsolete sense—the power of sight; vision.

p. 123, 2, l. 135. *impe*: insert, engraft upon. The term, when used in falconry, meant to improve the power of flight by engrafting feathers into a damaged wing. The aspiring human mind in quest of the beatific vision needs to begin by looking intently at the created universe, and deducing from it the goodness of its Creator. This will enable him to dismiss the world from his thought and turn all his attention to God Himself, just as the eagle according to traditional superstition was able to look directly at the sun. The result of this vision is, as the next stanza shows, not pride in achievement, but abject humility and an acute consciousness of sin and the need for redemption. Once more we see the divergence of Spenser from orthodox Neo-Platonism. The poet turns his attention to God, but he never actually sees Him, but only His surroundings, His encompassing light, and Sapience sitting in His bosom. It is interesting that from now on everything that Spenser says about God or wisdom is based on the Scriptures. Although he never explicitly says so, it looks as though the first part of the poem deals with what well-conducted natural reason can discover about God, the second part with the revealed truth which supplements but does not contradict it (cf. *supra*, pp. 32 ff).

p. 123, 3, l. 149. *the Lambes integrity*: the righteousness of Christ, the Lamb of God, whose self-sacrificing death fulfilled and superseded the ancient Jewish sacrifices and atoned for the sins of the whole world. Both Catholics and Protestants would have accepted these lines as orthodox; but the Protestants laid special stress on the doctrine that Christ's righteousness was imputed rather than imparted to believers.

p. 123, 4, l. 157. *the great Dragon*: Satan, see Revelation 12 : 9.

p. 123, 5, l. 163. *Titans*: the Sun's. Usually 'Titan' is a generic term, denoting one of the class of deities or giants who rebelled against Zeus. Vergil and Ovid sometimes use Titan as a name for the sun.

p. 123, 6, l. 168. *wisards*: sages rather than magicians (cf. Milton, *Nativity Ode*: 'The star-led wisards haste with odours sweet'). In Spenser's day the astrologer was not sharply differentiated from the astronomer.

p. 124, 1, l. 183. *There in his bosome Sapience doth sit*. Spenser's Wisdom has been identified with the Second Person of the Trinity, the Holy Spirit, the Virgin Mary, the Schekina of the Cabala, the Angelic Mind of the Neo-Platonists, and even with the most obvious prototype, the personified Wisdom of the Old Testament and Apocrypha. Not all of these theories are mutually exclusive. For instance, the Neo-Platonists themselves sometimes identified the Biblical Wisdom with the Angelic Mind. Henry Suso, a poetically-minded mystic of the fourteenth century, called himself 'the servitor of the Eternal Wisdom' and conducted much of his religious life as a kind of love-affair with a personified feminine wisdom, whom he nevertheless from time to time invoked as a masculine person, identical with Christ (cf. *The Life of Blessed Henry Suso, by himself*, tr. T. F. Knox, chapters iv and x). Even greater flexibility, though of a very different kind, appears in Dante's attitude to Philosophy or Wisdom, the heroine of his *Convivio*, 'a gentle lady', who—not without a struggle—superseded Beatrice in his affections and comforted him for her loss. Dante identifies her quite explicitly with the Biblical Wisdom of *Proverbs* and *Wisdom of Solomon*, and also with the Logos of St. John's Gospel and with the Incarnate

Christ. As Professor Wickstead puts it: 'Ultimately, then, Dante's "second love" is for Wisdom as a hypostasis in the Trinity. But the transition is easy to Wisdom as an attribute of Deity not identified with Deity itself. ... And the wisdom that thus exists primarily in the Creator exists in a secondary way in created intelligences angelic and human. ...' (cf. *op. cit.* Treatise III, chapters xiv and xv and Appendix II). My interpretation (see *supra*, pp. 53 ff.) is not inconsistent with the belief that Spenser may have taken a hint from his great predecessor. Those who wish to go further into the matter should consult *Spenser, Var* M.P., Vol. I, pp. 558–70, and Ellrodt, *op. cit.*, pp. 171–93, where they will find views different from those given here.

p. 125, 1, ll. 207–8. *Sparkled on her . . . goodly grace.* This statement is somewhat startling. How can Wisdom *independently* increase the beauty showered on her from God? It is to be noticed that this beauty is said to be showered *from*, not *by* God. I suppose that Spenser means that the Order of Creation both reflects something of the ineffable beauty of the Creator and has in addition a recognizable beauty of its own. Christianity, unlike Pantheism and some Eastern religions, insists on the *absolute distinction* between the Creator and the Creature, but is equally insistent on the total dependence of the Creature on the Creator, not only for its good qualities but for its very existence.

p. 125, 2, l. 211. *that Painter*: Apelles, a celebrated painter who lived in the time of Alexander the Great. His masterpiece was a picture of a sleeping Venus, Venus Anadymone.

p. 125, 3, ll. 219–24. *that sweete Teian Poet . . . be fraught*: Anacreon, a lyric poet of Teos in Ionia, who lived in the sixth century B.C. and whose odes are still extant. *Vaine*, vein, here is used in its figurative sense of 'special aptitude', 'particular genius'. *Idole* is derived from Greek ἔιδωλον meaning 'shape', 'image'; 'image in the mind'; 'image or portrait especially of a god'; hence 'idol', 'false god'. Spenser seems to have had all these meanings in mind. Had so gifted a poet as Anacreon seen even a glimpse of Sapience, the heavenly beauty that Spenser is trying to portray, he would have praised her rather than the false goddess of his imagination.

p. 125, 4, l. 230–6. *Ah, gentle Muse . . . so heavenly thing.* Spenser has invoked the Holy Spirit to inspire his verses, but here he is using Muse in the conventional way, as a synonym for his own poetic gift. These lines should be compared with the ending of H.L., where the poet undertakes to compose 'An heavenly Hymne, such as the Angels sing' in honour of human Eros-love. Spenser, like Dante, emphasizes his total inability to express in words the loveliness of Wisdom.

p. 126, 1, ll. 253–4. *None thereof worthy be . . . to receave.* These lines have been taken, perhaps rightly, as a proof of Spenser's belief in pre-destination. The belief was not confined to Calvinists and, of course, goodness and wisdom are bestowed on us by the grace of God. I find no trace in Spenser's works of concern with the grimmer aspects

ppalling doctrine; indeed, much of the *Faerie Queene* makes
if we deny freewill (see *supra*, pp. 33–5).

, 1, l. 274. *And that faire lampe*: the beauty of women which
he love of men. Some commentators remark on the fact that
Spenser does not mention this among the beauties of creation; but, of
course, beautiful women cannot be excluded from 'the endlesse kinds
of creatures' which inhabit the cosmos. But the lines are evidently a
deliberate retraction of H.B. 99–105 and do describe a deliberate
turning away from earthly love and apparently a denial of its value
(but see *supra*, pp. 61–3).

p. 127, 2, l. 293. *prief*: proof, experience; and so also the result of
experience and, in this case, experience of the falsity and unreliability
of earthly love for earthly beauty, a folly which has only resulted in a
belated repentance. The poet, therefore, exhorts himself to turn away
from an unsatisfying earthly, to the satisfying Divine beauty. As
St. Augustine said: 'Our hearts are restless until they rest in Thee.'
But even now the poet ends on a note of hope rather than of complete
achievement.

EPITHALAMION

p. 128, 1, l. 1. *Ye learned sisters*. Spenser is following the long-lived
convention, derived from Homer, of opening poems with an invocation to a Muse or to the Muses. The cult of the Muses seems to have
originated in Pieria on the borders of Thessaly and Macedonia. Their
various local titles suggest a connection with mountains, springs and
rivers, and it has been suggested that they were originally nymphs and
particularly associated with running water. Our first written mention
of them occurs in Homer who represents them as entertaining the
Olympian Gods and inspiring human poets. Originally, they appear to
have been three in number, but Hesiod (Theogony ll. 1 ff.) names nine
of them and, although there were occasional variations, his classifica-
tion on the whole prevailed. At first they functioned as an impersonal
choir, but gradually they became differentiated, and by the end of
antiquity the prevalent conception of their several functions and
insignia was as follows: *Clio*, History; *Euterpe*, Flute-playing; *Thalia*,
Pastoral Poetry and Comedy; *Melpomene*, Tragedy; *Terpsichore*, Dancing
and Lyric; *Erato*, Erotic poetry; *Polyhymnia*, Learning; *Urania*, Astronomy; *Calliope*, Epic poetry.

Belief in the Muses was originally connected with old and widespread
notions of possession and the ancients found it easier than we should
do, to regard the Muses both as a source of inspired poetic madness
and as daughters of memory and patronesses of learning, because to
them the function of the poet or minstrel was not so much to express
his inner feelings as to tell stories, to commemorate, to record the

past and sometimes even to foretell the future. The minstrel Demodicus made Odysseus weep because he was divinely inspired to sing of the Fall of Troy with historical accuracy (cf. Homer, *Odyssey*, Book 8, ll. 485-522). In the sixteenth century the poet's habit of referring to his muse was a literary convention; but in some ways his attitude was nearer to that of Homer than to that of the nineteenth or twentieth century poet. Spenser needed the help of the 'learned sisters' to enable him to praise his love with skill and eloquence and erudition. The same attitude is even more strikingly displayed by Spenser's contemporary, Samuel Daniel, who regarded the poet as the upholder of civilization and humane letters, the only defence against oblivion and barbarism.

p. 128, 2, l. 7. *And when ye list your owne mishaps to mourne.* The reference is almost certainly to Spenser's *The Teares of the Muses*, a poem of uncertain date, included in *Complaints*, a collection of some minor poems of Spenser published by Ponsonby in 1591. In this poem Spenser invites the nine Muses to rehearse to him the sad complaints made by the 'Springs of Helicone', for since the time when they all mourned the death of Phaeton and when Calliope mourned for her twin sons. 'Such mournfull tunes were neuer since inuented.' In response to this request each Muse in turn bewails the decadence of poetry and the neglect of learning and the arts in sixteenth century England. Erato laments that she, the inspirer of noble love poetry, is now exiled from court and school, 'Banisht by those that Loue with leawdnes fill'.

p. 128, 3, l. 16. *So Orpheus did for his owne bride.* Orpheus is not mentioned by Homer or Hesiod, but his legend was already current in the sixth century B.C. The son of a Thracian king and of the Muse Calliope, he was a hero, a magician, a musical poet of such remarkable skill that he could move natural and supernatural beings by his songs. He was said to have accompanied the Argonauts on their famous voyage, but the most renowned episode of his life was his marriage to the nymph Eurydice and his journey to Hades to recover her after she had died of a snake-bite; for Orpheus so charmed the Infernal Powers by his music that they allowed him to lead away his wife on condition that he did not look back at her until they reached the upper world. Unfortunately his resolution failed and he lost his bride for the second time. The story is told by Vergil in *Georgics* IV, ll. 453-527, and by Ovid in *Metamorphoses* X, ll. 1-147. Spenser's line may have been suggested by either or by both of these poets. Ovid's story opens with an account of Orpheus summoning Hymen to his wedding:

> Inde per immensum croceo velatus amictu
> Aethera digreditur Ciconumque Hymenaeus ad oras
> Tendit et Orphea nequiquam voce vocatur.
> Adfuit ille quidem, sed nec sollemnia verba
> Nec laetos voltus nec felix attulit ad omen.

[Thence through the boundless air, Hymen clad in a saffron robe, departed and took his way to the country of the Ciconians and was summoned by the voice of Orpheus though all in vain. He was present, it is true; but he brought neither the hallowed words, nor joyous faces, nor lucky omen.]

The idea of the poet singing of his beloved to himself alone may have been suggested by Virgil's moving account of Orpheus' lamentation after Eurydice's death:

> ipse cava solans aegrum testudine amorem
> te, dulcis coniunx, te solo in litore secum,
> te, veniente die, te decedente canebat.

[But he (i.e. Orpheus), solacing love's anguish with his hollow shell, sang of thee, sweet wife, of thee to himself, on the lonely shore, of thee as day drew nigh, of thee as day declined] (*Georgics* IV, 464–6).

p. 128, 4, l. 25. *Hymen is awake*. 'Hymen' originally signified the sign of virginity and certain features of Greek and Roman wedding ceremonies seem to be survivals of marriage by capture. The word Hymenaeus is first met with in Homer and Hesiod and denotes the joyous processional songs which accompanied the bride on her way to her husband's house. In some fragments of Sappho it is part of a refrain, and 'Hymen O Hymenaeus' frequently occurs as a traditional refrain in classical epithalamia and in the derivative epithalamia of the Renaissance. At an uncertain date the nuptial hymn became personified as Hymen, the God of lawful marriage, and the poets invented legends about him as the son of Aphrodite (Venus) and Dionysius (Bacchus). Together with other deities he is frequently invited by writers of epithalamia to take part in the wedding celebrations. In the first fifteen stanzas of Carmen 61, Catullus invites virgins to join with him in a long invocation to Hymen, in which the god is prayed to leave his haunts, to don gala dress and come to sing the nuptial song and bless the marriage of Manlius and Vinia. In Ronsard's *Epithalame de Monseigneur le duc de Lorraine et de Madame Claude Fille du Roy* Hymen is invited to leave Mount Parnassus in order that he may tear the bashful virgin from her mother's bosom and throw her into the arms of the cruel youth. This is imitative and anachronistic. Spenser keeps closer to the marriage customs of his own day. 'Maske' here denotes not a face-mask, but the procession of masked and disguised persons, accompanied by torch-bearers and musicians and headed by a Presenter or Leader, who arrived at a wedding or other social function to dance and also sometimes to present gifts to distinguished members of the company. Hymen frequently figured as a character in or as leader of wedding masques of the sixteenth and seventeenth centuries.

p. 128, 5, l. 27. *With his bright Tead . . . many a flake*: 'Tead' [Lat. taeda], a wedding torch; 'flake': a piece of ignited matter thrown off by a burning body.

p. 128, 6, ll. 31–3. *For lo . . . long delight.* These lines and line 243 suggest that difficulties had to be overcome before the marriage could take place. The nature of the difficulties is uncertain. *Amoretti* 86–9 have been interpreted as referring to a temporary breach between the lovers; but sonnet 86 need imply no more than a brief lover's quarrel, and 87–9 speak only of separation. It is to be noticed that here the poet speaks of the *bride's* 'paynes and sorrowes past'. I doubt whether he would have so spoken of a temporarily broken engagement; for it would have been more complimentary to his bride to ascribe the pains to himself.

p. 129, 1, l. 37. *Bring with you all the Nymphes that you can heare*: 'Bring with you all the nymphs that can hear your voices'.

p. 129, 2, l. 39. *. . . the sea that neighbours to her neare.* It is possible that Elizabeth Boyle was married from the house of her brother-in-law, Sir Richard Smith, whose house stood on the estuary where the river Blackwater flows into the sea.

p. 129, 3, l. 40. *wel beseene*: well-provided with, apparalled, good-looking.

p. 129, 4, l. 51. *diapred lyke the discolored mead*: 'diaper' meaning a textile fabric woven with a small pattern of threads crossed diamond-wise. 'to diaper' could mean 'to diversify the surface of anything with a small pattern', and then 'to adorn with diversely coloured details, to variegate', 'discolored' is used here in an obsolete sense, meaning particoloured, variegated and derived from the Latin adjective *discolor*, of various colours, the opposite of *concolor*, of the same colour.

p. 129, 5, l. 56. *Mulla*: Spenser's name for the river Awbeg, a tributary of the Blackwater, which flowed past the southern boundaries of his estate at Kilcolman. He invented the name from certain ruins called Kilnemullah, which he assumed to mean 'church on the Mulla'. Cf. *Colin Clout's Come Home Again*, ll. 104–55 and Professor Renwick's notes thereon in *Daphnaida* and *Other Poems*, pp. 183–4. Nearby rivers are frequently mentioned in epithalamia, as a compliment to the bride and bridegroom through whose grounds or native cities they flowed.

p. 129, 6, ll. 67–8. *And eke ye lightfoot mayds . . . towre.* For 'dere', the 1595 octavo edition and the first folio have 'dore'. O.E. deor, dior, M.E. deer, der, deor, could mean any kind of wild animal. Shakespeare, *Lear* 3, 4, 144 speaks of mice and rats as small deer. Although there is no authority in any early text for the emendation, it is probably correct especially as the charge is required for the rhyme and the 'lightfoot mayds' must be the nymphs of the huntress Diana. 'Towre', tower, stand high, mount aloft, soar (a term in falconry), Renwick (p. 205) glosses as 'climb', Van Winkle (p. 88) as 'perch high'. Spenser may be likening the swift movements of animals up a mountain-side to that of a soaring bird; or he may be thinking particularly of deer standing out impressively against the skyline. Cf. FQ. II, xii, 30: '. . . on th'other side an high rocke toured still', and FQ. VI, x, 6:

And in their tops the soring hauke did towre,
Sitting like King of fowles in majesty and powre.

p. 130, 1, ll. 74–5. *Wake, now my love, awake ... Tithones bed.* References in Homer and Hesiod, the epithalamia of Theocritus, Catullus, Statius and Claudian suggest that chanting takes place during the bridal procession and at the bridal chamber when the newly-wed are about to retire for the night. In Theocritus XVIII, twelve Spartan maidens sing and dance outside the bridal chamber of Menelaus and Helen and promise to return at daybreak. Du Bellay begins his *Epithalame* (cf. *supra* p. 68) with along dawn-song, but it is described by a 'Poet' as having been recited by Antoinette Deloine (she is a real person) as she rouses her three daughters to get ready to celebrate the marriage of Princess Marguerite. Du Bellay's composition is not, strictly speaking, an epithalamion, but the libretto for a masque-like performance. Spenser here, as elsewhere, combines classical and mediæval tradition and awakes his fiancée with an 'aubade', the traditional dawn-song, which the Provençal troubadours sang outside their mistresses' windows. Greek Eos, Latin Aurora, is the Goddess of Dawn, who fell in love with the Trojan prince Tithonus. Before the sun rises she sets out in a chariot drawn by white horses, pours dew on the earth and makes the flowers grow. The stock Homeric epithet for her is 'rosy-fingered'.

p. 130, 2, ll. 77–91. *And Phoebus ... eccho ring.* 'Phoebus' is an epithet of Apollo, derived from Greek φοῖβος meaning bright, radiant. Phoebus Apollo is both a sun-god and the leader of the Muses. The rising of the sun is accompanied by the dawn chorus of the birds. 'Mavis': the song-thrush. 'Ouzell': the blackbird. 'Ruddock': the robin. 'Consent' could mean either compliance or concord, and Spenser is making a poetic use of this ambiguity. The birds are singing to their several mates, but their songs are concordant and this dawn chorus, both 'love-learned' and harmonious, is in tune with the wedding merry-making and even suggests that the birds are participating in it. The list of song-birds was a mediæval poetic convention.

p. 130, 3, l. 95. *Hesperus*: the name given to the planet Venus, the planet of Love, when it appeared after the setting of the sun. When it appeared before the rising of the sun it was called Phosphorus. Hesperus is frequently mentioned in epithalamia and is welcomed as a prelude to the bridal night. Here it would seem more appropriate to compare the bride's eyes to the morning rather than to the evening star; but Spencer was no doubt influenced by the fact that Hesperus was the more familiar term.

p. 130, 4, l. 96. *Come now ye damzels, daughters of delight*: the Graces. (cf. FQ. VI, x, 15):

Those were the Graces, daughters of delight,
Handmaids of Venus, ...

and FQ. VI, x, 21:

> . . . all those Ladies, which thow sawest late,
> Are *Venus* Damzels, all within her fee,
> But differing in honour and degree:
> They all are Graces, which on her depend,
> Besides a thousand more, which ready bee
> Her to adorne, whenso she forth doth wend:
> But those three in the midst, doe chiefe on her attend.

Renwick considers that in *Epith.* l. 96, 'the phrase "daughters of delight" must apply generally to the bridesmaids', because the Graces are mentioned in l. 103. But surely in the context of the stanza, to mention *human* bridesmaids would be inappropriate, and if the reference is to mythical bridesmaids it seems simpler to identify the 'daughters of delight' with the Graces alone rather than with the Graces and Hours together. The poet summons the Graces to come quickly to help dress the bride, 'but', he adds, 'you Hours must come first, and you', turning again to the Graces, 'must help to adorn her'.

p. 130, 5, ll. 98–102. *But first come ye fayre houres . . . Doe make and still repayre.* Compare FQ. *Mutabilitie*, Canto VII, stanzas 44, 45:

> And after these, there came the Day and Night,
> Riding together both with equall pase. . . .

> Then came the *Howres*, faire daughters of high *Ioue*,
> And timely *Night*, the which were all endewed
> With wondrous beauty fit to kindle loue;
> But they were Virgins all, and loue eschewed,
> That might forslack the charge to them foreshewed
> By mighty *Ioue*; who did them Porters make
> Of heavens gate (whence all the gods issued)
> Which they did dayly watch and nightly wake
> By even turnes, ne ever did their charge forsake.

Compare also HHL, lines 24–6, and the note thereon.

For Professor Hieatt's theory that Spenser's Hours are sidereal hours and that the theme of *Epithalamion* is very similar to the theme of *Mutabilitie* cf. Appendix 2.

Greek ʾΩρα, Latin Hora, meant any limited period fixed by natural law, and like our word 'season' was particularly applied to a division of the year. The first known record of its use as a division of the day occurs in the works of Anacreon, a poet of the sixth century B.C. The mythological Hours are primarily personifications of laws governing vegetation and the meteorological phenomena which regulate all earthly life by their periodicity. The hours are regarded as beneficent and particularly associated with the spring-time. Homer treats them as divinities of material nature, who wait upon Zeus and open and close the gates of Heaven by gathering and dispersing the clouds and who also join with the Graces in dancing choirs attendant upon Aphrodite (cf. *Iliad* V, 749–51).

Hesiod (*Theogony*, 901–6) makes the Hours daughters of Zeus and Themis (the Goddess of Law) and names them Eunomia (good government), Dike (justice), Eirene (peace), and from his time onward they personify both the regular renewal of nature's gifts and also social qualities making for order and harmony. In spite of Hesiod's naming of them, the poets thought of them collectively until comparatively late times. As a triad the Hours were associated with the seasons which were usually regarded as three in number. Euripides, however, mentions the division into four seasons which was used by the Pythagoreans, but was never fully adopted until after the death of Alexander the Great. There is no classical authority for Spenser's account of the parentage of the Hours, though, as we have seen, Hesiod makes Zeus their father. In *The Mutabilitie Cantos* they are said to be the 'daughters of high *Ioue*' and since Jove or Zeus was a sky-god it seems probable that in *Epithalamion*, line 99, Jove and Day are to be identified. To speak of the Hours as the daughters of Day and Night might seem an obvious instance of allegorization; but the Neo-Platonists with their addiction to analogies and correspondences might well have regarded this affiliation as a particular example of a more general process, by which the created universe was born of the union of spiritual light and material chaos. However, it seems to me that in the *Epithalamion* Spenser is concerned with emotional experience rather than with cosmology; the Hours personify divisions of time and especially of one particular wedding-day and wedding-night. Perhaps he recalled Pico's explanation (*op. cit.* Bk. II, ch. xi) that the Angelic Mind was named Paradise by the Ancients, because Paradise means 'garden'; and the Angelic Mind is called the Orchard of Jove because ideas are planted there like trees in an orchard. The paradisal garden image, with its rich associations of new life, fertility and joyousness, may well have lingered in his memory; particularly since it was the birthplace of the God of Love and the Goddess of Beauty and since the Hours, like the Graces, were traditionally the handmaids of Aphrodite, and also were represented in contemporary pageantry. For instance, in 1591, Queen Elizabeth was welcomed into the park of Elvetham by six virgins, who first removed the blocks of Envy out of Her Majesty's path, and then 'walked on before her towards the house, strewing the way with flowers, and signing a sweete song'. 'Three of these virgins represented the three Graces, and the other three the Howres, which by the poets are fained to be the guardians of Heaven gates. They were all attired in gowns of taffeta scarcenet of divers colours, with flowerie garlands on their heads, and baskets full of sweet herbs and flowers upon their arms.'

(*The Honorable Entertainment given to the Queene's Majestie, in Progresse at Elvetham in Hampshire, by the Right Honorable the Earle of Hertford* 1591).

p. 130, 6, l. 103. *And ye three handmayds of the Cyprian Queene*. The three Graces in attendance upon Aphrodite or Venus. Greek χάρις, Latin *gratia*, means favour, grace, loveliness, charm, etc., and in mythology the χάριτες were the goddesses who dispensed all these blessings. Originally they were deities of Nature who made nature beautiful and fruitful; but although their connection with the natural world was never forgotten, the ancient poets regarded them as intimately connected with human life, conferring on it pleasure and graciousness. Since they lend charm to poetry, music and oratory, they are connected with the Muses and with them form part of the cortège of Apollo and take part in hymeneal songs and dances. They are frequently associated with other deities and particularly with nymphs and the Hours. According to Hesiod the Graces were three in number, Aglaia, Euphrosyne, Thalia, and daughters of Zeus by the ocean-nymph Eurynome. Homer speaks of them collectively and describes how they clothe and anoint Aphrodite (cf. *Odyssey* VIII, 362 ff; XVIII, 192–4). For the Renaissance attitude to the Graces see *Wind*, pp. 31–56.

p. 131, 1, l. 121. *O fayrest Phoebus, father of the Muse*. According to Hesiod, the Muses were the daughters of Zeus and Memory, and this was the generally accepted view, although the poets sometimes varied the parentage for their own poetic purposes. The Greek poet Eumelos (date uncertain, eighth century B.C. or later) makes Apollo the father of the Muses; but Spenser probably took the idea from *Comes'* familiar handbook of mythology: 'Fuerunt ... Musae in ejus tutela creditae quarum & dux & pater Apollo fuit existimatus' (Lib. IV, p. 351).

[... The Muses were believed to be under the protection of Apollo, who was supposed to be both their leader and their father].

p. 131, 2, l. 124. *boone*: prayer. The poet requests that for this one day he may be allowed that control of the weather which is the prerogative of Apollo as sun-god, and points out that as a poet he has some claim on the 'father of the Muse'. Throughout the poem there is a recurrent suggestion of an analogy between bridegroom and sun and between bride and moon.

p. 131, 3, ll. 131–4. *The pipe ... tymbrels smyte*; 'tabor': an early name for the drum. After the introduction of the word 'drum' in the sixteenth century, the word 'tabor' usually denoted a small drum which was chiefly used to accompany pipe or trumpet. 'Croud': an obsolete and dialectal term for a fiddle. Both word and instrument are of Celtic origin. There is a good example of a Welsh *crwth* in Sir John William's collection in the National Library of Wales. 'tymbrels': musical percussion instruments which could be held in the hand. Cf. Psalm 68. 25: 'The singers went before, the players on instruments followed after; among them were the damsels playing with timbrels.' Although classical imagery predominates Biblical imagery is by no means absent from this poem, and one is conscious of the pervasive influence of the *Song of Solomon* and of Psalm 45, which celebrates the marriage of a king to a foreign princess, describes her glorious bridal garment, her entry into the king's palace with 'the virgins her companions' and prophecies a magnificent future for the children of the married couple.

p. 131, 4, ll. 137–40. *The whyles the boyes . . . Hymen they do shout.* Both Homer and Hesiod speak of young men accompanying bridal processions with dance and song, and in ancient Rome the procession of the bride to the bridegroom's house was accompanied by young people chanting 'O talassio' or 'Io Hymen', etc., and singing jocular and usually very indecent songs known as *fescennina.* Cf. Catullus, *Carmen* LXI:

> Tollite, o pueri, faces:
> Flammeum video venire.
> Ite, concinite in modum
> Io Hymen Hymenaee io
> Io Hymen Hymenaee.
>
> Ne diu taceat procax
> Fescennina jocatio.

[Raise aloft the torches, boys: I see the wedding veil coming. Go on, sing in measure, Io Hymen . . . etc. Let not the merry Fescennine raillery be silent long.]

p. 132, 1, l. 148. *portly* (from Latin *portare*, to carry) meant 'dignified', 'of stately carriage', not, as with us, pompous, stout, etc. Spenser uses the word several times in the *Amoretti* to convey admiration of his lady.

p. 132, 2, l. 149. *Phœbe*: the feminine form of *Phoebus*, 'bright', and one of the names of the virginal Artemis in her function as Moongoddess. Artemis was the twin sister of Phoebus Apollo, the Sun-god. In the *Epithalame de Monseigneur le duc de Lorraine et de Madame Claude Fille du Roy* (which forms part of *La Bergerie*), Remy Belleau makes the nymphs of the Meuse compare the bridegroom to the sun, and the nymphs of the Seine compare the bride to the moon.

p. 132, 3, l. 155. *Perling*: derived from 'purl' meaning to twist, which is frequently spelt 'pearl'.

p. 132, 4, l. 158. *lyke some mayden Queene.* This may be an allusion to Queen Elizabeth, who was herself constantly referred to as the moon-goddess and is 'shadowed' as Belphoebe in *The Fairie Queene* and had the same christian name as Spenser's bride. Cf. *Amoretti* LXXIV, where Spenser praises the 'happy letters', forming the name of his mother, his 'sovereigne Queene most kind' and his 'love, my lives last ornament'. 'Ye three Elizabeths for ever live, that three such graces did unto me give.' In this context, however, the comparison with Queen Elizabeth would seem rash.

p. 132, 5, l. 173. *rudded*: reddened.

p. 132, 6, l. 175. *uncrudded*: uncurdled.

p. 133, 1, ll. 189-90. *And stand astonisht . . . mazeful hed*: 'Red', past tense of 'to read', used in the now obsolete sense of 'to see', 'discern'. 'Mazeful', amazing, bewildering, stupefying. Medusa was one of the Gorgons, three monstrous sisters who lived in the far west, close to the infernal regions. Her head turned anyone who perceived it into stone, and retained this power even after it had been cut off by Perseus, emissary of Athena (or according to some accounts by Athena herself) and affixed to Athena's shield where it served as a potent protective weapon.

In the second of his *Trionfi*, Petrarch identifies Laura with the goddess of Chastity, who triumphs over love and describes her as clothed in a white robe and having in her hand a Medusa-shield.

> Ell' avea in dosso il di candida gonna,
> Lo scudo in man che mal vide Medusa. . . .

(*Trionfo della Castita*, verse 40.)

Petrarch makes Medusa a defence of Chastity against Love; but du Bellay and Spenser make her a defence of virtuous love against vice. See *supra*, pp. 74, 75.

p. 134, 1, l. 228. *crimsin dyde in grayne*: dyed scarlet. Scarlet dye was made from the dried bodies of small insects which were gathered from evergreen oaks and mistaken for berries: hence 'grayne', grain [Lat. granum, seed].

p. 134, 2, ll. 229-31. *That even th' Angels . . . about her fly*. In the Anglican Communion Service before the prayers of Humble Access and of Consecration the officiating priest says: 'Therefore with Angels and Archangels, and with all the company of heaven, we laud and magnify thy glorious Name.' But Spenser's lines also suggest the Cupids who in classical art are seen fluttering about the bride (cf. *Epith.* ll. 357-64, and notes).

p. 134, 3, l. 240. *Singye sweet Angels, Alleluya sing*. We may compare with this and with the next stanza Spenser's description of the betrothal feast of Una and Red Crosse in FQ. I, xii, 38, 39:

> Then gan they sprinckle all the posts with wine,
> And made great feast to solemnize that day;
> They all perfumde with frankencense diuine,
> And precious odours fetcht from far away,
> That all the house did sweat with great aray:
> And all the while sweete Musicke did apply
> Her curious skill, the warbling notes to play,
> To drive away the dull Melancholy;
> The whiles one sung a song of loue and jollity.

> During the which there was an heauenly noise
> Heard sound through all the Pallace pleasantly,
> Like as it had bene many an Angels voice,
> Singing before th'eternall majesty,

In their trinall triplicities on hye;
Yet wist no creature, whence that heauenly sweet
Proceeded, yet each one felt secretly
Himselfe thereby reft of his senses meet,
And rauished with rare impression in his sprite.

p. 134, 4, l. 243. *Bring home the triumph of our victory.* In ancient Rome a great victory was celebrated by a 'triumphus', that is to say, a solemn and magnificent processional entry of the victorious commander into the capital city. In his *Trionfi*, Petrarch describes the triumphs of various allegorical figures, Love, Chastity, etc., and the word continued to be used in connection with processions and spectacular pageants performed during the Renaissance. The use of the word 'our' suggests that the homecoming of the bridal pair is a triumph celebrating their common victory over difficulties that had stood in the way of their marriage (cf. *Epith.* ll. 31–3).

p. 134, 5, l. 253. *And sprinkle all the postes and wals with wine.* In ancient Rome the bride on arriving at her husband's house anointed the door-posts before being carried over the threshold. Spenser, however, seems to expect the guests to do the sprinkling and his lines suggest revelry at the wedding banquet rather than a solemn ritual act.

p. 135, 1, l. 266. *Barnaby the bright*: a stock description of St. Barnabas Day, implying that it is the longest day of the year. St. Barnabas Day is June 11th, but (owing to an originally slight over-estimate of the length of the solar year in terms of days) by the sixteenth century the Julian Calendar made it coincide with the summer solstice, when the sun moving through the Zodiac leaves the house of the Crab and enters that of the Lion.

p. 135, 2, l. 282. *O fayrest Planet*: the sun which in the Ptolemaic system was reckoned as one of the planets. In classical mythology the sun is supposed to drive his chariot across the sky.

p. 135, 3, l. 290. *nightes dread*: the octavo edition has 'nights'; the folio editions emend this to 'nights sad dread' evidently for the sake of the scansion. Van Winkle and the editors of *Variorum* retain 'nights'. Other modern editors amend to 'nightes'.

p. 135, 4, ll. 296 ff. *Now ceasse ye damsels.* . . . Cp. Catullus:

> Claudite ostia, virgines:
> lusimus satis. at boni
> conjuges, bene vivete et
> munere assiduo valentem
> exercete juventam.

[Maidens, shut the doors, we have sported enough. But ye, happy pair, live happily, and in your office exercise joyfully your vigorous youth].

The final section of Spenser's poem corresponds to the last fourteen stanzas of *Carmen* LXI, where, after the bride has crossed the threshold, the epithalamian singers utter their final encouragements and compliments to the newly-wed and wish them a long, happy and fruitful marriage. Good wishes for the founding of a family are part of the epithalamic tradition; Spenser transfers these hopes from the lips of the well-wishers to the mind of the husband.

p. 136, 1, ll. 307–10. *Like unto Maia . . . Acidalian brooke.* These lines afford an example of *contaminatio*, the confusion of different myths. The Vale of Tempe was the scene of Apollo's pursuit of Daphne; but the nymph Maia, daughter of Atlas, bore the god Hermes to Zeus on Mount Cyllene in Arcadia. The incident is recorded by Ovid in *Fasti*, Book V, as part of a discussion between the Muses about the derivation of the name of the month of May, in which Calliope maintains that it is derived from Maia the most beautiful of the Pleiades. Perhaps her association with the flowery spring-time month of May led Spenser to number Maia among the attendants of Aphrodite; for according to Servius (ad *Aen.* I, 720) the 'Acidalian brooke' is a fountain in Boeotia, where Aphrodite and the Graces were wont to bathe and disport themselves and where, according to Spenser (cf. FQ. IV, v, 3–5), Florimel was brought up by the Graces and where she discovered the famous girdle of chaste love which Venus had 'left behind her in her secret bower'. In FQ. VI, x, 5 ff., Spenser gives us an enchanting description of the Mount Acidale of his imagination. It was there that Sir Calidore, the Knight of Courtesy, surprised Colin Clout as he was piping to his lady, around whom the three Graces were singing and dancing.

p. 136, 2, ll. 315–8. *Now welcome night . . . for aye*: 'defray' means 'pay for', 'discharge by paying'. Night brings the compensating reward for the long labour of the wedding day and has put an end to the anxieties felt during the period of wooing; for with the coming of night all these varied and painful love-longings are concentrated into one intense desire for union which is completely fulfilled as the marriage is consummated. Spenser's desirous Eros-Love is a creditor and the debt to him is discharged by the hymenaeal-Love of the wedding night.

p. 136, 3, ll. 328–9. *Lyke as when Jove . . . Tirynthian groome.* Zeus, having fallen in love with Alcmena, daughter of the King of Argos, gained access to her bed by disguising himself as her absent fiancé, Amphitryon. To delay the latter's return, he stopped the rising of the sun, so that his night with Alcmena was prolonged to three nights. The fruit of this union was the hero Hercules, who was brought up at Tiryns.

p. 136, 4, ll. 330–1. *Or lyke as when . . . begot Maiesty.* Does this refer to some liaison of Zeus with Night, derived from an as yet undiscovered source, or is it Spenser's own invention? If the latter supposition is correct, what is Spenser's meaning? He describes the Hours as daughters of Jove and Night, but why should he describe them as

N

'Majesty'? Majestas was a Roman goddess and Spenser may have had vague and confused memories of Polyhymnia's opening speech in Ovid's *Fasti*, V, and also of references to it made by later commentators, such as Cartari. Polyhymnia describes how even after Chaos had begun to give way to Order, there remained considerable confusion among the Gods and 'Themis was often relegated to the lowest place, until Honour and comely Reverence with her calm look united in lawful wedlock. From that union sprang Majesty who regulates the whole world, and who was great on the very day she was born. Without delay she took her seat high in the midst of Olympus.' When the rebellious Titans attempted to destroy this harmony, they were worsted by Jupiter's thunderbolts. 'These weapons of the gods protected Majesty well; she survived and has been worshipped ever since. Hence she sits beside Jupiter, she is Jupiter's most faithful guardian; she assures to him his sceptre's peaceful tenure.'

Spenser may have been misled into identifying Jupiter with Majesty's father Honour by some passages in Cartari: *Imagini de gli Dei Delli Antichi* (Padova M.DC.XXVI). On p. 132 of this edition there is an engraving of a marble image in Rome, representing a man and woman with a child joining their hands together. Underneath the illustration is written: 'Imagine della Fede significata per il Dio Fidio adorato anticamente. La Verità è rappresenta qui come Madre, l'Honore come Padre, l'Amore come legame,' i.e. 'Image of the Fidelity signified by the god Fidio who was adored in antiquity. Truth is represented here as Mother, Honour as Father, Love as the bond of unity.' All this comes under the heading of *Giove Horcio* whom Cartari identifies with *Dio Fidio*.

Verdi in the section on *Jupiter* in his augmented translation of Cartari gives Cartari's explanation of it and adds: 'Ovide en ses Fastes, faint que du marriage d'Honneur avec Reverence naisse Majesté, ce que Burchardus Pylades confirme en sa Theogonie.' Cf. *Antoine Du Verdier: Les Images de Dieux des Anciens, contenans les idoles, coustumes, ceremonies, & autres choses appartenans à la Religion des Payens. Lyon MDLXXX.*

Cartari (*ed. cit.*, pp. 113 ff.) says that according to Seneca the wisest of the ancients believed that Jove was the all-pervading Mind, who created, protected and governed the Universe. Natales Comes says that, although some of the ancients regarded Night as born of formless matter called Chaos, others regarded her as the oldest of the gods, because she occupied this chaotic matter before the birth of the gods. In the Orphic Hymns she is rightly described as the mother of gods and men (cf. *Comes*, Lib. III, *De Nocte*, Cap. XII, p. 231).

The Florentine Neo-Platonists equated the gods of Greek mythology with the Ideas produced in the Angelic Mind by love of Divine Beauty and regarded their appearance there as the first phase of the creation of cosmos out of chaos. In ll. 315-71 Spenser deals with the *ambivalence*

of Night and his appeal to her better nature may well have culminated
in a reminder of the occasion when, by yielding to Jove, she became
the mother of the ordered Universe.

p. 137, 1, l. 341. *Pouke*: Old Irish *puca*: Welsh *pwka*: Mid. Eng.
pouke a malicious sprite. The mediæval 'pouke' was a more sinister figure
than the mischievous Puck of *A Midsummer Night's Dream*.

p. 137, 2, l. 345. *Let not . . . the Storke be heard*. The inclusion of the
stork among the birds of ill-omen has caused some surprise; but
Spenser may have been thinking of Chaucer, *Parlement of Foules*,
ll. 358 ff.:

> The waker [i.e. watchful] goos; the cukkow ever unkynde;
> The popynjay, full of delicasye;
> The drake, stroyere of his owene kynde;
> The stork, the wrekere of avouterye [adultery];
> the hote cormeraunt of glotenye;
> The raven wys; the crowe with vois of care;
> The throstil old; the frosty feldefare.

With the possible exception of the goose and the raven, this seems
to be a group of dismal if not positively evil birds. The stork, it is
true, has strong moral principles; but for the 'avenger of adultery' to
make his voice heard on the wedding-night would be tactless to say
the least!

p. 137, 3, ll. 353–6. *But let stil Silence . . . playne*. The exorcisms of
the preceding stanza have been directed against night-fears and
disturbing night noises; now Silence is invoked as a true night-
watchman who can stand sentry against both of these evils.

Spenser makes frequent use of the adjective 'timely', but one cannot
always be sure of the precise meaning which he attaches to it. It seems
to mean both 'opportune' and 'temporary', that which occurs at a
given moment, that which is appropriate to the moment, that which
will pass when the moment passes. Here it would seem to mean
'opportune', but the following lines suggest that the lovers' slumber is
light and frequently and pleasantly interrupted.

'May poure his limbs forth' is a Latinism: Latin *effundo*, to pour out,
being sometimes used in conjunction with solid objects (cf. Vergil,
Aeneid V, 836–7):

> . . . placida laxabant membra quiete
> Sub remis fusi per dura sedilia nautae.

[The sailors, stretched (lit. poured out) on their hard benches under
the oars, relaxed their limbs in quiet rest.]

What does Spenser mean by 'playne', plain? 'Plain' was sometimes
used for the 'scene of battle', just as we speak of 'taking the field'. The
latent metaphor of the opening lines of this stanza is a military one.
Silence is a sentry standing on guard against hostile disturbances and

N*

thus enabling Sleep to bring a temporary respite even to the pleasing-painful encounters of husband and wife.

p. 137, 4, ll. 357–64. *little winged loves ... at will.* Winged Cupids and Venus' doves make frequent appearances both in Classical and Renaissance art and literature. For instance, du Bellay (*op. cit.*) describes how the chaste Venus attends the wedding of Marguerite de France.

'Et les petits Amours
Y volettent sans cesse
Autours de la Princesse
En mille & mille tours.'

The most curious instance occurs in Remy Belleau's *La Bergerie*, a fanciful description in verse and prose of the pictures and tapestries which adorned the rooms in the Chateau de Joinville. One of these pictures depicted a magnificent wedding and Belleau gives a detailed account of the embroidery on the bride's robe: 'C'est un Apollon jeune, beau ... la lyre en la main, autour de luy les Graces et mille petits Amours, il invite les Nymfes de la Seine et de la Meuse a chanter ce marriage et commence ainsi ...', and then follows *l'Epithalame de Monseigneur le duc de Lorraine et de Madame Claude Fille du Roy*, which Belleau supposes to be sung by the nymphs invoked by Apollo embroidered on the robe of the bride who is herself a figure in a painting! The nymphs of the Seine sing of the appearance of the evening star and the oncoming of the auspicious night:

Ainsi l'Estoile qui guide
Les petits Amours dorez
Avec Hymen, qui preside
A ces festins honorez,
Vous appelle & vous convie,
Tous deux au col vous saisir,
Pour savourer le plaisir
Le plus doux de nostre vie.

The room was not only remarkable for its tapestry. 'Cette chambre est plaine de petits oiseaux, non pas peints ou contrefaits mais vivans, et branlant l'aile. ... Et croy que c'est là qu'Amour couve ses amoureux changez et transformé en ces petits oisillons, compagnons du labeur de ces bergers, & fidelles secretaires de leurs plus secrettes pensees.' Thus in this strange work the little loves appear in three different guises, at three different removes from reality: they surround the embroidered Apollo, they follow the evening star in the poem that this Apollo is imagined to be singing, and it is suggested that they are embodied in the living birds that fly about a real room in the real Chateau de Joinville. Spenser almost certainly knew both these epithalamia and is working in the same convention, but whereas du Bellay and Belleau are merely inviting us to admire their ingenuity and delicate artistry,

Spenser is also inviting us to believe in the emotional situation suggested by his imagery. *La Bergerie* was first published by G. Gilles, Paris, 1565. The *Epithalamion* chanted by the Apollo depicted on the bride's robe was first published in 1559 under the title of *Epithalame sur le Mariage de Monseigneur le duc de Lorraine et de Madame Claude Fille du Roy, Chante par les Nymphes de Seine et de Meuse*. See Doris Delacourcelle, *Le Sentiment de l'Art dans la Bergerie de Remy Belleau*, Oxford, 1945, especially p. 38; also *Belleau*, vol. II, pp. 88–98; *La Bergerie*, pp. 62–72.

p. 138, 1, ll. 374–81. *Is it not Cinthia . . . thee wrought.* Artemis (Lat. Diana) was, in one of her three aspects, a Moon-goddess and surnamed Cynthia because together with her twin-brother Apollo (a sun-god) she was born on Mount Cynthus in the island of Delos. Although Artemis was a virgin, and a zealous patroness of virginity, in her character as Moon-goddess she was a protectress of married women and especially of women in labour. Stories of her own love-affairs are late in date. The most famous of them relates how she fell in love with the shepherd Endymion, sleeping naked on Mount Latmos and came down night after night to enjoy his company. According to Vergil (cf. *Georgics* III, 391–3), the fleece of wool was given her, not by the 'Latmian Shepherd' but by Pan:

> munere sic niveo lanae, si credere dignum est,
> Pan deus Arcadiae captam te, Luna fefellit,
> in nemora alta vocans; nec tu aspernata vocantem.

['Twas with gift of such snowy wool, if we may trust the tale, that Pan Arcadia's God charmed and beguiled thee, O Moon, calling thee to the depths of the woods; nor didst thou scorn his call']. Spenser is not contaminating the story of Endymion with that of Pan; he is accepting the authority of Servius who, commenting in the above-quoted lines, says 'mutet fabulam: nam non Pan sed Endymion ammasse dicitur Lunam'. [He is changing the fable; for it is not Pan but Endymion who is said to have loved the Moon.]

p. 138, 2, ll. 390–5. *Juno . . . women in their smart.* Juno (identified by the Romans with the Greek Goddess Hera, sister and wife of Zeus) was the feminine counterpart of her husband, the sky-god Jupiter, and was particularly concerned with the sexual and maternal functions of women. She was regarded as the Guardian Spirit of women from birth to death and as the Goddess of lawful and fruitful marriage. In this latter capacity she frequently appears in plays and marriage masques of the sixteenth and seventeenth centuries.

In Spenser's day there was a distinction between the betrothal and the wedding ceremonies; but a betrothal was more solemn and committing than a modern engagement. Una is betrothed, not married to the Redcross Knight at the end of the first book of the *Fairie Queene* (cf. *supra*, pp. 181–2). The word 'religion' here seems to retain something of its original meaning of binding force.

p. 138, 3, l. 398. *Genius* [Lat. 'genius' (from 'gigno', beget, produce, cause)]: the productive power; the superior or divine nature in created beings. The 'genius' of each man is born with him and its function corresponds more or less to that of the guardian angel; although, unlike the guardian angel of Christian belief, it was not regarded as external to its protégé, but was sometimes considered as the divine part of him that could survive death. The 'genius' was not always attached to a human being; the Romans could speak of the genius of a place, a city, etc. The 'genius' was masculine, the guardian spirit of a woman was called her Juno. *Lectus genialis* ('genial bed') was a Roman technical term for the marriage bed.

p. 138, 4, l. 404. *timely.* The word here seems to have a future reference. Fruit is the appropriate result of the sowing of the seed, but it has to mature through time.

p. 138, 5, l. 405. *And thou fayre Hebe, and thou Hymen free* (cf. HL. l. 283 and note; also *Epith.* l. 25 and note).

p. 139, 1, l. 409. *And ye high heauens . . . gods* (see *supra*, pp. 167-8).

p. 139, 2, l. 425. *And cease till then our tymely ioyes to sing.* 'Tymely' here seems to mean 'temporal'. Does 'till then' refer to the birth of children into this world or to their entry into Heaven? Perhaps it implies both. The birth of children, it is hoped, will bring future joy both to themselves and to their parents; but as husband and wife look at the starry sky, time loses its character and stretches out into Eternity.

p. 139, 3, ll. 427-33. *Song . . . endlesse monument* (see *supra*, pp. 81-3).

APPENDIX I

THE TEXT

ON November 19th, 1594, William Ponsonby entered in the Stationer's Register 'A booke entituled Amoretti and Epithalamion written not longe since by Edmund Spenser'. In 1595 appeared a small octavo volume (the sheets may have been cut down) entitled '*Amoretti and Epithalamion* written not long since by Edmunde Spenser. Printed for William Ponsonby. 1595'. The printer was Peter Short. No other edition appeared during the poet's lifetime and since he was absent from England at the time of its publication it is to be presumed that he did not revise it for the Press—the text is very faulty, and the punctuation, which is based on a rigidly metrical system, is frequently careless and inconsistent.

The first collected edition of Spenser's poems is the folio volume entitled: 'The Faerie Qveen; The Shepheard's Calendar; Together with the other Works of England's Arch-Poet, Edm. Spenser. Collected into one Volume, and carefully corrected. Printed by H.L. for Mathew Lownes. Anno Dom. 1611, fol'. The editor was conscientious and did his best to emend some errors, but his corrections have no independent authority and are not always happy. The punctuation of the Folio version of *Epithalamion* is on the whole heavier and less rigid than that of 8° but the attempted compromise between metrical and logical punctuation is not wholly successful.

There is no entry of *Fowre Hymnes* in the Stationers' Register. In 1596 there appeared a Quarto volume containing 'Fowre Hymnes made by Edm. Spenser. London, printed for William Ponsonby. 1596', together with a second edition of *Daphnaida*, based, with only minor alterations, on the first quarto edition published by Ponsonby and printed by Thomas Orwin under the date 1591. The quarto volume of 1596 was printed by Richard Field. The first two Hymns are entitled: 'An Hymne in Honour of Love', with running-title: 'An Hymne of Love'; 'An Hymne in Honour of Beautie', with running-title: 'An Hymne of Beautie'. The titles and running-titles of the last two Hymns are 'An Hymne of Heavenly Love' and 'An Hymne of Heavenly Beautie'.

Spenser was in England when the 1596 Quarto appeared, but there is no indication that he revised the 2nd Quarto of *Daphnaida*; it seems likely, however, that he prepared *Fowre Hymnes* for the Press for the text is unusually good and the punctuation presents fewer difficulties than does that of other early editions of his poems.

The text of this present edition is that of the earliest quartos as prepared by Professor W. L. Renwick for *The Works of Edmund Spenser*, published by Basil Blackwell for the Shakespeare Head Press, 1930. I have drawn attention to variant readings only when they affect the sense. Fuller textual information is to be found in *Daphnaida and other Poems*, ed. W. L. Renwick, pp. 237–41; *Spenser's Minor Poems*, ed. E. de Sélincourt, vol. I, Introduction, pp. xv, xvi, xxi-xxvi; *The Minor Poems, vol. I*, Appendix VII, pp. 712–14; vol. II, Appendix X, pp. 697–9, 704–5, 720–21; in *The Works of Edmund Spenser, A Variorum Edition*.

APPENDIX II

NUMBER SYMBOLISM IN EPITHALAMION

IN *Short Time's Endless Monument*, Professor A. Kent Hieatt has offered a fascinating and original interpretation of *Epithalamion* which no editor of that poem can afford to disregard; and has also suggested a new line of approach to Elizabethan poetry which has already proved fruitful. His position is powerfully supported by D. Alistair Fowler who in *Spenser and the Numbers of Time* describes a 'numerological pattern' in the *Fairie Queene* similar though more complicated than that discovered by Professor Hieatt in *Epithalamion*.

Professor Hieatt's theory may be summarized as follows: Beneath the literal surface of the marriage ode, lies concealed an elaborate numerical symbolism referring to the diurnal and annual movements of the sun, which produce the cyclic rhythm of the seasons and so make natural life possible. *Epithalamion*, therefore, has two levels of meaning: there is (1) the overt description of the poet's particular wedding-day; there is (2) a covert symbolism conveying general reflections on Time and Eternity similar to those expressed more openly in the 'Garden of Adonis' stanzas and the 'Mutabilitie cantos' of *The Faerie Queene* (cf. FQ.III, vi and FQ.VII, vi, vii.) The central theme which links the literal and the symbolic senses together is that of the compensation for mortality and impermanence provided by recurrence. *Epithalamion*, 'as a marriage ode and a register of time', expresses the paradox that in spite of change and death 'the individual, mortal life of man is renewed in generation, just as the insufficiency of the sun is recompensed in its annual journey, with all the recurring, time-given variety so created' (p. 51).

Professor Hieatt produces much learned and impressive evidence in support of this reinterpretation of *Epithalamion*. The ramifications of his argument are too intricate and extensive to be considered here in detail, and to give even his main positions the careful examination they deserve, it is necessary to keep constantly in mind the nature of the astronomical ideas which Spenser is using and, of course, to think in Ptolomaic not Copernican terms. The chief points to be remembered are as follows:

1. The earth is the fixed centre of a nest of concentric spheres. The outermost celestial sphere, the sphere of the fixed stars, revolves round the earth in 24 hours carrying with it the other spheres, to each of which a planet is attached and each of which has also its own individual motion. The sun and moon are regarded as planets and it is the sun's diurnal rotation with the celestial sphere that creates the divisions of day and night.

2. While it is being carried round the earth by the diurnal revolution of the celestial sphere, the solar sphere is also engaging in a rotation of its own in the opposite direction and this necessarily slows down its diurnal movement; so that while in slightly less than 24 solar hours the celestial sphere has completed its full revolution of 360° round the earth, the sun during the same period has only completed 359° of the circle. Since the sun is daily retarded by $\frac{1}{365}$, almost one degree of a circle, it takes it 365 days to complete its individual rotation round the earth and so to create the solar year.

3. The retardation of the sun involves it in a continuous change of position in regard to the fixed stars, a change which can be described as the following from west to east of a circular pathway through the zodiac. This orbit of the sun through the zodiac cuts the celestial equator at an angle and by so doing causes seasonal variations of the position of the sun in the sky and in the lengths of day and night.

4. The movements of the sun are related not only to the fixed stars, but also to the Hours, both to the diurnal Hours which divide day and night into 24 equal periods of time and to the sidereal Hours, which by imaginary lines drawn between the two celestial Poles, divide the Celestial Sphere into 24 equal spaces comprising 15° or $\frac{1}{24}$ of a circle and also by their diurnal rotation with the fixed stars define the spaces and periods within which the heavenly bodies (including, of course, the sun) rise and set (cf. HHL ll. 22 ff.). In its diurnal movement, therefore, the sun can be regarded as travelling with a particular Hour though at a slightly slower pace; in its annual movement it passes every fifteen or sixteen days from the realm of one Hour to that of the Hour immediately to the east of it, until after the lapse of 365 days it has risen and set in each of the Hours in turn and finally returned to the one from which it started.

5. This constant change of the Hour in which the sun rises and sets necessarily involves a constant interchange between the Hours which emerge above the horizon during daylight and those which do this at night. To put it another way, the same position of the sky will be exposed during daylight at the beginning and ending of any period of 12 months and this will be true also of the night sky.

Thus at the summer solstice in Southern Ireland, during the period from dawn to dusk, sixteen and a fraction Hours will rise with their stars above the eastern horizon and at sunset give place to the seven and a fraction hours which will emerge with their stars during the ensuing night. At the winter solstice the position is reversed: the seven and a fraction night Hours become the seven and a fraction day-Hours, and the sixteen and a fraction day-Hours become sixteen and a fraction night-Hours. At the vernal and autumnal equinoxes the interchanging night-Hours and day-Hours are both 12 in number.

The sidereal hours still play a part in modern astronomy, but they are more useful to the poet when set in the Ptolemaic universe, for in that context it is easy to personify them as female figures stationed at equal distances from one another all round the celestial sphere, revolving diurnally round the earth together with the fixed stars and interchanging their daily and nightly duties of shepherding the rising and setting of the appropriate Heavenly Bodies. This according to Professor Hieatt is how FQ. VII, vii, 45 and the 24 'matching stanzas' of *Epithalamion* are to be interpreted.

6. The *simple*, uniform movement of the Celestial Sphere bears a closer resemblance to eternal duration than do the more *complex* and therefore more *imperfect* movements of the sun and other planets. This idea, which can be traced back to Plato's *Timaeus*, was still current in the sixteenth century. Spenser alludes to it in the 'Mutabilitie Cantos' (cf. FQ. VII, vii, 58) and, although he does not explicitly mention it in *Epithalamion*, it is the presupposition which, according to Professor Hieatt, provides the key to the meaning of the poem.

Professor Hieatt begins his argument by calling attention to certain peculiarities of *Epithalamion* which require explanation:

1. The Bride is the only character in Spenser's works to be attended by the Hours, who possess creative and restorative functions and represent both the familiar diurnal hours and also the seasonal hours of classical antiquity (cf. *Epith.*, ll. 98–102).

2. *Epithalamion* is the only poem of Spenser's in which the stanzas vary in length, rhyme-scheme and metrical structure without any apparent reason.

3. There seems to be no known parallel for the form of the final stanza, and this stanza, which fills the rôle of the traditional envoy or tornata, is oddly phrased and obscure in meaning.

4. Another alleged peculiarity of *Epithalamion* is that by means of resemblances or striking contrasts, widely separated pairs of stanzas are matched together in such a way that stanzas 1–12 correspond in order to stanzas 13–24 and so divide the poem in half.

Professor Hieatt contends that all these peculiarities can be explained as parts of an elaborate system of covert astronomical symbolism expressing the poem's central theme: namely, that procreation and seasonal recurrence are means by which deficiencies are remedied and

3

temporal existence is made 'eterne in mutabilitie' (FQ. III, vi, st. 47). The requisite combination of annual and diurnal symbolism is effected by the numerical organization of the poem, and the systematic matching of the paired stanzas.

If we include the Envoy, *Epithalamion* contains 24 stanzas, 365 long lines and 68 short lines. If we exclude the Envoy, the marriage ode contains 23 stanzas, each consisting of groups of long lines—pentameters and a concluding hexameter—divided (with two exceptions) by 3 short lines, which (again with the two exceptions) are trimeters. Stanzas 15 and 23 contain only 2 short lines: the number of long lines contained in the 23 stanzas varies from 15 to 16; consequently these stanzas vary in length from 17 to 19 lines. The Envoy consists of 6 pentameters and one tetrameter.

The 24 stanzas symbolize both the diurnal and the sidereal hours. The 365 long lines symbolize the 365 days which make up the year and the daily retardation of the sun by $\frac{1}{365}$ of a circle as compared with the rate of the celestial sphere. That each of the 23 stanzas contains either 15 or 16 long lines may refer to the fact that the sun takes 15 or 16 days to pass from the region of one sidereal hour to another. In all these ways the long lines signify *duration* of time.

The function of the short lines is to mark *divisions* of time. The fourfold subdivision of most of the stanzas suggests that Spenser is symbolizing the quarter-hourly as well as the hourly periods of his wedding day and night, and it is certainly interesting that if we accept this quarter-hourly symbolism we find that night falls (cf. *Epith.*, l. 300) at the time it would have fallen in Southern Ireland at the summer solstice, according to the calculations of certain authorities with whom Spenser was almost certainly familiar (Hieatt, *op. cit.*, pp. 10 ff.).

Although the quarter-hourly symbolism may have been intentional, it was not consistently carried out. To produce the required 96 quarters of an hour we need 72 short lines and *Epithalamion* provides only 68. Professor Hieatt's explanation is that Spenser wished to attach annual as well as diurnal significance to his short lines, and since the annual sum of seasons, months and years amounts to 68, he was obliged to omit 4 short lines and content himself with a merely 'dominant auditory image' of elapsing quarter-hours punctuated by the tripping sound of trimeters and ending at the hour with the word 'ring'. The transition from day to night is marked by the change from positive to negative refrain.

Astronomical symbolism furnishes an explanation of the final stanza, which consists of 6 long lines and one short one and shares the ambiguity of the traditional *tornata*, which addressed itself directly to an already completed poem, while at the same time contributing to its total poetic effect. If we regard Spenser's Envoy as outside the marriage ode we have only 359 long lines, whereas if we regard it as within it we have 365, and this is particularly interesting because, as we have seen, when the hours and the celestial sphere have completed their diurnal circle of 360°, the solar sphere has only moved through 359° and it is by this 'declining daily by degrees' that the sun creates the year of 365 days. Professor Hieatt's contention is that 'Spenser wishes to communicate the relationship between the daily short-comings of the sun and the total measure of 365 days created by this shortcoming, and between the 359 long lines of the full-size stanzas and the 365 long lines complete with envoy' (p. 44).

Professor Hieatt suggests that this relationship is communicated by the meaning as well as by the length of the envoy and discovers beneath the literal sense which regards the 'song' as a marriage ode composed in honour of the bride, an astronomical sense in which the 'song' is regarded as a celebration of the movement of the sun.

It is impossible here even to summarize the multiple meanings which Professor Hieatt suggests as possible interpretations of the envoy, but his main point is that the fourth line refers to untimely birth and the last three lines refer to the compensation for this untimeliness. Without the Envoy, *Epithalamion* is a description of the passage of one particular day and night but as such it is incomplete, for it finishes at the end of its twenty-third stanza 'having accreted only 359 long lines, just as the orbit of the sun is incomplete having amounted only to 359°, at the time when the starry sphere has closed its circle'. When the Envoy is included in *Epithalamion* it compensates for this incompleteness by adding a twenty-fourth stanza and the extra six lines which enable the poem to symbolize both the day and the year.

The first 23 stanzas arrive incomplete born before their due time, and 'the sun similarly does not "stay" to await its "dew time", for, embarked on another journey, it will not stand fixed with the stars in their sphere to be carried around the circle in their due time of a sidereal day' (p. 50). Just as the insufficiency of the song celebrating a particular wedding day is recompensed by the Envoy, 'which the ostensible insufficiency of the song itself calls forth', so the daily insufficiency of the sun is recompensed by the cyclic recurrence of the seasons which is caused by that same insufficiency. 'The poem is a monument to short time in the sense that it celebrates the cyclical measures of time created by the sun . . . and in the sense that it celebrates short time over against Eternity' (p. 56).

Spenser symbolizes the mutability theme not only by the Envoy but also and in an even more abstruse and complicated way by the device of the matching stanzas. If the stanzaic series 1–12 corresponds to the series 13–24 it follows that the members of each matching pair are separated from each other by the length of half the poem and can thus symbolize the fact that on the celestial sphere any one of the sidereal hours is situated precisely opposite another hour, which is twelve hours or one hemisphere away from it and that in relation to the sun, and the lengths of day and night, they exchange positions with one another in exactly half a year. Obviously Spenser could have made the same point by beginning his series at any stage of the poem; he could, for instance, have matched a series 7–18 with a series 19–24, 1–6 'conceiving the poem as a circle [*sic*] with its tail in its mouth'. Why then did he split his poem in half by matching series 1–12 with series 13–24? The answer is that the poet wanted to symbolize the four seasons of the year. According to the literal sense, the coming of night at stanza 17, which is marked by the change of refrain, is a particular moment on the poet's wedding-day; on the symbolic level it could equally well refer to the situation of the sidereal hours in relation to the sun and the length of day at the time of the summer solstice. On the same principle the midway break at the end of stanza 12 could refer to the situation at the vernal equinox. Since at the beginning and ending of any period of six months the situations of the sidereal hours in relation to the sun are *reversed*, it follows that the divisions at the ends of stanzas 12 and 16 can be held to mark the transitions from night to day, as well as from day to night, and so symbolize the vernal and autumnal equinoxes and the summer and winter solstices. As Professor Hieatt puts it: 'Spenser's symbolic intent here was to indicate the position of the heavens in relation to the sun at the four seasons of the year and the lengths of day and night at the four climatic points of the sun's annual progress' (p. 40).

Professor Hieatt states very clearly that recognition of the covert symbolism involves not merely a fuller appreciation of the overt annual references in stanzas 6 and 15, but also a reinterpretation possibly even a reappraisal of *Epithalamion*; for it turns the celebration of a unique event into a meditation on mutability. 'We must think of the substance of the poem as the substance of time itself—duration with its divisions— and we must see a year as a day, as God does. Finally we must see how man and the universe mirror each other, and what paradoxical boon is granted to all of us: that though we may not endure individually, our mortality and the insufficiency of all created things is, by grace, only one aspect of a total situation of which cyclical return is the other face, until such time as time shall cease' (pp. 80, 81). This is so beautifully and persuasively put that it seems ungracious to raise any doubts and yet Professor Hieatt's thesis does pose some puzzling questions as to the way in which symbolism works; and the nature of the relationship between the literal and symbolical meanings of the poem.

According to Professor Hieatt, in order to understand *Epithalamion* aright we have to execute the following manoeuvres. First we must attend to the 'shimmering surface' of Spenser's wedding-day (a surface which, as I have tried to indicate in my introduction, has its own *depth* of thought and feeling and a powerful, forward flow), and then we must dissolve the 'surface' in order to replace it by a model of the cosmos based on astronomical knowledge and numerical calculations. The task is far from simple. Not only must we count the stanzas and the long and short lines, but we must so memorize the imagery, etc. of the individual stanzas, that as we follow the second half of the poem we can keep on pairing each stanza with its twin situated 12 stanzas back, and draw further inferences, based on our knowledge of astronomy. Having equated the stanzas with both the diurnal and sidereal hours we locate the equinoxes and the solstices and reflect that they are caused by the complicated movement of the sun, indicated by the number and arrangement of the long and short lines. The process culminates in the last two stanzas where we see the bridegroom looking at the sky and hoping to found a family and the Envoy helps us to understand that the procreation theme unites the two senses of *Epithalamion* by showing how man mirrors 'the larger scheme of nature in continually recreating and regenerating himself according to the harmony of the natural plan' (p. 32).

Can this or any other poem be experienced *as a poem* when read in this manner?

It might perhaps be argued that an Elizabethan reader would have answered: 'Yes.' Spenser's contemporaries were apt to find a mystic significance in numbers; they were not unacquainted with the numerical organization of works of art and not astonished to find philosophy concealed beneath fables and different levels of meaning in the same poem. The four senses of the Bible had been recognized for centuries and the same method of interpretation was at times applied to secular literature. Dante, for instance, begins his exposition of the polysemous character of *The Divine Comedy* by expounding the four senses of a Biblical text, and, having explained that the three 'mystic senses . . . may all in general be called allegorical since they differ from the literal and historical' continues 'When we understand this we see clearly that the *subject* round which the alternative senses play must be twofold . . . The subject of the whole work [i.e. *The Divine Comedy*] then, taken in the literal sense only, is "the state of souls after death" without qualification, for the whole progress of the work hinges on it and about it. Whereas if the work be taken allegorically the subject is "man, as by good or ill deserts, . . . he becomes liable to rewarding or punishing justice" ' [cf. *Dante, Latin Works*, pp. 347, 348]. Nearly three centuries later we find Fairfax justifying his interpretation of Tasso's *Jerusalem Delivered* on the same principle of dual significance: 'Heroicall Poetrie (as a living creature wherein two natures are conjoyned) is compounded of *Imitation* and *Allegorie*; with the one she allureth unto her the minds and cares of men and marvellously delighteth them; with the other either in virtue or in knowledge, she instructeth them'.

For the full understanding of polysemous poetry it is undoubtedly requisite that several operations should be performed simultaneously;

but these operations are not incongruous. The two senses of *The Divine Comedy* can easily be apprehended simultaneously and, indeed, it is almost impossible to dissociate them because 'the state of souls after death' is a state of rewards or punishments for deeds done on earth, and this is constantly explained and illustrated by characters in the literal narrative; particularly, of course, by Dante's official guides, Virgil and Beatrice. Again in *The Fairie Queen*, Arthur, seeking Gloriana, is easily recognizable as an exemplary Christian gentleman seeking to win honour by the exercise of virtue, and he and the other knights do not have to step out of their fairy tale in order to suggest to the reader that the chivalrous ideals of the Round Table will one day be partially realized at the court of Queen Elizabeth and finally perfectly fulfilled in the Kingdom of Heaven. In fact, Dante and Spenser and even translators such as Harrington who read their own allegorical interpretations into their texts, are all following the traditional principle that the allegorical senses may legitimately deepen the meaning and extend the application of the Biblical history or the poetic fiction, but not radically alter our understanding of the literal sense. As Aquinas puts it in *Summa Theologica* Q. 1, 17 Art. 10, p. 17, the 'spiritual sense . . . is based on the literal, and presupposes it . . . all the senses are founded on one—the literal—from which alone can any argument be drawn and not from those intended allegorically'. Aquinas, of course, is speaking as a theologian but in a more secular context, Dr. Fowler allows 'that numerological analysis will seldom alter our evaluation of a poem; nor is it likely to overthrow our previous understanding of its meaning' (*op. cit.*, p. 248). Again, 'The significance of formal numbers is properly in the nature of a correspondence. No numerological interpretation can carry conviction, therefore, unless the text supports it (*op. cit.*, p. 252). Even the intricate system of numerical astronomical symbolism discovered by Dr. Fowler does not interfere with the narrative and pictorial aspects of the *Fairie Queene*. For instance, Book II is concerned with the principle of 'the Dyad' which is especially manifest in the physical-spiritual duality of human nature, and consequently its hero is 'confronted by pairs of enemies, whom he attempts to restrain rather than kill. . . . So regular is the arrangement of characters in complementary pairs, in this book, that one might almost think it a direct translation of the number symbolism into purely formal terms—a kind of Pythagorian literary ballet. Two by two the *personae* are marshalled: Mordant and Amavia, Hudibras and Sans Loy . . .' (*op. cit.*, pp. 11, 12).

It is, however, one thing to appreciate 'a kind of Pythagorean literary ballet', but another to enjoy a poem while doing mental arithmetic. I find it difficult to believe that even the most numerically-minded Elizabethan could *experience* the number of lines and stanzas as part of his *immediate experience* of *Epithalamion*. Nevertheless, since he tended to value a poem as an *artifact* rather than as 'a spontaneous overflow of powerful feeling' he could be expected to admire the ingenuity by which the poet had fitted format to subject matter and paid a compliment to his bride by having taken such pains for her sake. He might take pleasure in discovering that the numerical pattern illuminated the deepest meaning of the text. But it would have to illuminate, not obscure or dissolve it; for it is hard to see how a poem could possess any unity at all if its different levels of meaning contradicted one another and the numerological interpretation was unsupported by the text. Such a poem might be read either as a poem or a cryptogram, but it could hardly be read as both at once.

To what extent does the text support Professor Hieatt when he turns a paean of praise into a message of consolation by an argument drawn from an allegorical interpretation of the matching stanzas and drawn chiefly by a process of abstract calculation because, 'the direct bodying forth of meaning through imagery . . . is denied in this mode'? The question cannot be evaded; but it does not admit of a simple answer.

Much of the temporal symbolism discovered by Professor Hieatt is supported by the text and provided with at least one simple explanation by the poet himself. Why do some people keep the anniversaries of their marriage and celebrate their silver and golden weddings? What could be more significant to a poet than that the most important day of the most important year of his life occurred at the summer solstice?

> Never had man more joyfull day then this,
> . . . This day is holy; doe ye write it downe
> that ye forever it remember may.
> This day the sunne is in his chiefest hight. . . .

If from another point of view it may seem inappropriate to be married on the longest day of the year, that is only because, although the day is holy, the night is holier still. Whichever way you look at it, the emphasis is not on imperfection but on fulfilment, not on cyclic movement, but on the unique significance of a particular year and day. Professor Hieatt's more complicated exegesis of the temporal symbolism depends chiefly on his interpretation of the matching stanzas, the Envoy and the final meditation of the Bridegroom. By the matching of the stanzas Spenser has, he believes, introduced a covert circular movement into the *Epithalamion* symbolizing the seasonal cycle which results from and compensates for the complicated and therefore imperfect movements of the sun. Here again the text supports him, for by speaking of the sun as 'declining by degrees' and informing us that the Hours are begotten of Day and Night and also

> . . . doe the seasons of the yeare allot
> And al that ever in this world is fayre
> Doe make and still repayre. . . .

Spenser certainly introduces the notion of seasonal renewal and reparation; but that does not prove that he intended to symbolize this by means of 'a complex system of divisions and matchings' dependent on a circular movement which the reader can only deduce from a vividly descriptive narrative that marches him straight forward through the events of one particular day while the actual text so far from helping him to perform this difficult double operation is often positively misleading. For instance, one would expect the narrative to indicate the crucial break at the end of stanza 12, by which the poem is to be divided into two halves. But does it do so? In stanza 12 the church doors are opened and the bride walks to the altar; in stanza 13 she remains standing there while the ceremony is performed. After she has given her hand to the bridegroom we hear no more of the proceedings within the church, and the opening line of stanza 14:

> Now al is done; bring home the bride againe

suggests not only a lapse of time between stanzas 13 and 14 but also a transition from sacred to secular celebrations. This seems a curious way of inviting us to pause at the end of stanza 12, and the parallelism and matching of the paired stanzas would surely have to be striking and unmistakable in order to counteract the movement and visual imagery of the narrative, and this in my opinion is far from being the case.

Professor Hieatt's thesis, however, does not depend on the matching stanzas; for to an educated Elizabethan the textual references and the numeration of lines and stanzas would suffice to *suggest* the seasonal cycle caused by the sun without distorting the flow of the narrative.

The meaning of the Envoy is not, I believe, as obscure as is sometimes supposed; but Professor Hieatt succeeds in demonstrating that the literal text *can* be given an interpretation that supports the solar symbolism and stresses the theme of compensation for deficiency. Even so, it is odd that in the Envoy, as in the Ode, Spenser seems to be deliberately putting his readers off the scent by producing an *imaginative* impression which obscures even if it does not contradict the symbolical meaning. The literal sense suggests that the Ode (or its writer) *hurries up*, the symbolic sense suggests that the sun slows down. The literal sense suggests that the Ode compensates by its intrinsic excellence for the hurried wedding preparations by providing the bride with 'an endlesse monument', an image which conveys the idea both of *Stability in space and endurance throughout time*: the symbolic sense suggests that the sun compensates for *its own* deficiency by producing seasonal recurrences through its ceaseless *circular movement through space and time.*

From Professor Hieatt's reinterpretation of *Epithalamion* it seems to follow that the literal and symbolic senses conflict not only in the movement and structure, but also in the mood and tone of the poem as a whole; for while apparently rejoicing wholeheartedly in the fulfilment of his love, Spenser is really chiefly concerned to console us for our mortality and point out a compensation for the imperfections of temporal existence.

If so, it seems strange that he has taken so little trouble to explain himself. In the first stanza, Spenser states, in mythical terms indeed, but quite unambiguously, that he intends now to abandon 'sorrowfull complaints' about death and other misfortunes and sing the praises of his love. In the ensuing Ode he celebrates the bride's beauty and virtue, he emphasizes the religious and secular value of the 'lovely bond' which unites her to him, he exults in the joy and holiness of the wedding day which cancels all their past pains and offers them a vista of enduring future happiness. There is not one sigh of regret for the transience of human pleasure; all the changes mentioned are changes for the better and even death is only envisaged as an ascent from prolonged earthly joys to everlasting happiness in Heaven.

If the literal sense fails to suggest the 'mutability theme', the supposed symbolic sense fails to interpret the daylight proceedings of the wedding. It discovers no cosmic significance in the figure of the bride or the feelings of the bridegroom or the mutual love which is consecrated in the church and consummated in the bridal chamber, and discovers symbolic value not in the marriage relationship as a whole but only in procreation. And that brings us to the bridegroom's final meditation.

That parents can, in a sense, defeat physical death by living on in their children has always been a familiar idea, but it is markedly absent from the bridegroom's nocturnal meditations. He expresses no desire that he and his wife should survive in their offspring and seems chiefly preoccupied with the wellbeing of his descendants for their own sakes. He shows no particular interest in the 'renewal of the mortal life of men' but hopes that by raising a large posterity he will increase the number of immortal individuals who, after long and prosperous lives on earth, will increase the population of Heaven. The movement of *Epithalamion* is not that of a round dance, but of a procession that proceeds onwards and upwards until it passes beyond our range of vision. On the other hand, Spenser does suggest a means whereby temporal mutability may be defeated even in this life, but it is not by procreation or seasonal renewal, it is by poetry. Both the first and the last stanzas state explicitly that the bridegroom is thinking of himself as also a poet. Elizabethan poets never tired of reminding their patrons or their mistresses that they could confer immortality upon them and that, unlike stone or brass, words could be shaped into an 'endlesse monument'.

I should like to emphasize that although I find myself in disagreement with Professor Hieatt on certain points, I am very far from denying the importance of his discovery. His prophecy that 'in time many poems of the Renaissance will be discovered to possess a symbolism resembling that of *Epithalamion*' has already begun to be fulfilled. His exposition of the numerical symbolism has thrown valuable light on Spenser's artistry, deepened our awareness of the cosmic significance of the poem, and afforded us a new insight which can, I believe, be used so as to enrich our enjoyment and understanding of *Epithalamion*, while strengthening rather than weakening the impact of the verbal text.

Taken together, numerical symbolism and textual references serve to set Spenser's marriage into its context of space and time, of the flowering earth and the rotating spheres. The poet's wedding-day is not, I suggest, 'the shimmering surface' but the whole body of his poem including its heart; for the substance of *Epithalamion* is surely not 'Time itself' but Love itself, 'the Love that moves the Sun and other stars' to renew the seasons; that moves all living creatures 'to multiply the likeness of their kind'; that can work within the human mind to overcome time, not only through time and beyond time, but within time, by inspiring a poet to endow a particular day and year with eternal significance and to embody it in a monument of immortal verse.

Addendum: The Matching Stanzas

Professor Hieatt reaffirmed his belief in the 'matching stanzas' in 'The Daughters of Horus: Order in the Stanzas of Epithalamion', an article included in *Form and Convention in the Poetry of Edmund Spenser*, ed. William Nelson, 1961. Here, as in his former work, he acknowledges that the evidence for pairing the series 1–12 with the series 13–24 varies in convincingness and, since his theory of systematic matching is admittedly not so fully proven as his theory of numerical symbolism, he suggests that its degree of probability might usefully be tested by an independent investigator 'attempting an alternative matching'.

In response to this invitation I propose the following system:

Alternative Proposals for 'Matching Stanzas'

1 = 7, 24	13 = 9, 22
2 = 8, 14	14 = 2, 8
3 = 17	15 = 7
4 ——	16 = 23
5 = 19	17 = 3, 18
6 = 18	18 = 17
7 = 1, 15, 21	19 = 5
8 = 2, 14	20 = 13
9 = 13	21 = 7
10 ——	22 = 12, 13
11 ——	23 = 16
12 = 22, 23	24 = 1

Since it is impossible here to produce my evidence in full, I shall confine my exposition to the crucial stanzas 1, 13, 12, 24 and those who would look further into the matter should consult Professor

Hieatt's admirably lucid exposition of his own system (pp. 86–109) and ask themselves whether equally plausible reasons could not be produced for pairing the stanzas in the way suggested above. His text should also be consulted in order to supplement my necessarily abbreviated summary of his arguments. My comments on these arguments are placed in square brackets. I have marked with an asterisk those passages which Professor Hieatt prints in italics to mark a lesser degree of probability. In my own system, I have followed Professor Hieatt's plan of matching on a basis of either resemblance or striking contrast. For instance, Professor Hieatt makes *Stanza* 8 with its 'noise, minstrels', etc. correspond to *Stanza* 20 with 'silence, sacred peace, sleep' (cf. pp. 100–101), and on the same principle of contrast I pair *Stanza* 5, where the bride is bidden to awake and listen to the birds' dawn-chorus with *Stanza* 19 where the bridegroom prays that no ill-omened birds may interrupt the 'gentle sleep' of himself and his wife.

EXAMPLES OF PROFESSOR HIEATT'S SYSTEM

Stanza 1 = *Stanza* 13

1.a. The Muses have honoured the greatest in Spenser's poetry.
13.a. The Angels round the Altar serve the greatest.
1.b. At the poet's bidding, the Muses are to change their theme and praise his bride.
13.b. The Angels forget their proper service and fly about the bride. The poet bids them sing 'Alleluia'.
1.c. *The Muses aid the poet.
13.c. *The Angels aid the priest.
1.d. *The poet will praise his bride.
13.d. *The priest blesses the bride.
1.e. *'Orpheus sang of his own bride (to the powers of Hell so as to recover her); Spenser will sing her praises to himself.'
13.e. *Spenser's bride will not allow 'one look to glance awry which may let in a little thought unsound', but 'Orpheus lost his bride by doing just this'. The Christian allegorical interpretation of this myth is found in Boethius and Henryson. [Notice that the text of *Epithalamion* only mentions Orpheus' rescue of Eurydice; the reason for his subsequent loss of her has to be *inferred* by those readers who know the story and its interpretation.]

Stanza 12 = *Stanza* 24

12.a. Occurrence of words: 'due', 'endless'.
24.a. Occurrence of words: 'due', 'endless', 'duly'. (The words are used in the poem only in Stanzas 12 and 24.)

12.b. Temple gates to be opened wide, posts to be adorned, pillars to be decked to give due honour to the bride.

o

24.b. 'The bride should duly have been decked with many ornaments for which this poem is a recompense.'

12.c. 'The sacred ceremonies making endless matrimony.'

24.c. 'The endless monument made by the poem to short time.'

12.d. Awe before the Almighty (cf. ll. 210–4).

24.d. The relation between Time and Eternity (cf. l. 433).

EXAMPLES OF ALTERNATIVE SYSTEM

Stanza 1 = Stanzas 7, 21, 24

1.a. Spenser makes a request to the Muses and refers to his past poetic work.

7.a. Spenser makes a request to Phoebus, 'father of the Muse', and refers to his past poetic work.

1.b. Spenser deprecates possible envy of his 'owne love's prayses' which he intends to 'resound'.

7.b. *Spenser prays Phoebus not to disgrace his bride's beauty by shining too brightly* (not a very convincing parallel).

21.b. Spenser prays Cinthia the moon-goddess:

> . . . do thou not envy
> My love with me to spy.

[The words 'envide', 'envy' occur only in Stanza 1 and 21 respectively.]

1.c. Spenser expects the woods to echo a song to be sung directly by himself alone.

7.c. Spenser expects the woods to echo a song to be sung directly by himself alone.

[There is no other instance of this in the poem.]

1.d. Spenser, by implication, identifies himself with Orpheus, poet and musician.

7.d. Spenser, by implication, identifies himself with 'Phoebus, father of the Muse'.

1.e. In the *Invocation*, Spenser stands *outside* his marriage Ode and prepares to compose it.

24.e. In the *Envoy*, Spenser stands *outside* his marriage Ode and presents it to his bride.

Stanza 13 = Stanzas 9, 20

13.a. The bride *blushes* as she stands before the altar.

9.a. The bride *blushes* as she proceeds to church.

13.b. The angels peep and *stare* at her but she keeps her eyes 'still fastened on the ground . . . with goodly modesty'.

9.b. The onlookers watch her walk to church, while

> Her modest eyes abashed to behold
> So many gazers, as on her do *stare*,
> Upon the lowly ground affixed are.

20.b. The bride is to go to sleep, while 'little winged loves' fly and flutter round her bed. (The behaviour of the 'loves' is very like that of the 'angels' and in both cases the bride is apparently unaware of the presence of her supernatural admirers.)

Stanza 12 = *Stanzas* 22, 23

12.a. The bride enters the temple and shows a becoming reverence as she goes into the 'holy place' and before 'the Almighties view' in order to partake of the sacred ceremonies which make 'endlesse matrimony'.

22.a. This stanza gives us an allegorical, pagan counterpart to stanza 12. The bridal chamber is regarded as a chaste, holy place where spiritual powers are present to bless the married couple, and Juno, patroness of the laws of wedlock and of the sacred rites which solemnize betrothal, is invoked: 'eternally bind thou this lovely band'.

23.a. In this stanza the 'temple' is greater than either the church or the bridal chamber; it is the 'high Heaven' inhabited by the gods, the powers, who are invoked to bless the marriage.

12.b. The bride enters through the 'temple gates', opened to receive 'the saynt with honour due'.

23.b. The descendants of the married couple are foreseen mounting up to the 'temple of the gods' to swell the ranks of 'the blessed Saints'.

12.c. The bride comes 'with trembling steps and humble reverence' into the presence of the Almighty and up to the altar where she partakes of 'endlesse matrimony'.

23.c. The married couple regard themselves as 'wretched earthly clods', praying to be illumined, influenced and blessed by the celestial powers, so that their union may result in the temporal and eternal happiness of their *posterity*.

Stanza 24 = *Stanza* 1

Stanza 24 can be paralleled with Stanza 1, in that both Envoy and Invocation are outside the marriage Ode proper.

I do not claim that my system supplies an adequate means of matching stanzas, but only that it is as convincing as that of Professor Hieatt. I suspect that other equally plausible systems could be produced. I do not believe that any system could indicate correspondences of conceits, images, etc. sufficiently striking to enable a reader to perform the difficult feat of memorization required for the pairing of widely-separated stanzas. Professor Hieatt's main thesis does not, however, depend on the matching stanzas.

BIBLIOGRAPHY

Aquinas. *Basic Writings of Saint Thomas Aquinas.* 2 vols. An English translation; edited and annotated with an introduction by Anton C. Pegis. New York and London, 1945.
  St. Thomas Aquinas: Philosophical Texts. Selected and translated with notes and introduction by Thomas Gilby. O.U.P. 1951.
Armstrong, A. H. *An Introduction to Ancient Philosophy.* London, 1947.
Augustine. *The City of God* (De Civitate Dei). Tr. John Healy, 1610. Edinburgh, 1909.
  An Augustine Synthesis. Arranged Erich Przywara, S.J. London, 1939. *La Bergerie.* ed. Doris Delacourcelle, 1954.

Belleau, Remy. *Oeuvres Completes.* 3 vols. Edited A. Gouverneur. Paris, 1867; See also Delacourcelle.
Bembo, Pietro. *Gli Asolani.* Tr. Rudolph B. Gottfried. Indiana Univ. Press, Bloomington, 1954.
Benivieni. *Opere.* See Pico della Mirandola.
Bruno, Giordano. *The Heroic Enthusiasts* (Gli Eroici Furori) by Giordano Bruno. Tr. L. Williams. 2 vols. London, 1887.
  Des Fureurs Héroïques (De gl'Heroici Furori). Texte établi et traduit par Paul-Henri Michel. Paris, 1954. (Italian text with French translation.)
Buttet, Marc-Claude de. *Les Oeuvres Poétiques de Marc-Claude de Buttet.* ed. A. Philibert-Soupe. Lyon, 1877.

Case, R. H. *English Epithalamies.* London, 1896.
Castiglione. *The Book of the Courtier*, by Count Baldassare Castiglione. Done into English by Sir Thomas Hoby. Anno, 1561. Everyman Edition.
Catullus. *The Poems of Gaius Valerius Catullus*, with an English translation by Francis Warre Cornish. Cambridge, 1904.
Claudian. Latin text with English translation, by Maurice Platnauer. 2 vols. Loeb Classical Library.
Comes, Natalis. *Natalis Comitus Mythologiae sive explicationis Fabularum.* Francofurti, 1584.
Cornford, F. M. *Plato's Cosmology.* The *Timaeus* of Plato, translated with a running commentary. London, 1948.

Dante. *The Convivio of Dante Alighieri.* Edited and translated P. H. Wickstead. Temple Classics.
  A Translation of the Latin Works of Dante Alighieri. A. G. Ferrars-Howell and P. H. Wickstead. Temple Classics.
  Italian text and English translation of *The Inferno of Dante Alighieri*:

The Purgatorio of Dante Alighieri: The Paradiso of Dante Alighieri. Temple Classics.

For English translation of *Vita Nova*, see D. G. Rossetti.

D'Arcy, M. C., S.J. *The Mind and Heart of Love.* A study in Eros and Agape. London, 1946.

Daremberg and Saglio. *Dictionnaire des Antiquités Grecques et Romaines.* 5 vols. Paris, 1873. Revised 1919.

Delacourcelle, Doris. *Le Sentiment de l'Art dans la Bergerie de Remy Belleau.* Oxford, 1945.

Di Benedetto, Luigi. *Rimatori del Dolce Stil Novo.* G. Guinicelli, etc. Scrittore d'Italia 172. Bari, 1939.

du Bellay, Joachim. *Oeuvres Poétiques.* 6 vols. Edited Henri Chamard. Paris, 1908–1931.

Ellrodt, Robert. *Neo-Platonism in the Poetry of Spenser.* Geneva, 1960.

Ficino, Marsilio. *Marsilio Ficino's Commentary on Plato's Symposium.* Text and English translation S. R. Jayne. In *University of Missouri Studies,* Vol. XIX, No. 1 (1944).

Fowler, Alistair. *Spenser and the Numbers of Time.* London, 1964.

Hesiod. *The Poems and Fragments.* Tr. A. W. Mair. Oxford, Clarendon Press, 1908.

Theogony. Edited M. L. West. Oxford, Clarendon Press, 1966.

Homer. *The Iliad.* Text and translation A. T. Murray. 2 vols. Loeb Classical Library.

Hooker, Richard. *The Works of that learned and judicious Divine Mr. Richard Hooker with an account of his life and death* by Isaac Walton. 2 vols. Oxford, 1850.

Kristeller, P. O. *The Philosophy of Marsilio Ficino.* Tr. Virginia Conant. New York, 1943.

Leone Ebreo. *The Philosophy of Love* (Dialoghi d'Amore). Tr. F. Friedeberg-Seeley and Jean H. Barnes. London, 1937.

Lewis, C. S. *The Allegory of Love.* A Study in Mediæval Tradition. Oxford, 1938.

English Literature in the Sixteenth Century. Oxford, 1954.

Luther, Martin. Martin Luther on *The Bondage of the Will.* A new translation of *De Servo Arbitrio* (1525). Martin Luther's reply to Erasmus of Rotterdam, by J. I. Packer and O. R. Johnston. London, 1957.

Reformation Writings of Martin Luther. Tr. Bertram Lee Woolf. Vol. I. *The Basis of the Protestant Reformation.* London, 1952.

Nelson, J. C. *Renaissance Theory of Love.* New York, 1958.

Nygren, Anders. *Agape and Eros.* Pt. I, Pt. II in 2 vols. Tr. P. S. Watson and A. G. Herbert. S.P.C.K.

Petrarch. *Le Rime di Francesco Petrarcha,* di suo gli originale. Commentate da Giosuè Carducci e Severino Ferrari. Firenze. G. C. Sansone Editore. 1924.

Petrarch's Secret; or, the Soul's Conflict with Passion, three Dialogues between himself and S. Augustine, translated from the Latin by W. H. Draper. London, 1911.

The Sonnets and Stanzas of Petrarch. Tr. C. B. Cayley. London, 1879. See also Tatham.

Pico della Mirandola. *A Platonick Discourse upon Love, by Pico della Mirandola.* Ed. Edmund G. Gardner. The Humanists Library VII. Boston, 1914. (This is a reprint of a translation of Pico and Benivieni made by the seventeenth-century writer, Thomas Stanley. The translation is sometimes misleading and incomplete).

Opere di Girolamo Benivieni Firentino . . . con una canzona dello Amore celeste e divino coll commentate dello Ill. S. Conte Giovañi Pico Miradolano. distinto in Libbri III. Venice, 1522.

Plato. *Plato.* With an English translation. Vols. I–X. Loeb Classical Library. See also Cornford.

Plotinus. *Plotinus, The Enneads.* Tr. Stephen MacKenna. 2nd edition revised by B. S. Page. London, 1956. See also Armstrong.

Porter, H. C. *Reformation and Re-action in Tudor Cambridge.* Cambridge, 1958.

Robb, Nesca A. *Neo-Platonism of the Italian Renaissance.* London, 1935.

Ronsard, Pierre de. *Oeuvres Complètes.* 17 vols. Edited Paul Laumonier. Paris, 1914-1959

Rossetti, D. G. *The Early Italian Poets, together with Dante's Vita Nuova.* Tr. D. G. Rossetti. Temple Classics.

Ruysbroeck. *John of Ruysbroeck.* Tr. C. A. Wynschenk. Dom. Edited Evelyn Underhill. London, 1916.

Shaw, J. E. *Guido Cavalcanti's Theory of Love.* 'The Canzone d'Amore' and other Related Problems. Toronto, 1949.

Smyth, H. W. *Greek Melic Poets.* London, 1900. (Gives a brief account of the Hymn and the Marriage Song).

Souchay, l'Abbe. *Discours sur l'origine et le caractère de l'Epithalamion.* In Acad. Roy. des Inscriptions, etc. Tome IX, Paris, 1736.

Spenser, Edmund. Editions: *The Works of Edmund Spenser. A Variorum Edition.* 10 vols. Edited E. Greenlaw, C. G. Osgood, F. M. Padelford, R. Heffner, H. G. Lotspeich. Including *The Minor Poems,* 2 vols., and *The Life of Edmund Spenser* by A. C. Judson. The Johns Hopkins Press.

The Fowre Hymnes. Edited Lilian Winstanley. Cambridge, 1907. (Pitt Press Series.)

Epithalamion by Edmund Spenser. With introduction and notes by Cortlandt Van Winkle. New York, 1926.

Daphnaida and Other Poems by Edmund Spenser. Edited W. L. Renwick. London, 1929.

Spenser's Minor Poems. Edited Ernest de Sélincourt. Oxford, 1960.

Spenser, Edmund. Studies: William Nelson: *The Poetry of Edmund Spenser*. New York, 1963. (Chapter I, entitled 'Prince of Poets', gives an admirable summary of the known facts of Spenser's life; Chapter IV, 'Love creating', deals with *Amoretti, Epithalamion* and *The Fowre Hymnes*.)

Epithalamion. Studies: A. Kent Hieatt. *Short Time's Endless Monument*. The symbolism of numbers in Edmund Spenser's *Epithalamion*. New York, 1960.

James A. S. McPeek. *The Major Sources of Spenser's Epithalamion* in JEGP. Vol. XXXV (1936), pp. 183–213. (Some helpful references but his treatment of the theme is not very convincing.)

The Fowre Hymnes. Studies: E. M. Albright. *Spenser's Cosmic Philosophy and his Religion* in PMLA. Vol. XLIV, ii. (Sept., 1929), pp. 715–59.

C. G. Osgood. *Spenser's Sapience* in SP. Vol. XIV (1917), pp. 167–77.

For Neo-Platonic interpretation of the Hymns: J. W. Bennett. *The Theme of Spenser's Fowre Hymnes* in SP. Vol. XXVIII (1931), pp. 18–57 and also *Addenda*, SP, Vol. XXXII (1935), pp. 131–57;

J. B. Fletcher. *Spenser's Fowre Hymnes. A Study in Renaissance Mysticism* in PMLA, Vol. XXVI (1911), pp. 452–75; and *Benivieni's Ode of Love and Spenser's Fowre Hymnes* in MP, Vol. VIII (1911), pp. 545–60. (This article contains an English verse translation by Fletcher of Benivieni's Ode.)

For Calvinistic interpretation of Hymns: F. M. Padelford. *Spenser and the Puritan Propaganda* in MP, Vol. XI (1913), pp. 88–106. *Spenser and the Theology of Calvin* in MP, Vol. XII (1914), pp. 1–18. *Spenser and the Spirit of Puritanism* in MP, Vol. XIV (1916), pp. 31–44. *Spenser's Fowre Hymnes: A Re-survey* in SP, Vol. XXIX (1932), pp. 207–32.

Statius. Latin text with English translation by J. H. Mozley. 2 vols. Loeb Classical Library.

Tatham, E. H. R. *Francesco Petrarca*, The First Modern Man of Letters. His Life and Correspondence. Vol. I. London, 1925.

Tillyard, E. M. W. *The Elizabethan World Picture*. London, 1943.

Whitaker, V. K. *The Religious Basis of Spenser's Thought*. Stanford University Publications in Languages and Literature, Vol. VII, No. 3, Stanford Cal., 1950.

Wind, Edgar. *Pagan Mysteries in the Renaissance*. London, 1958.

Yates, Frances A. *Giordano Bruno and the Hermetic Tradition*. London, 1964.

INDEX TO NOTES ON INTRODUCTION

INDEX TO NOTES ON TEXTS

212